MANNERISMS

The Five Phases of Manfred Mann

GREG RUSSO

CROSSFIRE PUBLICATIONS
P.O. Box 20406
Floral Park, New York 11002-20406 U.S.A.

"Mannerisms: The Five Phases of Manfred Mann" was conceived on September 9, 1992 and completed July 29, 1995.

Layout and design by Greg Russo.

All photos are from the collection of Greg Russo unless otherwise noted.

First edition - August 1995.

Printed and manufactured in the United States of America.

Special thanks: John Arkle, Jean Pegg, Graeme Yates, Dennis Sedita, Peter Heller, Ron Furmanek, Steve Kolanjian, Joseph F. Laredo, Fernando L. Gonzalez, Richard Peters, Don Pedini, Andy Taylor, Vincent DiFrancesco and Mark Roberts.

This book is dedicated to the memory of my grandfather, Michael Russo.

For further information, please address all correspondence to:
Crossfire Publications, P.O. Box 20406, Floral Park, NY 11002-20406. Fax: (516) 352-3037.

ISBN: 0-9648157-1-0

Table of Contents

So beginnen Karrieren!

THE WORKHOUSE STUDIOS

488/490 OLD KENT ROAD.
LONDON, SE1 5AG
TELEPHONE: 071 237 1737/8
FAX: 071 231 7958

28-7-95

Many thanks for your support and continued interest. I never thought that anyone would remember or even care about what we did over the years.

Greg Russo has worked extremely hard on 'Mannerisms' over a long period of time.

Its a book full of immense detail, personally I dont believe there are many people interested in all these facts and sub-facts, but Greg has convinced me otherwise.

I'd like to thank you all once again, and of course Greg Russo, for all his hard work.

ALL THE BEST.

Manfred Mann.

PETBROOK LTD
DIRECTOR: M. LUBOWITZ
INCORPORATED LONDON 919764   VAT NO. 236 3944 50   REGISTERED OFFICE: 26 GILBERT STREET, LONDON. W1

Introduction

When considering the musical career of Manfred Mann, questions immediately arise whether a book length document is required, or even necessary. The answer in both cases is a definite "yes," and the reasons are mainly twofold: the previous spread of misinformation and Manfred's lack of proper recognition. Concerning the first issue, to most people Manfred Mann is an enigma, and a frustrating one at that. Due to Manfred's avoidance of publicity, even those familiar with the sixties pop group that carried his name misidentified Manfred as singer Paul Jones! This is because an insufficient amount of information has been presented on Manfred for music fans to make an informed analysis of his entire body of work.

Over the years, quite a lot of misleading Manfred Mann information has been presented in publications and liner notes due to their authors copying information from past, incorrect articles. After years of turning the other way, the '60s members of Manfred Mann have now justifiably expressed their displeasure with this flawed information, even if they have chosen the wrong forum to do so (i.e. concerts).

By thorough and independent research, this book endeavors to accurately present the definitive history of Manfred Mann (the musician) and his band members. To do this, interviews and conversations were undertaken by myself and the other main contributors of the Manfred Mann fan club publication Platform End. These informal interviews took place by telephone, in studios, backstage at concerts, and even by having members answer written questionnaires. Thanks must go to the musicians that graciously provided their time to answer questions that they must be tired of by this point, besides answering the questions that kept them interested in providing Manfred Mann fans more accurate information. They are: Manfred Mann, Paul Jones, Mike Hugg, Mike Vickers, Tom McGuinness, Mike d'Abo, Mick Rogers, Noel McCalla and Clive Bunker. It is, after all, their story that is being presented here.

On the second front, recognition has been an important point for Manfred Mann fans. Certainly, Manfred's low profile has been the major roadblock for widespread acknowledgement of his career accomplishments. However, being a viable contributor to the music industry over a long period of time, as Manfred has, he deserves recognition and respect, even from his detractors. Again, the purpose of this book is to redress the balance and fairly state why Manfred's career is more than just a long string of hit 45s. Rather, it is a collection of treasured performances that have transcended time parameters and musical fashions.

Even if you are only interested in Manfred's '60s music, there is plenty here to enjoy. Without question, different trains of thought are required to appreciate all five phases of Manfred's career. These phases are the separate R&B and pop periods of the '60s Manfred Mann group, the free-form jazz of Manfred Mann Chapter Three, the progressive Manfred Mann's Earth Band, the more worldly "Plains Music" project and the reformations of the Earth Band and The Manfreds.

This book divides all of Manfred's career phases. So, if you just want to examine the '60s version of the group for example, you can just look at the first two sections. In addition, all of the most notable Manfred Mann group members went on to accomplish some distinguished work after leaving the band. Mini-profiles of each of these members follow the main Manfred Mann discography.

My Story

As for myself, how I got involved with Manfred Mann is a story in itself. In 1975, at the age of 13, I was a little late to be discovering music. Nevertheless, that's when I started. Without delay, I immersed myself in Top 40 AM radio stations in New York. In December 1976, I heard "Blinded By The Light" for the first time over a friend's house. I told my friend, "That song is awful, but I bet you I'll end up liking it." Since Top 40 stations were (and still are) notorious for playing the same song every three or four hours, I kept hearing "Blinded" over and over as the days went by. Wouldn't you know it, as it got more airplay, the song started growing on me! Just after the turn of the new year, there I was in the record store buying a 45 of "Blinded By The Light" on the Warner Brothers label. As was usual with Warner Brothers singles, it was very noisy, but this would not damper my newly found enthusiasm in this Manfred Mann guy. I had a thing with the 45s I bought (and I bought lots of them) that I had to play the B-side following the A-side, because occasionally I found some pretty interesting stuff there. After playing "Blinded," I played "Starbird No. 2," and after hearing the amazing singing and rapid fire solos played in succession by the Earth Band on this B-side, I remained there with my mouth open! I had to buy the album, and for me, it was a luxury, since the only albums I previously obtained were The Beatles' "Hey Jude" and "Love Will Keep Us Together" by The Captain And Tennille!

In February, I bought "The Roaring Silence" from the sale rack at Record World for $2.99 (ah, the good old days), and played it to death. The one thing I didn't do was check the album section for Manfred Mann, but since I was not used to checking this section, I still had a lot to learn. After nearly wearing out the album, I found myself in a Sam Goody record store looking for more. As I went through the Manfred Mann section, I said to myself, 'This guy goes back to 1964!' (I was close, but for a fourteen year-old, this was a revelation!) I had heard "Do Wah Diddy Diddy" on those AM stations, but I didn't make the connection at first.

I started going backwards, buying "Nightingales And Bombers" first, and I played it every day for 30 straight days until I bought the rest of the available catalog. This included all of the US Earth Band albums and a '60s "best of." When I graduated high school in 1980, I made my first trip to Greenwich Village, the mecca for record collector's shops in New York City. At a store called Farfel's on West 4th Street, I went up to the counter and asked the guy, "Do you have any Manfred Mann singles?" He said that they had some there (which he pulled out) and that he had extras in his collection that he wanted to sell. This obviously intelligent person with unquestionable taste was Steve Kolanjian. Over the next two years, I visited Steve every week and discussed all things Manfredian. Putting this knowledge down on paper, I wrote my first Manfred article in Steve Kolanjian's Aware magazine.

It was now time to visit England. I had to get all the British records that I found that I now needed, and I wanted to meet Manfred, my new hero, personally. Well, the day before I was to come back home, I received a birthday present of sorts. On May 25, 1982, just three days before my 20th birthday, I met Manfred and spent five hours with him in the studio. That day, Manfred was very busy and I was understandably very nervous, but it was the start of a mutually appreciative relationship that has lasted to this day. Even now, Manfred and I still laugh about our first meeting!

Special Note for Record Collectors and Other Scholarly Fanatics!

For those desiring precise details about specific records or points raised in the text of this book, this information has been referenced by numerically indexed endnotes which follow the sessionography. Please read at your own risk!

I heartily welcome any Manfred Mann-related material for the second edition of this book. Please send these items to the address shown elsewhere. Thank you for your interest.

Manfred with the author - 5/25/82

Manfred with the author - 9/9/92

The Paul Jones (HMV) Era - Chapter One

Manfred Mann - The Beginning

Manfred Mann (born Manfred Lubowitz[1]) was born to a wealthy family in Johannesburg, South Africa on October 21, 1940. The Lubowitz household had a piano in their house, played by Manfred's mother. At the age of six, Manfred became interested in the family's piano and started to learn how to play it. From this time, Manfred became miserable and frightened with the racist conditions in South Africa, and unhappiness set in quickly. Using Manfred's term, he became an "anti-racist" when he was about eight or nine, and his greatest nightmare was rearing children in South Africa that were racist. Piano became Manfred's refuge, and he practiced in earnest, as much as five hours per day.

Manfred was sent to Meyerton College, a boarding school in the South African countryside (known as the Transvaal), between the ages of nine and fourteen. By the time he completed his subsequent studies at Highlands North High School in Johannesburg, Manfred was exposed to jazz and was soon playing at school dances. In his eighteenth year, he was appearing at local coffee bars.

Within the restrictive confines of South Africa, Manfred concluded that his talents could not be fully developed and utilized. Manfred had also worked for his father in the printing business, but that work was not meant for him. As a 19-year old, Manfred studied classical music at Johannesburg's Witwatersrand University under the tutelage of Professor Hartman. The American jazz pianist John Mehegan, known in jazz circles for his playing ability and the high quality of his instructional piano guides and LP liner notes, also taught Manfred on the jazz end while visiting South Africa. In fact, Manfred had some lessons with Mehegan in a four-piece band, and Hugh Masekela (later known for "Grazing In The Grass") and Jonas Gwangwa were two of the other three players.

However, it was another long-forgotten US musician that fully recognized Manfred's talents. Manfred relates the story: "An American jazz player, whose name I forget, came to South Africa. I saw him playing a concert at the Johannesburg University, and thought he was great. Then, one night I was playing in a coffee bar, and he came in. He told me (that) he thought my playing was great. I thought, 'Fantastic. He thinks I can play.' I suppose around then I realized that I could play, but I never thought I'd earn a living as a player - maybe as a teacher."

By this point, Manfred's practicing increased to eight hours per day, and his jazz exposure widened through the works of John Coltrane, Miles Davis, Horace Silver, Cannonball Adderley, Ornette Coleman, Charles Mingus, Dave Brubeck, Bill Evans and others.

In late 1961, Manfred decided that further development of his talents (i.e., putting musical theory into practice) had to take place outside South Africa. South Africa had just left the British commonwealth and there was a one-year grace period for South African nationals to get work permits in the UK. This was the last chance for South Africans to obtain these permits, so Manfred left home and boarded a boat for England. To maintain permanent residence in England, Manfred played jazz piano and taught music and harmony theory. While in England, Manfred took this one step further by writing for the publication Jazz News under the name Manfred Manne. Manfred's nom de plume was derived from another jazz performer, the well-known drummer Shelly Manne. Shortly, Manfred would remove the "e" from this pseudonym to become Manfred Mann.

Manfred's passport photo

Money was getting tight, but Manfred's skills became known to the groups that he played with in England. However, Manfred's eagerness to impress got him in trouble with club owners, who fired him regularly! In 1962, Manfred was the first jazz musician to ever play at The Bull's Head in Barnes, London, a club known for its jazz entertainment even to this day. Manfred's stint at The Bull's Head lasted for about nine months, when the club's management fired him in order to showcase different players during the week. An early success for Manfred was the jazz quartet that he played in at a Butlin's holiday resort in Clacton, England. It was at this location that Manfred met Mike Hugg, who was experiencing the same financial hardship.

Drummer/vibes player Mike Hugg was born Michael Hug on August 11, 1942 in Andover, Hampshire, England. Like Manfred, he was also jazz-oriented. In 1962, Hugg's jazz quartet had problems due to the instability of their pianist. Hugg's band, which included ex-Alexis Korner organist Graham Bond, also made the rounds at the Clacton-based Butlin's. Hugg and Bond spotted Manfred playing piano at this resort, and Bond asked Manfred if he could play on their weekend gigs. Bond was handling three weeknights, and the band had one weekday off. Since Manfred was teaching during the week and had little weekend work, he jumped at the opportunity. The weekend lineup with Mann and Hugg was very successful with club goers, and lasted throughout the 1962 summer club season. Around this time, Manfred married his wife Susan, with whom he would have two children, Sara-Jane (born 1963) and Nina (born 1965). With these new responsibilities, Manfred needed regular work to survive.

Mike Hugg

Intermediate late 1962 lineup:
(left to right: Tony Roberts, Ian Fenby, Mike
Hugg, Dave Richmond, Paul Jones, Mike
Vickers, Manfred Mann)
(photo credit: Glenn Baker)

The Crossover

Throughout 1962, British clubs were crossing over from traditional ("trad") jazz to rhythm and blues (R&B). This was an unusual occurrence, since R&B was a previously ignored commodity in England, and now R&B became the commercial factor for the success of jazz-based groups. Through his time with Alexis Korner, Graham Bond became one of the biggest proponents of this crossover. Bond soon formed The Graham Bond Organisation with bassist Jack Bruce, Ginger Baker (drums) and sax player Dick Heckstall-Smith. In addition, Bond fully communicated his musical vision with Manfred Mann and Mike Hugg, who in turn reflected this jazz/R&B fusion of sorts in a new band concept.

Manfred Mann and Mike Hugg wanted to create a four-piece band that combined the style of jazz and the excitement of R&B. As Mike Hugg described it, he and Manfred intended to produce "a distinctive hardhitting jazz and blues" sound. The name of this band was The Mann-Hugg Blues Brothers. Their jazz grounding was firm, with influences by Charles Mingus and Roland Kirk. However, they still needed to develop their R&B background. In the latter part of 1962, the group played the Marquee, The John Dankworth Club, and the main London jazz clubs. The lineup at this point was Mann, Hugg, Dave Richmond on bass, and Mike Vickers, a multi-instrumentalist who concentrated on guitar. Although some horn players like tenor saxman Alan Skidmore played fleetingly with the band, three horn players were permanently added to the band to maximize their crossover potential: Tony Roberts (tenor sax), Don Fay (baritone sax) and trumpeter Ian Fenby.

Now a seven-piece band, The Mann-Hugg Blues Brothers were still lacking the knockout punch: a vocalist with the right R&B credentials. That vocalist was Paul Jones.

Paul Jones

Born Paul Pond in Portsmouth, England on February 24, 1942, Paul Jones was a veteran of numerous groups. In the early spring of 1962, vocalist/harp player Jones and pianist Ben Palmer formed the Oxford-based Thunder Odin And The Big Secret. Throughout the existence of this group, Jones met with two guitar players that would enjoy future success: Tom McGuinness and future Rolling Stones member Brian Jones, then known as slide guitarist Elmo Lewis. When not rehearsing with Lewis, Paul Jones and Ben Palmer played with Tom McGuinness' group, which also included Ned Lunn (guitar) and a long series of drummers (there was no bass player).

Paul Pond and Elmo Lewis' main goal was to use Alexis Korner, the kingpin of the British blues scene, to get them a job at The Ealing Club. To do this, they sent some demos to Korner. This method failed, so both young musicians visited The Ealing Club and managed to sit in with Korner's group, Blues Incorporated. At this point, Pond felt that he could never achieve fame as Paul Pond, so he took the common last name Jones to become P.P. Jones (Paul Pond Jones).

After his Alexis Korner experience and name change, Paul Jones was known as Paul Peterson in the summer of 1962 when he vocalized for the Top 20 cover band Gordon Reece And The Adelphians. This group originated from the Slough area. Jones then moved to London and worked for Esquire Records. He had also spent a short time in school at Oxford, but studying was not for him. Still, Jones wanted a more rewarding musical experience than playing someone else's hits.

Mike Vickers was born in Southampton on April 18, 1941. After being discovered by Mann and Hugg, he and Manfred shared a flat in England's Forest Hill area. Vickers played guitar, alto sax and flute, all within blues and jazz formats. He also had a jazz background, but with heavier pop leanings than the others. He was also interested in classical music, and cited Bach as one favorite. In addition, Vickers had aspirations to arrange and conduct from the very beginning.

Mike Vickers

Getting the Act Together

Meanwhile, The Mann-Hugg Blues Brothers established themselves at London's Marquee, and Mann and Hugg made it known to Marquee staff that they were looking for the right singer to complete their act. In December 1962, Bill Carey from the Marquee introduced Paul Jones (then known as "Blue Boy Jones") to the band, and The Mann-Hugg Blues Brothers invited Jones to their audition at the Carnaby Street ska club The Roaring 20's.

To everyone's surprise, Jones was the only candidate to audition! Since this was the case, Mann and Hugg made it clear that Jones would fill in until they found a vocalist that was more in line with their musical vision. The first band rehearsal took place in Manfred's flat in Forest Hill in December 1962, and Manfred was in his pre-organ days, playing piano. As it turned out, Jones' enthusiasm was infectious, as was his taste of R&B. Mann and Hugg found themselves moving toward Jones' R&B direction, apparently by osmosis! Fan reaction to the band's initial performances with Jones was extremely positive and The Mann-Hugg Blues Brothers started to pick up respect within the musical community. With Jones fronting the band, Mann and Hugg and company solidified their London residencies at the Marquee, the Crawdaddy (both locations) and Studio 51 in London. In fact, their early appearances revolved around clubs on the south coast of England, where Hugg and Vickers lived and had some influence.

Manfred tells where he and the band were headed: "I was just going wherever I could earn a living, to be honest. We were flat broke as jazz musicians, and getting mixed in with the blues guys was kind of a good combination, with Paul Jones and eventually Tom McGuinness (on bass; Dave Richmond's replacement). Tom was only there from late 1963, so Paul mainly was a kind of blues influence. That influence didn't come from me. I thought blues was Ray Charles and stuff. This kind of blues material that we were drawing as a source was stuff that Paul knew about that I didn't know, although I might have had a hand in choosing what to do."

R&B completely took over British clubs by the spring of 1963, especially since the one night per week trials of R&B groups at jazz clubs worked tremendously. While at The Hambrough Tavern in the West London locality of Southall, they were spotted by a London publicist, Kenneth Pitt. Upon meeting the band, Pitt convinced the group that a manager would be necessary in order for them to go any further. In no time, Pitt set the wheels in motion. As it turned out, the shrewd Pitt had a lot of influence in the music scene. According to Manfred, the three horn players (Roberts, Fay and Fenby) left on their own soon after in May 1963.

A very opportunistic manager, Pitt arranged for band auditions for Pye, Decca and EMI. The unsuccessful Pye audition consisted entirely of instrumentals, and Decca was not interested in the more vocal-oriented presentation that the band gave. The May 23, 1963 audition for EMI was a combination of the two approaches. This method worked, and the band was signed to EMI's His Master's Voice (HMV) label. The group was also assigned Adam Faith's producer, John Burgess, who would prove to be the shaper of their crisp sound.

John Burgess, with image in mind, wanted a more direct group name. Among other names, Manfred wanted the band to be called The Driving Wheels! Since Burgess was faced with a lack of choices for the band's title, he felt that Manfred's own professional name, Manfred Mann, was the best available name. This did not go over well with the band, including Manfred. Burgess and Pitt solved the situation by convincing the band that HMV's marketing would stress that <u>all</u> of the band members were Manfred Mann. This proved to acceptable to everyone involved. Still, the Manfreds (as they became known) wanted to ensure their individuality on record.

Manfred gives his views on the band's moniker: "I was dead against the name 'Manfred Mann,' partly because I felt embarrassed. I was both right and wrong. The name became a source of friction years later, and was part of the reason that Paul Jones eventually left. I was wrong because the name was brilliant for a group, and very memorable."

At the EMI audition, six different titles were recorded, four vocals ("I Don't Want To Know," "Let's Go," "Tell Me What Did I Say" [later known as "Don't Ask Me What I Say"] and "Without You") and two instrumentals ("Why Should We Not" and "Brother Jack"). Despite strong original songs from Paul Jones and the generally rough but exciting performances laid down, the two instrumentals, "Why Should We Not" and "Brother Jack," were released as the respective top and bottom sides of their debut single in July 1963. Talk about a blow to Jones' ego!

"Why Should We Not" equally represented each member's instrumental talents, while "Brother Jack" was a jazz-oriented arrangement of the children's song "Frere Jacques." Despite strong airplay, sales did not follow. Mike Hugg recounts the musical intent of the band in the early days: "We were still very much into the music at that point. We weren't into image or being commercial. In fact, we were trying to be quite different. That element helped in the end."

"Why Should We Not" was apparently too different to the record buying public, although music papers of the day noticed. The second single, "Cock-A-Hoop," was the first released Paul Jones vocal performance and composition. Released in October 1963, "Cock-A-Hoop" used the R&B style of "call-and-response" to create a catchy record. The American Heritage Dictionary has defined the term <u>cock-a-hoop</u> as being "in a state of elation or exultation," and the energy of the single made it very clear what it was about. Also, "Cock-A-Hoop" marked the first time that Jones inserted mentions of the band within his compositions. Later examples were "5-4-3-2-1" and "The One In The Middle." The B-side was another Jones original, the humorous "Now You're Needing Me."

Sales didn't equate to airplay or interest, but Manfred Mann was quickly invited to appear on the ITV program "Ready Steady Go." After their appearance for "Cock-A-Hoop," the band was hired to write a new "Ready Steady Go" (RSG) theme song, replacing "Wipeout" by The Surfaris. It's unfortunate that none of the band members remembers exactly why they were hired to do this! Still, Manfred Mann was on the upswing, scoring heavily through their club appearances. These appearances occupied every night of the week, even at this early point. An amateur video of a 1963 live club performance of "Cock-A-Hoop" (when Dave Richmond was still in their ranks) illustrates their early command over their growing audience, further exemplified by their turnout at the 1963 National Jazz and Blues Festival in Richmond.

The song Mann, Hugg and Jones came up with was "5-4-3-2-1," and it became the RSG theme and their third single. Mike Hugg explains the song: "'5-4-3-2-1' had all of the R&B elements of what we were doing at the time. Since it was a signature tune for 'Ready Steady Go', that obviously had a bearing on what it turned out to be. I quite like it, it's a little bit off the wall and quite a bit silly. It's certainly not something to be taken seriously!"

One thing that <u>was</u> taken seriously was the bass slot of the group. Dave Richmond had great difficulty in making the transition from jazz to R&B, and ended up playing everything in a jazz mode. A few days after the recording of "5-4-3-2-1," ex-Roosters member Tom McGuiness (professionally known as Tom McGuinness) replaced Dave Richmond on bass.

Tom McGuinness, a guitarist by trade, was born in Wimbledon, England on December 2, 1941. Tom describes his inspiration this way: "For me, it all began with skiffle and Lonnie Donegan, as it did for a million other people. Then it was Buddy Holly, because he wore glasses, and suddenly I realized you didn't have to look like Elvis or Tony Curtis. Then it was Hank Marvin (of The Shadows), because he wore glasses and he was English, and I realized that you didn't have to be American!"

Tom McGuinness

Tom had played R&B in numerous groups since 1962, the most notable being The Roosters with Eric Clapton. The Roosters even supported The Mann-Hugg Blues Brothers at the Marquee, but had difficulty getting paid! After meeting Paul Jones in 1962 through a Melody Maker blues musician advert placed by Ben Palmer, McGuinness sometimes crossed paths with Jones. On these occasions, they informed each other of their progress.

In 1963, McGuinness became aware of Dave Richmond's inability to play R&B bass with the Manfreds, so he brought the matter up with Paul Jones. Tom was moving furniture at the time, so he decided that he had to stretch the truth with Jones to get Richmond's position. During their conversation, Tom McGuinness told Paul Jones that he was now playing bass, and was available. One thing led to another, and McGuinness was soon being interviewed (pre-gig) by Mann and Hugg at St. John's Ambulance Hall, Chigwell, Essex for the bassist position. At this interview, Manfred and Mike asked McGuinness, "Will you promise to play . . . simply?" Since he didn't have to actually play, McGuinness said, "Yes, I promise to play simply" and he was in. What McGuinness didn't know was that Richmond was taken in the next room by Mike Vickers while this was going on! The band played that night with Richmond, and after some early morning decision making, Mann and Hugg agreed that McGuinness was their new bass player. The next night (Saturday, December 21), the band played at The Ealing Club, and McGuinness borrowed a bass from the club before anyone in the band noticed. At Ealing, McGuinness made his band debut and his bass debut, all in the same night!

The Hitmaking Begins

The cross-promotion of radio and TV shot "5-4-3-2-1" onto the British charts, and it peaked at the #5 position.[2] With this success, the Manfreds moved toward a more commercial (i.e., singles) direction. The American record industry also took notice of this success. However, EMI's American counterpart, Capitol Records, had right of first refusal. Since Manfred Mann had produced only one hit, Capitol had no interest in the group.

"5-4-3-2-1" then became Manfred Mann's US debut single on Prestige Records, a jazz label. For the group, Prestige Records seemed like the perfect fit, but the record did not make any impact. Manfred's recollection of the Prestige arrangement is fuzzy at best, so the Manfreds could not have profited from this record.

The B-side, "Without You," was a strong blues track with a solid rhythm laid down by Tom McGuinness and Mike Hugg, and solos on flute (Mike Vickers) and vibes (Hugg) were classy inclusions. This version was a re-recording of their demo session take.

To the band's credit, "5-4-3-2-1" succeeded before its use on "Ready Steady Go," and the Manfreds started to put together their tour plans of England. By this time, the group's weekly grind was as follows: the Marquee (Monday), Portsmouth (Tuesday), Southampton (Wednesday), Bournemouth (Thursday) and The Ealing Club on Saturday. They were now graduating to the big time.

Their first real tour of duty was to duplicate the Phil Spector "wall of sound" behind The Crystals in a live setting, and they pulled it off. The success of "5-4-3-2-1" enabled Manfred Mann to get its own up-front position on the tour. Also on the show's list of acts was Joe Brown and Johnny Kidd And The Pirates, a group whose singer was an idol of Paul Jones.

The frenetically paced "Hubble Bubble (Toil And Trouble)" became the next A-side, and a rare group-written one at that. "Hubble Bubble" cracked the UK charts in the spring of 1964, cresting at #11. In recent years, the band has distanced itself from "Hubble Bubble," citing their dissatisfaction with its cluttered arrangement as the reason why it is the least favorite of their A-sides. As a result, the '90s touring group of ex-Manfred Mann members known as The Manfreds have avoided playing "Hubble Bubble" in their set. The B-side of "Hubble Bubble" was "I'm Your Kingpin," a track that perfectly illustrated how adept Manfred Mann was at fusing jazz and R&B elements.

As you get to know Manfred, you'll find out that he is a master of understatement at times. When speaking about "I'm Your Kingpin," Manfred called it "a bit of a B-side," but it was much more than that. This Jones/Mann composition was the quintessential jazz fusion experiment: a hot rhythm section, with vibes, sax, and piano solos taking turns between Jones-led verses.[3]

With two hit records to the band's credit, HMV released an EP, "Manfred Mann's Cock-A-Hoop With 54321." This extended play record was made up of the A-sides of their first three singles and "Without You," the B-side of "5-4-3-2-1." The record just missed the New Musical Express (NME) EP chart.

US "Hubble Bubble" promo 45

In the US, the British Invasion was in full force, and every American record company was on the lookout for British artists to give The Beatles competition. After the American record industry ignored the band a few months earlier, US United Artists became so interested in Manfred Mann that they signed them almost immediately to their Ascot subsidiary label. Unfortunately, Ascot's speed in signing Manfred Mann did not immediately result in any commercially released records.[4]

"Blue Brave" - the US version of "Why Should We Not"

 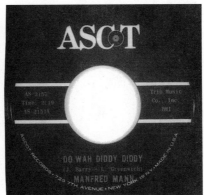

"Do Wah Diddy Diddy"

In June 1964, the Manfreds submitted the tapes for their next single to EMI. Included in these recordings was the Jeff Barry/Ellie Greenwich song "Do Wah Diddy Diddy," and HMV and Ascot knew they had a hot single in the making. Performing the song as a straight R&B number under its original title "Do-Wah-Diddy," the mostly female R&B vocal group, The Exciters, enjoyed only minor success. However, the Manfreds would not imitate another artist's arrangement.

What HMV and Ascot did not know was that although "Do Wah Diddy Diddy" was an obvious single, it was not so obvious to the band how the song was going to come together. Most of the Manfreds hated the song, but they were convinced into recording what became a million seller in many countries. Mike Hugg explains: "Most of the outside material was coming from within the band, and Paul Jones was into that type of American music. At the time, 'Do Wah Diddy Diddy' was OK. We just went into the studio and did it. As a group, we trimmed the rough edges off it."[5]

The single of "Do Wah Diddy Diddy" was released as quickly as possible, and HMV and Ascot celebrated its #1 placing on both sides of the Atlantic during the summer of 1964. The success of "Do Wah Diddy Diddy" fully illustrated the band's stylish yet simple and memorable arrangement, and its irresistibility has successfully crossed generations of listeners. Very few '60s records have accomplished that feat! As a result, Manfred Mann's "Do Wah Diddy Diddy" has justly become a classic and their most familiar song.[6]

The single's B-side was not a throwaway either. The Jones/Mann-written "What You Gonna Do?" was another jazz/blues fusion with spicy contributions on harmonica, organ and guitar from Jones, Mann and Vickers respectively.[7]

"The Five Faces Of Manfred Mann"

Most groups would have difficulty following up a major hit, but the Manfreds had been preparing for this since Tom McGuinness' arrival in December 1963. From that time, the band had been making journeys to the recording studio at regular intervals to lay down tracks for their first album. The title of their delivered album to EMI, "The Five Faces Of Manfred Mann," was devised to illustrate and exemplify the band's five discrete musical talents. Furthermore, the convergence of these talents on the album created an even greater collective musical expression.

"The Five Faces Of Manfred Mann" marked the intersection of jazz, R&B and pop, and was performed effortlessly and masterfully. Music fans have widely recognized the uniformly high quality of the songs on this classic album, and it climbed to the #3 position on the UK album chart. [8] All the Manfreds charted equally well on their performances on the album.

As for the "Five Faces" album itself, it was a powerful collection of blues, pop and jazz covers, original material and strong B-sides. The blues aspect was represented by "Smokestack Lightning," "I'm Your Hoochie Coochie Man," "Down The Road Apiece," "Got My Mojo Working" and "Bring It To Jerome."

"Smokestack Lightning" brought the intensely focused harmonica playing of Paul Jones to the forefront on this Chester Burnett (aka Howlin' Wolf) classic. [9] The Willie Dixon-penned "I'm Your Hoochie Coochie Man" (incorrectly shown as "Hoochie Coochie" on the album) was a Jones tour de force with outstanding vocals and harmonica. The band's choice of "Down The Road Apiece" illustrated that their blues knowledge wasn't limited to recent vintages - Don Raye's original recording of the song dated back to the 1940s. With their consistently solid performances of blues numbers, Manfred Mann made the process look deceptively simple.

"Got My Mojo Working" (also shown incorrectly on the album - "I've Got My Mojo Working") was a popular and effective "call-and-response" blues from Muddy Waters. In the hands of the Manfreds, it was played enthusiastically with a fight-'m-out solo of guitar, harmonica and piano. The same lighthearted approach was also used on "Bring It To Jerome." The Jerome referred to in the song was Bo Diddley's maracas player, Jerome Green, and "Bring It To Jerome" [10] was an extension of the theme Diddley and Green used for Diddley's Top 20 hit in 1959, "Say Man."

The Manfred Mann takes of "It's Gonna Work Out Fine" and "Untie Me" covered the pop/R&B categories very well through Manfred and Paul Jones' interactions. "It's Gonna Work Out Fine" was a #14 US hit in 1961 for Ike And Tina Turner, but Jones' vocal and Manfred's organ contributions equally captured the essence of the song. The Joe South-written "Untie Me" [11] was a mid-sized 1962 hit for The Tams. This time on piano, Manfred classily embellished the emotions conveyed by Jones.

The Manfreds' personalization of "Sack O' Woe," the Julian Edwin "Cannonball" Adderley instrumental, was another jazz/blues hybrid. This included using the theme of the former style and the chord structure of the latter. Solos abounded during the song, but Manfred's singing along with his piano solo is the most priceless part of the recording. During his piano and organ solos during the sixties, Manfred would sing along in delight. Listen closely!

Even the original material was influenced by the blues. "Don't Ask Me What I Say" [12] was another re-recording of an EMI demo and a spirited Jones blues song that shared more band enthusiasm. The blues pattern made famous by revered US bluesman Sonny Boy Williamson was the source for the group-composed instrumental, "Mr. Anello." Paul Jones got another opportunity to express his harmonica skills, and Tom McGuinness took a rare lead guitar solo. [13] Just as effective was "You've Got To Take It," another unrelenting blues original. [14] The icing on the cake was the album's inclusion of the noted B-sides, "Without You," "I'm Your Kingpin" and "What You Gonna Do?," the flips of their last three singles.

"The Manfred Mann Album"

US promo EP

HMV canceled the stereo version of their album, with one reason being Manfred's dissatisfaction with the stereo mixes. However, most of these "rejected" mixes would only be used on stereo copies of the US Ascot long player "The Manfred Mann Album." [15] Also issued in September 1964, "The Manfred Mann Album" became a #35 US hit. Fans buying the Ascot album were surprised when they discovered that it was not filled with pop songs like "Do Wah Diddy Diddy." Fortunately, the surprise for American fans was a pleasant one. Since Ascot was promoting the band as an instrumentally and vocally balanced unit with wide-ranging influences, the Manfreds had a strong reputation from the outset in the US.

Live!

Once firmly established, Manfred Mann built on its status as an exciting live draw. The Manfreds came to the US just once in the sixties - a three-week tour of one-nighters and TV appearances in December 1964. The most notable appearances were those on the ABC-TV program "Shindig!" (These television performances are shown in the discography.) For live shows in the States, the group was packaged with British duo Peter And Gordon and Travis Wammack. Wammack was a Muscle Shoals, Alabama session guitarist touring on the moderate success of his recent instrumental "Scratchy." While in New York, the Manfreds met with "Do Wah Diddy Diddy" writers Jeff Barry and Ellie Greenwich. In Manfred's opinion, this was the only highlight of their time in the States: "We did not enjoy the US tour, and we made no money. Touring conditions were awful in the early 1960's, and we were a long, long way from home."

Manfred gives his take on the early live shows: "At the beginning, we were a jazz/blues band and then we gradually changed. Manfred Mann was a good live band when it was just a blues band. In addition to the hits, 'Smokestack Lightning,' 'Got My Mojo Working,' 'Sack O' Woe,' 'Without You' and 'I'm Your Hoochie Coochie Man' were things we did live as a blues band, and they were very successful in those days. The second Manfred Mann in the mid-'60s (with Mike d'Abo) wasn't as good as the years went by, as it became more of a pop band. In fact, until Manfred Mann's Earth Band, the band with Paul Jones was the best live band."

After this taste of US live success, offers started to come in for further visits. Unlike their contemporaries, Manfred Mann declined to return to the US. They felt that the months required to fully develop themselves in the US could be better spent by concentrating on the global picture. In addition, the Manfreds knew that they would have to keep spending this time to maintain their exposure in the States. In the band's opinion, it was too great a risk, and they were fully prepared for a lower profile in the US as a result. Manfred Mann continued their TV appearances in England, Germany and throughout the world to keep themselves on view. Other countries they visited included Finland, New Zealand, Singapore and Hong Kong, and they were Britain's first pop group to perform behind the "iron curtain" in Czechoslovakia.

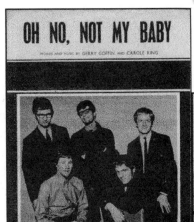

Consolidating Their Success

To build on their enormous success, the Manfreds looked to another female US R&B group, The Shirelles, as the source for their next single - "Sha La La." The Shirelles had a small degree of success in 1964 with the song, but Manfred Mann took it one step further. Another sing-along song, "Sha La La" illustrated the breezy pop that the band was masterful at. "Sha La La" was full of hooks: Manfred's piano duplicating Paul Jones' choruses, and the interaction during the breaks by Manfred and Mike Vickers. "Sha La La" was a UK #3 record, and did well in the US (a #12 placing). The record's B-side was "John Hardy," a tight performance of the Alan Lomax-discovered country blues song about a jealous man convicted of murder.

Since their formula was successful, Manfred Mann relied on outside material from Jones' record collection or song publishers for their single A-sides, but Manfred expressed why this was the case: "In the early '60s, I decided very early on that we weren't good enough songwriters. Even though I wasn't in charge then, I must have held some sway with the guys because most of the stuff we played we didn't write, and yet there were songwriters in the band." The band's original material then became readily available for B-sides and LP tracks.

Next up was another EP, "Groovin' It" and "Did You Have To Do That" fine harmonica and organ work by other hand, "Groovin'" was a blistering blues standard from the album "Apollo Hugg laid down the hot rhythm track vibes rebounded. This EP also included

With Manfred Mann." "Can't Believe were slow, simmering blues cuts with Jones and Mann respectively. On the jazz-oriented cover of the Ben E. King Saturday Night." McGuinness and off which vocals, piano, guitar and "Do Wah Diddy Diddy," which inevitably helped it reach its #3 peak on the British New Musical Express (NME) EP chart.

From late 1964 to early 1965, Manfred spent his free time producing sessions for The Yardbirds (both versions of Major Lance's "Sweet Music"), John Mantell, and the R&B outfit The Mark Leeman Five. On the Yardbirds track, Manfred played piano and Paul Jones sang backing vocals. Shortly after Manfred produced the "Portland Town" single for Mark Leeman's group, Leeman died in a car accident. The Mark Leeman Five continued after Leeman's death and the group's output has gained quite a lot of respectability in recent times.

HMV and Ascot started 1965 with their next single release - "Come Tomorrow." Again, the song was drawn from an American R&B source - Marie Knight's 1961 OKeh label single. Paul Jones' uplifting vocal performance on this enlightening song was endowed with a sensitive musical backing by the rest

of the band. The flip was "What Did I Do Wrong," a slow blues with nice vibes and sax solos. Apparently, the song was not taken seriously, since talking and laughing are going on throughout it! For their efforts, Manfred Mann was rewarded with a #4 UK hit, but only a #50 US placing. The effects of not touring the States began here, and the group would not return to the US hit parade in a big way until the next year.

With quite a lot of UK Manfred Mann hit records available in their homeland, Ascot in the States decided to release a compilation album of recent UK hit singles ("Hubble Bubble," "Sha La La" and "Come Tomorrow"), EP tracks and other material that had not been released on a US album. This February 1965 collection was confusingly dubbed "The Five Faces Of Manfred Mann." Of the new material, "Dashing Away With The Smoothing Iron" and "Watermelon Man" represented the jazz side of their talents and "She" illustrated their pop sensibilities. Despite its contents, the album peaked at a disappointing #141 position.[16]

Canadian "The Manfred Mann Return" LP

The way Paul Jones' vocal slid across "Dashing Away With The Smoothing Iron" exemplified how proficient he became in carrying off an original and humorous jazz-flavored tune, and Manfred's piano playing was also a highlight. The Manfred Mann treatment of Herbie Hancock's "Watermelon Man" also mixed this kind of humor with extremely tight jazz ensemble playing. Mongo Santamaria hit the US Top 10 with the song in 1963, but the Manfred Mann version was derived from the John Hendricks vocal version of the same vintage. Two performances to relish on "Watermelon Man" were Hugg's solid drumming and the way Mike Vickers' sax line mimicked Jones' vocal. "Watermelon Man" also appeared in the US first, but it soon surfaced on the UK "The One In The Middle" EP. "She" was another melodic but jazzy pop song, and its unavailability in the UK enabled British group Tony Rivers & The Castaways to record it as an unsuccessful single in 1965.[17]

For the German market, Paul Jones backing tracks of the songs "She" and now entitled "Sie" and "Weine Nicht" bottom sides of a German single. German, "Weine Nicht" was sung in a

recorded German vocals to the existing "Come Tomorrow." These versions, (Pretty Baby)," formed the top and While "Sie" was entirely recorded in combination of German and English.

The next 45, "Oh No Not My Baby," was issued the next month. This time, the song was a cover of a Maxine Brown single. "Oh No Not My Baby" made it to #11 in the UK, but Ascot opted for "I Can't Believe What You Say" b/w "Poison Ivy."[18] Again, Ascot's record was canceled before national release. "What Am I Doing Wrong," not be confused with "What Did I Do Wrong," was the underside of the British single and a breezy jazz/blues combination with an unusual fade-in introduction.

During 1965, Manfred Mann embarked on extensive tours with The Kinks and The Honeycombs. Some countries covered in these trips were Hong Kong, Singapore, Australia, New Zealand, France and Germany. Of these, the Manfreds were tremendously popular in Germany, and Manfred's overwhelming popularity there has continued to this day.

In the UK, Manfred Mann's headliner status was coupled on tours with fellow R&Bers The Yardbirds, and pop artists Bill Haley And His Comets, Jet Harris and Brenda Lee. On the shows with Haley, the Manfreds were embarrassed to find out that the Haley-oriented crowds found Haley more interesting than Manfred Mann! To avoid further problems, the two acts took turns headlining.

Another source of difficulty for Manfred Mann was their participation on the Burt Bacharach/ Hal David song "My Little Red Book (All I Do Is Talk About You)" for US single release and the "What's New Pussycat?" soundtrack LP. The band was never happy with the song, as Mike Hugg states: "We had a problem with recording that track. Burt Bacharach was very specific about the feel he wanted - all of his songs have got this very pronounced piano, and we found great difficulty in achieving that American feel. It was alien to us. We managed to get the basic feel, but I'm not sure about the piano track. First, Manfred played piano, then Burt Bacharach played piano, then Manfred and Burt played together. As a result, we don't look on that as a real Manfred Mann track, as that was just for the soundtrack."

Manfred's recollection of "My Little Red Book" is even less charitable: "The problem was me. Burt (Bacharach) wanted the chords (one to each beat) to be played with no accent whatsoever. I found this difficult, and ended up accentuating on '2' and '4.' Burt was terribly nice and should have just said, 'Let me do it,' but he slowly and tactfully edged me out, finally using the phrase: 'Manfred, why don't I play it, and you can tell me if it's O.K.?'"[19]

Despite the band's unhappiness with the results, the long player went up to #14 in the States. The single, however, did not even make the Top 100 (at #124). An edited version of "What Am I Doing Wrong" appeared as that record's B-side.[20]

original LP   reissue LP   first single release   second single release

THE ONE IN THE MIDDLE

WORDS & MUSIC BY PAUL JONES

RECORDED BY MANFRED MANN
ON H.M.V. POP

COOPER MUSIC LTD.
71, Denmark Street,
London, W.C.2

2/6

"The One In The Middle"

Success was coming on all fronts for the Manfreds, and UK HMV considered the band's next few EPs strong enough to have them compete on the <u>singles</u> chart. The first (and most successful) EP in this category was "The One In The Middle." This EP made #6 on the British NME singles listing, a feat that very few EPs of the time accomplished. "The One In The Middle" spent an amazing 38 weeks on the NME EP chart, nine of which at #1. The contents of the EP were equally impressive.

The title track was written by Paul Jones for Keith Relf, vocalist for The Yardbirds, to sing with his group. Jones was inspired to write the song after catching The Yardbirds at their most successful location, Richmond's Crawdaddy club. The female contingent in the Crawdaddy audience was enamored with Relf and expressed it vocally during the concert. Although Keith Relf was physically fronting the band, all of The Yardbirds presented themselves equally on stage. Because of this and Relf's unpretentious nature, the song was turned down. With some rewriting, Paul Jones took the opportunity to turn the song around so it referred to the Manfreds, but the most generous references were reserved for himself![21]

The EP also illustrated another trend that Manfred still relies on - a cover version of a Bob Dylan song. The EP's Bob Dylan tune was "With God On Our Side," a serious 4+ minute song about how people use God as justification for their evil deeds. This track, as well as the title recording, received quite a lot of TV exposure. Dylan's seven-minute version appeared on his album "The Times They Are A-Changin'."

Originally considered as the follow-up to "Come Tomorrow," the EP track "What Am I To Do" was a Phil Spector/ Doc Pomus pop song originally done by The Paris Sisters in 1962. Completing the EP was the aforementioned jazzer "Watermelon Man."

The Dylan Connection

original UK sheet music

Exactly what was Manfred Mann's connection with Bob Dylan? Well, it helped that their manager Kenneth Pitt just happened to be Bob Dylan's publicist in England. Therefore, this arrangement tremendously benefitted the Manfreds, as they potentially had the inside track on Dylan material in England.

The back cover of the EP "The One In The Middle" said that Dylan himself came to the Marquee in May 1964 to catch the band, and he stated that the band was "real groovy." Obviously, the feeling was mutual, as Hugg states: "We all liked and respected what Dylan was doing. We felt sort of an affinity with the material. It seemed that whenever we did his songs, it seemed to work out. The elements that went into those songs produced something worthwhile. <u>We</u> wish that we had written his songs!" Still, Dylan made it no secret that Manfred Mann's performances of his songs were the best.

The band's Dylan motif was continued when Bob's "If You Gotta Go, Go Now" was issued by HMV in September 1965. This song was a coup for the band, since Dylan's own version was not issued until an extremely rare Dutch single in 1967. The group composition "Stay Around" was the B-side in England, but Ascot felt that "The One In The Middle" would make a stronger flip. The record failed in the US, but "If You Gotta Go, Go Now" made it all the way to #2 in England - Manfred Mann's best showing since "Do Wah Diddy Diddy."[22] "Stay Around" was a slower jazz number with one of Manfred's patented piano/vocal breaks and a muted Hugg vibes solo.

Again, Manfred seized an opportunity by grabbing "If You Gotta Go, Go Now" at just the right moment, as he recounts: "Dylan did it in a concert. And what staggered me was the whole of Britain was interested in Bob Dylan; he was a great songwriter everybody knew. He did this song and <u>nobody</u> followed it up! I think it was Tom and I who discussed it and we then contacted the publishers and said, 'Can we have a copy?' and then we did it. And you would have thought with all these people looking for songs to record, there it is on television and nobody is paying any attention! So we did it. Lovely, lovely song."

Internal Conflict

The hits were coming in quickly, but the band was suffering from a lot of internal tension. Band members felt that they were losing their identity since they were now being identified as hitmakers under one name instead of the five eclectic musicians they actually were.

Nothing sums up the Manfreds' disappointment better than Manfred Mann's personal view: "One of the sadnesses about the band in the early stages was that we never managed (and this is something that's been a feature of me as well) to find commercial success with aspects of music that have appeared on albums. For some reason or other, it's been hard for me to find that commercial success, even though you can listen to an album and there's some really nice things on it. I really think 'The Five Faces Of Manfred Mann' is a really good album, as well as some of the B-sides we did, but we never managed, which The Rolling Stones could do, to somehow get the better of our stuff to be also the successful stuff. I'm not at all putting down what we did, as people always imagine, but the best stuff we did was not the hit records. We just were never able to bridge that gap, and that's been a feature of my recording all the time. The best stuff's been on albums and EPs and some of the singles have been very good, which is not to say that there isn't some very bad stuff on the albums. Generally, there's always been this dichotomy."

Mike Vickers had enough of this frustrating situation and gave in his notice in September 1965. His last recording session with the band was on the 13th of September, and he left the next month. Vickers finally actualized his dream of arranging, conducting and composing movie and TV themes.

In addition, Paul Jones was not happy with the "five faces of Manfred Mann" concept either, as he describes: "There was a degree of animosity going on. Mike Vickers made it easy for me because he handed in his notice in September 1965, and I said, 'Actually, while Mike's about it, I also want to go.' And they said, 'Well, you can't - there's a legal responsibility...' I said, 'All I'll do is stay until you find somebody else.' I didn't know they were going to take 11 months to find somebody else!"

Jones continues: "My main reason for leaving was that, here I was having all these hit records, and one by one they were being gradually notched up to someone called Manfred Mann, and I was not Manfred Mann!"

Jones was getting most of the attention, press and otherwise, so his decision to move on should not have been any surprise to the band. His unlimited enthusiasm and self-confidence made him one of the standout vocalists of the era. Besides, he had quite a lot of potential still to realize on his own. The immediate prediction of the time was that Manfred Mann was finished as a band without Jones, but Jones' reluctant agreement with the band neutralized any negative consequences.

The Rebuilding Process

After Jones' "going solo" announcement and promise to temporarily remain with the band were made in September 1965, some arrangements had to be made about replacing Vickers. Mann and Hugg's old friend Graham Bond recommended Jack Bruce, who went on to John Mayall's Bluesbreakers after leaving Bond's group. Bruce accepted the Manfred Mann gig, but he had to serve out his one-month notice with Mayall before he could join. During this period, Pete Burford and David Hyde served as interim bass players to satisfy Manfred Mann's live commitments, each player lasting for two weeks.

Jack Bruce was finally on board in December 1965, and to McGuinness' relief, Tom moved back to lead guitar! More changes were in store for the band, as a two-man horn section was added: Lyn Dobson (sax) and Henry Lowther (trumpet). Shades of The Mann-Hugg Blues Brothers! With this personnel change, Kenneth Pitt was removed of his managerial duties and was replaced by Gerry Bron.

Mann and Hugg were becoming bored with the pop rat race and their jazz tendencies were ready to materialize again with these new enlistments. Though all these musicians had solid jazz training, this lineup would only last for about four months.

During all of this personnel activity, some records made their way to record shops. The first of these was the US LP "My Little Red Book Of Winners!". This was Manfred Mann's third US album and

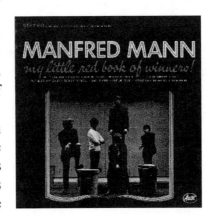

second compilation of scattered and some prized unreleased the unissued songs, they were One exception was the Mike For Me," repeated on the band's "My Little Red Book Of Gave Me Somebody To Love" appeared as a British single in originally recorded by the Dreamlovers. "Poison Ivy" was staple for British R&B groups Ascot single "I Can't Believe Ike And Tina Turner 1964 tracks from singles and EPs, material appeared as well. Of mainly strong R&B covers. Vickers composition, "You're next album "Mann Made." The Winners!" LP version of "You was different than the one that 1966, and the tune was American vocal group The the old Coasters tune, and a in the early '60s. The canceled What You Say," a cover of the chestnut, was another LP track that received a US preview before its UK release. Another cut, the Martha And The Vandellas gem "A Love Like Yours (Don't Come Knocking Every Day)" has still not appeared in the UK.

Next up was the only '60s Manfred Mann album whose contents were the same in the UK and US: "Mann Made." Using a similar formula as their debut LP, "Mann Made" was a wide-ranging collection of pop and R&B covers, with some originals and instrumentals mixed in. It was also a big seller in the UK, achieving a highest resting place of #7.[23]

US LP   Canadian LP

"As Long As I Have You," the third album by American R&B artist and labelmate Garnet Mimms (known for "Cry Baby") was the original source of two solid Manfreds covers on the album: "Look Away" and "I'll Make It Up To You." More pop-oriented songs came in the shape of "Since I Don't Have You" (originally by The Skyliners), "The Way You Do The Things You Do" (The Temptations' success) and the oft-covered "Hi Lili, Hi Lo,"[24] taken from the 1952 film "Lili," starring Leslie Caron. Jazz was well represented by "Watch Your Step" (the Bobby Parker hit) and the originals "The Abominable Snowmann" and "Bare Hugg" (original title: "D.D."), written by Vickers and Hugg respectively. On the blues side, Earl "Fatha" Hines' blues classic "Stormy Monday Blues" meshed well with an overwhelming version of the Ray Charles hit "You Don't Know Me." The band's blues compositions were Jones' mover "I Really Do Believe" and the McGuinness cut "L.S.D.," whose guitar figure was derived from Willie Dixon's "Wang Dang Doodle."

 After the success of their last EP, Manfred Mann released another one: "No Living Without Loving." HMV also promoted this September 1965 EP as a single, and it was a #1 EP for 7 weeks.[25] The record included the beautifully arranged and orchestrated "There's No Living Without Your Loving," covered less successfully by Peter And Gordon. A very unusual aspect of "There's No Living Without Your Loving" was its inclusion of female backing vocals by the UK Columbia recording act The Three Bells.[26]

promo single

The blues essentials "Let's Go Get Stoned" (an Ashford and Simpson composition first done by The Coasters) and "I Put A Spell On You" (the Screamin' Jay Hawkins classic) countered the all-out guitar attack of Paul Jones' "Tired Of Trying, Bored With Lying, Scared Of Dying." This was without question the heaviest rock song the early lineup recorded.

In January 1966, disaster struck when the car that the Manfreds were riding in was involved in an accident. Jones and Mann suffered serious injuries - a broken collarbone and severely bruised ribs, respectively. Manfred's hospital stay was brief, but Paul Jones' condition required a longer recuperation period. Without Jones to fulfill their recording plans, the rest of Manfred Mann concentrated on recording instrumentals until he recovered totally.

35

Before this accident, Manfred Mann era: "She Needs Company." It was a driving rhythm track, and the lyrics single people could really relate to. Company" only appeared as a US A- before its use on the later "Machines" Company" was Manfred Mann's last

had recorded a classic pop song of the perfect marriage of Jones' vocal and a described a rich/poor situation that Despite its strength, "She Needs side (backed with "Hi Lili, Hi Lo") EP in England.[27] "She Needs release on the US Ascot label, as the

band switched over to parent company United Artists for their next releases.

The most successful output from the augmented Manfred Mann lineup of the mid-'60s was "Pretty Flamingo." The song was a #1 smash in England and even brought the Manfreds back into the US Top 30 for the first time (at #29) since "Sha La La." For many, this swansong for the band was their finest hour, perhaps because everyone knew the finale was coming.[28] For the B-side of "Pretty Flamingo," the blues-oriented "You're Standing By"

used Lowther and Dobson effectively again, and the flute solo and violin chart were also reasons to recommend this flip side.

The band's final EP to reach #1 was also released at this point: "Machines." The unusual Mort Shuman title track[29] was packaged with the pop classics "Tennessee Waltz" (by Patti Page), The Everly Brothers' "When Will I Be Loved" and "She Needs Company." "When Will I Be Loved" later became the band's second and final single on United Artists, released after Jones left the group.

The wild and exciting outcome of Manfred Mann's short instrumental period (during Jones' hospitalization) was the "Instrumental Asylum" EP in June 1966, a #3 charting EP. The whacked-out jazz versions of recognizable 1965 hits ranged from Sonny And Cher's "I Got You Babe" to fellow British acts The Rolling Stones ("[I Can't Get No] Satisfaction"), The Yardbirds ("Still I'm Sad") and The Who ("My Generation"). Understandably, the EP put off quite a few pop fans who liked the original hit versions, but jazz fans had quite a lot of enjoyable playing to savor.

With the chart-topping success of "Pretty Flamingo" and the triumph of the recent EP added to his resume, Jack Bruce left Manfred Mann to form Cream with Eric Clapton and Ginger Baker.

Crisis Time

Mann and Hugg clearly had to take stock and decide on how to proceed, and both were not happy with EMI. Surprisingly, they discovered that this feeling was mutual, despite their many hits. In addition to locating a new vocalist and a new bass player, they had to obtain a new record deal quickly to maintain their popularity. HMV, perhaps feeling that the end was near, signed Paul Jones as a solo artist. Their feeling was that Jones would be the remaining creative and commercial force of the band. However, Manfred and Mike did not want to give it all up since they felt they still had more to prove musically. And, as in 1963, the brass section was eliminated, and Lowther and Dobson both went on to successful session stints.

To attack the vocalist problem first, Manfred and Mike decided to compile a list of vocalists to audition, regardless of their availability. Included in this list were Rod Stewart, Long John Baldry and Wayne Fontana, but the British popularity of these three made them hopelessly out of reach. After months passed, Manfred and Mike started getting more realistic about whom to approach for the vocalist slot. Eventually they spotted A Band Of Angels and their vocalist Michael d'Abo on the British TV program "A Whole Scene Going" doing the song "Invitation." The song "Invitation" was ignored commercially upon release in February 1966, but as Mike d'Abo tells it, "Little did I know it at the time, but actually that song ('Invitation') didn't fall on deaf ears when Manfred Mann were doing a TV appearance on a thing called 'A Whole Scene Going,' and we did that and apparently I got added to the list of possible replacement contenders for Mr. Jones, who'd got solo plans."

According to Mike Hugg, the Manfreds also caught d'Abo performing the same song on a "Radio Luxembourg" night at EMI. Manfred also remembers bringing Tom McGuinness along to see d'Abo at a Chelsea Town Hall gig. After some discussion and very few auditioned vocalists, lead singer/keyboardist Mike d'Abo became the new "one in the middle."

Paul Jones was literally left in the dark, as he tells it: "Nobody in the group would tell me anything. In fact, when we stopped to watch ourselves on television on the way to a gig somewhere and we saw A Band Of Angels doing that song ("Invitation"), I looked around the room at the rest of the guys in the group and they're all exchanging glances, I swear it. And, I thought, well, either they've also noticed that that bloke would be pretty good, or he's already in, or what's going on. I asked Tom McGuinness, who was sort of the person I communicated most with, I suppose, and nobody would say anything about what was happening."

The lack of communication between Jones and the rest of the band made for some interesting events, as Manfred describes: "I actually remember driving to our last gig with Paul when 'Just Like A Woman' was played on the radio - it was really awkward. We actually had our first single with d'Abo being played before the last gig with Paul was finished. No one said a word. At that time, there was a really bad vibe in the group. We felt that our whole career was over because of Paul's decision to leave. As it turned out, we were completely wrong about this."

With Mike d'Abo now in their ranks, things for Manfred Mann started to fall into place. Seasoned bass player Klaus Voorman (formerly of Paddy, Klaus And Gibson) also joined up. Voorman hung around with The Beatles in their Hamburg days and continued his ongoing connections with that band by designing their "Revolver" album cover. Another Voorman cover design was The Bee Gees' LP "1st," their debut album outside of Australia.

Manfred Mann signed to Fontana Records (Mercury Records in the US and Canada, and Philips in Australia), and on June 8, 1966, they recorded their first session with Mike d'Abo. Shel Talmy, known for his production work with The Kinks, The Who and many others, did the honors on Manfred Mann's early Fontana sessions.

When HMV discovered that Manfred Mann signed with Fontana, they scoured their tape archives to beat Fontana to the punch. And they succeeded, as the HMV single "You Gave Me Somebody To Love" preceded the debut Fontana disc "Just Like A Woman" by exactly four weeks. The song was recorded in 1965, and was far superior to the version released on the US "My Little Red Book Of Winners!" LP. Its superiority came from its female backing vocals (presumably also by The Three Bells) and its revised "wall of sound"-inspired production. During the summer of 1966, "You Gave Me Somebody To Love" b/w "Poison Ivy" hit #36 in the UK, a fair showing for an older track.

In the middle of this mayhem, Mike Hugg had placed his unrecorded song "You're A Better Man Than I" (co-written with his brother Brian) with The Yardbirds, who released it as the British B-side of their "Shapes Of Things" single.[30] The Manfred Mann/Mike Hugg composition "House On The Hill," another previously unrecorded Manfred Mann tune, was released as a single A-side by Lulu's former backing group, The Luvvers, in June 1966.

Meanwhile, United Artists felt that the success of "Pretty Flamingo" warranted the release of another Manfred Mann compilation album. The "Pretty Flamingo" LP was a collection of tracks from 45s, the "Machines" and "No Living Without Loving" EPs, and two new tracks: "Driva Man" (by jazzmen Oscar Brown Jr. and Max Roach) and the horn powered, group-written song "It's Getting Late." Additionally, the track "Did You Have To Do That" was repeated for apparently no reason. Following up (but not included) on this LP was the United Artists single release of the "Machines" EP track "When Will I Be Loved." "Did You Have To Do That" was this record's other side.

In September 1966, HMV's "Mann Made Hits" collection featured all of Manfred Mann's hits plus the unreleased instrumental "Spirit Feel." "Spirit Feel" was another hot jazz piece plucked from John Hendricks' repertoire. In short order, "Mann Made Hits" (which acknowledged Jones' departure and potential as a solo act through its cover billing of "Manfred

Mann with Paul Jones") made it to #11. HMV also cashed in with the "As Was" EP, a collection of previously unreleased tracks in the UK. The US premiere tracks "I Can't Believe What You Say," "Driva Man" and "It's Getting Late" appeared here with the Jeff Barry/Ellie Greenwich pop composition "That's All I Ever Want From You Baby."

Canadian "Soul Of Mann" LP   US LP   Canadian LP

Two more cash-ins completed this phase of the band's career: United Artists' "Manfred Mann's Greatest Hits" and HMV's "Soul Of Mann" compilation. The former was a cross-section of the Manfreds' US hits with some EP and LP tracks mixed in, while the latter was identified as a collection of instrumentals (except "L.S.D." - a vocal!) spread evenly throughout the band's HMV career. Sales for these albums were not spectacular, with only "Soul Of Mann" charting, a solitary week at #40. "Soul Of Mann,"[31] issued in January 1967, included the entire "Instrumental Asylum" EP and two further unreleased instrumentals: "Tengo, Tango" and "God Rest Ye Merry Gentlemenn." As expected, "Tengo, Tango," the Cannonball Adderley tune, was done by the Bruce/Lowther/Dobson lineup in an outstanding jazz tango arrangement. The 1965 recording "God Rest Ye Merry Gentlemenn" was the traditional Christmas song arranged in a jazz style by Mann, Vickers and Hugg similar to that used by The Modern Jazz Quartet a few years before.

The Mike d'Abo (Fontana) Era - Chapter Two

On the Hit Track Again

With all of their difficulties now aside, Manfred Mann could now get down to making hit records again. Manfred Mann had been recording with Mike d'Abo since early June 1966, but the official departure of Paul Jones did not take place until that August. Jones then tallied up two major solo hits: 1966's "High Time" and "I've Been A Bad Bad Boy" (1967). The latter appeared in "Privilege," a film in which Jones had the lead role.

In late July 1966, Fontana's first Manfred Mann single was issued, the Bob Dylan "Blonde On Blonde" tune "Just Like A Woman." Mike Hugg looks back on the song as a safe choice for the band, but Manfred has always disagreed with this. In any event, they were unsure about how they were going to be perceived in their new guise. Manfred certainly felt the heat: "The release of 'Just Like A Woman' was the most stressful event in my whole musical career. At the beginning, the record was not being played, and I was in a really bad state over it."

Through Tom McGuinness' guitar tremolo effects, the band's treatment of "Just Like A Woman" was a very commercial and pop-oriented one. This enabled them to just break the UK Top 10. In the US, the single just missed the singles chart at #101, but the band was happy with the results and picked up enthusiasm. The B-side of this record was "I Wanna Be Rich," d'Abo's hummable tune about his overwhelming desire of money and his plans for spending his untold wealth!

"Just Like A Woman" was another in Manfred's long line of successful Dylan covers, and Manfred expressed why the band's treatments worked so well: "We never tried to do Dylan's songs in his style or in that sort of way, and we would change things if we didn't like them! I remember somebody saying to me with 'Just Like A Woman,' - 'You can't change Dylan!,' and I just said, 'Well, watch us!' We took the middle of the song out because he was singing about amphetamines, and actually it was a very nice bridge. But, I figured out that somebody was going to ban that on the radio, and I didn't want to make a record that wasn't going to get played. We took stuff out, we changed things, we did them in a different style if we wanted to, and maybe that's why they succeeded."

With the addition of d'Abo, all of a sudden, the whole band sang! Manfred and Hugg, practically silent before, could now be heard on backing vocals on selected tracks. McGuinness also contributed more vocally, and Klaus Voorman was very helpful in vocal arrangements. While they did not sound that different at first, the Manfred Mann group on Fontana was a completely different band with different influences using different equipment.

A further addition to the band was Manfred's acquisition of a mellotron, the wonder instrument of the sixties that accomplished the amazing feat of reproducing string effects without the cumbersome and expensive hiring of an orchestra. Manfred used the mellotron on every opportunity that presented itself, including the jazz number "Autumn Leaves" (it's odd but it works amazingly!). Manfred's playing also changed, since his R&B/jazz style was augmented by a pumping 4/4 keyboard rhythm on mellotron and organ. This additional style gave the band's pop songs the necessary drive to carry them over the top. After 1969, the mellotron had pretty much worn out its welcome and Manfred retired it.

In France, where the 4-track EP was the standard form for 45RPM records, the "Just Like A Woman" EP was released. In addition to both sides of the title single, the EP featured the orchestrated "Let It Be Me," which was a hit for The Everly Brothers in 1960 and Betty Everett and Jerry Butler four years later. This song has not been reissued anywhere. Also among the EP's ranks was "Trouble And Tea,"[32] a d'Abo tune that modified the guitar riff from The Beatles' "Day Tripper."

The song "Semi-Detached Suburban Mr. James" made its way to shops in October 1966. Written by popular songwriter and New Vaudeville Band mastermind Geoff Stephens with partner John Carter, "Semi-Detached" was a #2 smash. However, it was roundly ignored in the US, and Mercury Records had great difficulty presenting the song's title properly on their record! On the record, Manfred's mellotron produced a horn effect that made the song very catchy.[33] The tune's original title was "Semi-Detached Suburban Mr. Jones," and to illustrate that the Manfreds meant no harm, its name was modified to avoid any backlash by Paul Jones. In fact, the '90s touring Manfreds (which <u>do not</u> include Manfred himself) have expressed this point frequently in their recent concerts. On recent Manfreds performances of this song, both Jones and d'Abo join in the fun, so no bridges have been burned here!

On the B-side in England was "Morning After The Party," a humorous song about the drunken aftereffects of a party. In North America and Australia, the perfect pop song "Each And Every Day" was the underside. Manfred's mellotron and horn effects accompanied this very memorable song, also a popular cover tune.[34]

Recorded by THE MANFRED MANN GROUP on MERCURY 72770

MIGHTY QUINN
(QUINN THE ESKIMO)
Words and Music by BOB DYLAN

Published by
BOB DYLAN WORDS AND MUSIC, INC.

75¢

Distributed by

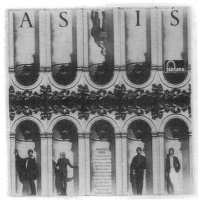

"alcove" cover

"As Is"

rare "locomotive" cover

Coincidental with the "Semi-Detached Suburban Mr. James" single was Fontana's distribution of Manfred Mann's "As Is" LP.[35] Also including the hit single "Just Like A Woman" and the previous B-side "Morning After The Party," the album was another eclectic mix of song styles. However, "As Is" marked a heavy decline in album sales for the band, with only a #22 peak in the charts. Other than "Just Like A Woman," the collection's contents remain unavailable in the US. As further promotion, two of the album's tracks formed a single in Sweden: "You're My Girl" and "Box Office Draw." The former had a haunting backing track, but it was hampered by double-tracked lead vocals, both of which were imprecise. "Box Office Draw" was the more successful side and described the rapid rise and fall of a stage performer. To promote this special single, the band even made a European TV appearance.

"As Is" still presented the R&B side of the group, although in different styles. "Dealer Dealer" was a gritty blues about a card-playing gambler, but unfortunately half of the backing vocals on this song were not used since they contained mistakes. The Ray Charles-styled "As Long As I Have Lovin'" had hot vibes and keyboard charts, and the song "Superstitious Guy" was more of a pop/R&B hybrid.

More than ever, pop abounded on the record. "Each Other's Company" was another brilliant example of this style, as was "A Now And Then Thing," a tender ballad starting with a d'Abo *a cappella* section before being joined by Manfred's mellotron.

The song that defied any categorization was "Another Kind Of Music." Its introduction was an outtake from an unspecified session, and its middle section alternated between pop and mock-operatic choruses. The end of the song was a snatch of the unreleased Voorman guitar solo "Acoustic Guitar Instrumental."

The jazz department was represented by the 1955 Roger Williams classic "Autumn Leaves." One of the band's most scorching jazz performances, the session pitted Dave Richmond's reappearance on string bass against piano solos, organ, mellotron, and jazz rimshots.

Other Directions

Keeping in the jazz vein, the band retained Dave Richmond for the UK-only "Instrumental Assassination" EP. Basically a side project without any d'Abo involvement, the EP was a slice of hysteria with wild versions of the Troggs hits "Wild Thing" and "With A Girl Like You," Bobby Hebb's "Sunny" and the Georgie Fame success "Get-Away." Just for this record, Klaus Voorman put down his bass for a recorder. "Instrumental Assassination" sold very poorly, and alienated even more people than the previous "Instrumental Asylum" EP. Luckily for the band, their fans had short memories!

The band tapped Tony Hazzard's songwriting talents for their next single in March 1967, the #4 hit "Ha! Ha! Said The Clown." Despite its strong pop nature and hooks (that driving keyboard again!), the song proved to be another hard one to put together, with edits galore.[36] Manfred describes his contributions to the song and how the band discovered it: "We would have got a demo. I remember it very clearly, it was from Tony Hazzard, and I didn't like the song at all and didn't want to do it. But Lillian Bron (then wife of manager Gerry Bron) kept going on and on and on, and in the end I thought, 'Well, perhaps it's better than it seems.' So we did it. I didn't want to do it at first. Mellotron, if you talk about the '60s, that was new then. So we used mellotron all the time. The flute sounds, and the trombone and string sounds in the middle (bam, bam, bam) were all mellotron. Yeah, it was a nice instrument. In fact, I think ours was the first use of mellotron (on record), before The Moody Blues."[37]

This is an important point, especially since the success of the mellotron-friendly LP "As Is" and the "Ha! Ha! Said The Clown" single definitely predated the September 1967 breakthrough of The Moody Blues' "Days Of Future Past" LP. However, The Moody Blues' use of the mellotron has received more notoriety since its use was directly related to the massive success of that band's albums, and Manfred Mann's mellotron success and publicity was mainly limited to singles.

Since "Ha! Ha! Said The Clown" was a complete failure in the US, The Yardbirds recorded it solely for US single release. The Yardbirds ended up with a #45 chart record for their efforts. The flip of Manfred Mann's single version, "Feeling So Good," was an experiment with Mann and Hugg on lead vocals. Tom McGuinness' lead guitar tore through the mix, and Voorman provided low vocals and the laughing on the song's introduction. This experiment was not repeated.

The French "Ha! Ha! Said The Clown" EP took both sides of the single, the US B-side "Each And Every Day" and another track exclusive to France: "All I Want To Do." This featured a rare Hugg vocal along with his vibes and Voorman's excellent backup vocals, most of which were not used in the final mix.

French EP

Swedish 7"

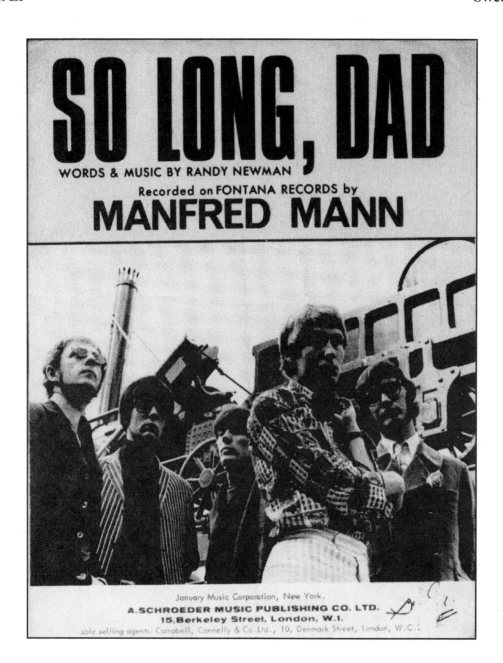

Difficulties

Many instrumentals were being recorded, and two of them, "Sweet Pea" (the Tommy Roe hit) and the group-written "One Way," formed the next single in May 1967. This single was chosen by Fontana, as the band did not want these tracks released as a follow-up to "Ha! Ha! Said The Clown." The band was proven to be correct, since this single only hit #36 and resulted in a loss of momentum. Again, "Sweet Pea" had to rely on editing to make it happen.[38] "One Way," on the other hand, was a complete and strong jazz performance. Solos from Hugg on piano and Manfred on organ made "One Way" another fine instrumental, and a McGuinness guitar solo took the song to its conclusion. This record was also not released in the US.

The problems that the band was having with their recordings were not related to playing difficulties - the arrangements themselves were becoming more complicated. More tracks were required to produce each song, and the result of this work sounded very full. Sometimes it proved to be too full, and editing was needed to save and sequence the best moments to make the strongest, most cohesive performance.

The Formula

Starting from this point, the band's perfected vocal trademark included extremely memorable d'Abo leads and overlapped, multi-layered backing vocals. Nearly all of Manfred Mann's later Fontana output used this formula, which matched catchy pop melodies with Manfred's forceful keyboard playing.

"So Long, Dad" became release in the late summer of rising composer Randy UK success of Alan Price's take Amazing Dancing Bear." To Long, Dad" missed the chart since "Cock-A-Hoop" that one dubious honor.

Manfred Mann's next British 1967. The song was written by Newman, enjoying the Top 10 on his "Simon Smith And His Manfred Mann's surprise, "So entirely! This was the first time of their 45s claimed this

"So Long, Dad" certainly had keyboards (tack piano, organ, surrounding d'Abo's humorous

its strong points, with plenty of harpsichord and mellotron) lead vocals and strong sing-along choruses. The unfortunate part was that the recording went through three poorly mixed recording stages and ended up sounding very tinny. While the late Denny Cordell was supposed to produce the record and received credit on the record for doing so, the record was actually produced by Cordell's underling, the Brooklyn, New York-born Tony Visconti.[39] Since Cordell was unavailable, the Manfreds were unhappy with this arrangement and the results bore this out. While the record was tailor-made for listening on a transistor radio, home enjoyment proved to be unsatisfying.[40]

To most fans, the band-composed flip, "Funniest Gig," was the favored side. "Funniest Gig" was as psychedelic as the band got, with swirling d'Abo vocals and tape loops of "Ha! Ha! Said The Clown" and "So Long, Dad" floating around dreamy keyboards, vibes, recorder, bells and Hugg's use of brushes on the drums.[41]

After the failure of "So Long, Dad," the band took a two-month break in recording from the end of August 1967 to the end of October. During this time, Mann and Hugg spent some of their free time looking ahead and they started dabbling in songwriting for TV commercials. This phase of their career, which ran parallel with their band activities, continued into the early '70s and is described in the next chapter.

Mike d'Abo notched up his first major songwriting success with a song he placed outside of the Manfred Mann camp - "Handbags And Gladrags." Chris Farlowe had British Top 40 success with the song, and more recently, the song has been associated with Rod Stewart.

To hold Dutch fans over until the next Manfred Mann release, Fontana released a compilation of previously released material entitled "One Way." This album included the entire "Instrumental Assassination" EP and many Fontana singles tracks up to that point. The album did not sell particularly well, but is interesting nevertheless.[42]

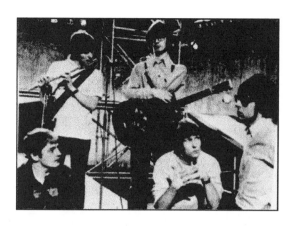

"Mighty Quinn"

Manfred Mann was on the downswing commercially, and help was needed immediately. Again, Manfred got hold of an unreleased Bob Dylan song, the "Basement Tapes" era song "Mighty Quinn" (also known as "Quinn The Eskimo," "The Mighty Quinn" or a combination of the two). As with Manfred Mann's biggest hits, it was a chore for the band to assemble the song in November 1967. Mike Hugg fills us in on what happened: "We had a lot of problems with 'Mighty Quinn.' We just couldn't finish it. We kept going back into the studio to try different things. It took us ages to get it right, but it was very worthwhile. It gave the band a new injection of life, not just in terms of being a hit, but it was a bit more on the playing side - it wasn't just a pop record."

However, Manfred reveals that it was even more involved than what Hugg described: "When we first recorded the backing track (to 'Mighty Quinn'), I was convinced it would be a hit record, but when we did the first mix, I listened to it at home and rejected it. The others just accepted my rejection. Several months later, Mike d'Abo called me and said that he'd played an acetate (rough pressing) of it to Lou Reisner of United Artists, who was convinced it would be successful. I reiterated what I felt. d'Abo said that he agreed with Reisner and asked for everyone to go to his house to listen to it. When it was played at Michael's house, it sounded very good, and I felt pretty foolish. I just couldn't believe that I could have made such a mistake. Then I asked Michael whether his turntable could have been running fast, and we checked and found that his record turntable was running a semi-tone fast. We then went into the studio and did the work that Mike Hugg referred to. We speeded up the record a semi-tone for release."

During the early stages of "Mighty Quinn"'s life, the song's arrangement was very simple. After a couple of trips to the studio, a Klaus Voorman recorder track was placed at the beginning of the song, and then the rest of the song was pieced on afterwards. While Hugg's drum overdubs provided an irresistible hook, what is unclear in the final mix is how well d'Abo's double-tracked vocals and the band's vocal backup flowed with the strong organ and piano chording.[43]

Above: The six US label variations of the "Mighty Quinn" single

"Mighty Quinn" was released in England in January 1968, and it put the band back on the map in England, rising to #1 in short order. In the US, the song also rose very quickly, reaching #10 on the singles listings. This was their best showing since "Do Wah Diddy Diddy."[44] After "Mighty Quinn" took over in the US, Manfred received an offer to tour the States in mid-April 1968, but he turned the deal down.

For a #1 record, what was even more shocking was its B-side - "By Request - Edwin Garvey." This hilarious and deliriously bad song was the first instance of d'Abo's alter ego, Edwin Garvey, singing in a 1920s style "vo-de-o-do" nasal voice. If anything, the song prepared Manfred Mann fans for a Garvey onslaught - something they had to deal with, whether they liked it or not!

Soundtracks

An ambitious project was on tap next - the soundtrack to the Paramount film "Up The Junction," with the junction being that of London's Clapham Junction. With unspecified assistance from former member Mike Vickers, the music that Mann and Hugg composed for the film was written entirely in a studio environment without viewing the picture. Being a recording made specifically for a film soundtrack, Manfred and Mike felt that the material was not to be used for any other purpose - including the issuance of singles. Fontana Records thought otherwise and released the edited "Theme - Up The Junction" as a single anyway. With very little interest in the music or film trades, the film, album and single all died very quick deaths.

As for the "Up The Junction" album itself, it was a daring blend of styles and tape effects (backwards and otherwise) which extended the boundaries of the concept set forth by the song "Funniest Gig."[45] The title song, about the mad dash of a commuter traveling to work, was recorded in five different ways. The vocal A-side version had another rare Hugg lead vocal, shared this time with Mike d'Abo. The song was also presented in two fiery jazz takes (one with a backwards piano tape), and another that featured a lovely McGuinness wah-wah guitar solo leading to sweeping tape loops of the main title theme and the pop song "Walking Round." The fifth version, which was the most psychedelic of the lot, is still in the vaults.

The orchestrated instrumental Love Theme" was cut twice for the album, and the jumpy jazz numbers "Sheila's Dance," "Belgravia" and "I Need Your Love" captured Klaus Voorman's fretless bass playing in full flight with Manfred's piano solos. The relaxed "Just For Me" and Hugg-vocalized "Sing Songs Of Love" also worked extremely well. On the other hand, the poorly edited and dissonant "Wailing Horn" could not stand up on its own without the assistance of viewing the film.

Also recorded at the album session was Up The Junction"'s other side, "Sleepy Hollow."[46] This simmering Tom McGuinness jazz/blues original was inexplicably excluded from the album. In addition to its unavailability on album, the unique Edwin Garvey makes a cameo appearance near the end of the song!

Another obscure songwriting Hugg at the time was the song custom single pressing by Dutch Group. The February 1968 single versions of "Jolita" was only issued Fontana attempted to keep interest failure of "Up The Junction" by "What A Mann," an album similar project for Manfred Mann and Mike "Jolita," recorded and released for a R&B legend Rob Hoeke's R & B featuring instrumental and vocal in Holland. Meanwhile, UK in Manfred Mann going after the issuing the unsuccessful collection to the Dutch "One Way" LP.[47]

Manfred and the band kept busy meanwhile by recording the title track for the obscure picture and soundtrack album "The Charge Of The Light Brigade." The song was Tennyson's poem of the same name set to music. Even though the song is definitely played by Manfred Mann, Manfred and Mike Hugg do not even remember it! Manfred himself got involved with another unreleased Dylan song, this time producing Zimmerman's "You Ain't Goin' Nowhere" and its Byrds spoof B-side "So You Want To Be A Blues-Player" for fellow popsters Unit 4+2.

The Manfreds' next single also came from a film, but their version was not the one that appeared on celluloid. The film was "You Are What You Eat" and Manfred Mann covered the song "My Name Is Jack." The writer of the song, John Simon, performed it for the film. "My Name Is Jack" was a humorous storytelling song about a wayward boy, adorned with a fun arrangement. British fans also appreciated its humor by bringing it to #8 on the singles chart. In the US, its #104 sales peak was not impressive at all, and the song's lyric "here comes Superspade" was replaced by "here comes Superman" to avoid any flare-ups of the racial unrest present in 1968. The record's flip was a very strange and droll Tom McGuinness song, "There Is A Man." This song was the story of a child who imagines a man doing strange things, and was a melange of jazz and spoken/sung pieces.

"Mighty Garvey!"

With the success of "Mighty Quinn" still fresh in people's minds, US Mercury and Fontana in England wanted to incorporate the hit on an LP. The albums they issued, "The Mighty Quinn" (US/Canadian Mercury, Australian Philips) and "Mighty Garvey!" (UK Fontana), featured this hit, and "Ha! Ha! Said The Clown" and "Each And Every Day" (making its first UK appearance). Otherwise, the two collections had very similar contents. The main difference between them was that only the US LP included "Semi-Detached Suburban Mr. James" and the British album featured four exclusive tracks, "Harry The One-Man-Band" and three different versions of the Edwin Garvey masterpiece, "Happy Families."[48] Still, neither album sold well, with the US collection making it to only #176 and the UK disc failing to chart entirely.

Both albums were full of fine pop songs: "The Vicar's Daughter," "Everyday Another Hair Turns Grey," "It's So Easy Falling," "No Better No Worse" and Tom McGuinness' contribution, "Cubist Town." Mike Hugg's harpsichord playing on his "Everyday Another Hair Turns Grey" provided a perfect match for the band's layered vocal blend,[49] and "The Vicar's Daughter" was Mike d'Abo's tune of wondering about what happened to his first love.[50]

Other songs had more wide-ranging influences. "Big Betty" (also known as "Black Betty") was a Leadbelly (aka Huddie Ledbetter) blues turned into a rocker, and the gypsy-influenced "Country Dancing" was a positive step in another direction for the band. On the other hand, "Harry The One-Man-Band" was a track with a long history. Stretching over sessions from 1966 to 1968, "Harry" was a song about a man that is down on his luck. It was pieced together from the best parts of these sessions, which included vocal goofing near the song's end.

The Mike d'Abo written/Edwin Garvey-sung showcase "Happy Families" was recorded under three different guises: a rock version (by Eddie "Fingers" Garvey), a jazz version (shown as Ed. Garvey & The Trio) and a sing-a-long pub song (by Edwin O'Garvey And His Showband). The first one was a rocking number, with blazing piano and a snatch of "Yakety Yak" thrown in for good measure. Recording for this version started in late 1966 and was not resumed until 1968. The jazz take featured standard and scat vocals, Garvey wisecracks and a spoken introduction leading into "Mighty Quinn." Unbelievably, Edwin O'Garvey And His Showband recorded and finished their version in 1966! On this one, the nasal Garvey invited his audience to "take a limp down memory lane."[51]

When I asked about who Garvey was, Manfred answered: "He was just a mythical character that we made up. It was just a joke. d'Abo played the role of Garvey. We were going to do Ravi Garvey, a sort of Indian one, Mento' Garvey (Mantovani) . . . it was just fun at the time." Exactly!

The Home Stretch

In October 1968, the band could be found touring Vienna, Austria with fellow labelmates The Rattles. At this stage of Manfred Mann's history, Hughie Flint was providing percussion for the band. Flint would figure prominently in Tom McGuinness' future.

Fontana closed out 1968 with the release of an experiment: the cassette EP. Two cassettes were released, one solely with Manfred Mann hits and another that shared Manfreds successes with hit 45s by Dave Dee, Dozy, Beaky, Mick & Tich.

Tony Hazzard came to the rescue again for the Manfreds' next single. The Manfred's organ made "Fox On The Mike Hugg's B-side "Too Many lyrical and musical message. Hugg and d'Abo's lead this time, and the second toned McGuinness note run with nice  by contributing his "Fox On The Run" band's strong layered vocals and Run" another top-notch performance. People" was another song with a strong Mann provided backing vocals to half of the song featured a heavy fuzz-keyboard accompaniment.[52]

 For nearly all of their past releases, the band could rely on each of their singles hitting the UK singles chart the week after its release. Since "Fox On The Run" was released on November 29, 1968, the band was expecting it to chart in the next available issue on the 11th of December. They were following up a major hit, so the Manfreds got very worried when they did not see their record among the Top 50. Even when the record finally charted the next week, it was not as high as they had expected. In fact, "Fox On The Run" was their slowest moving single, and it was not until early 1969 that it really took off and reached #5. In the US, the disc only made #97 and became their final charting single. The public reaction to "Fox On The Run" made Manfred and company think a lot about their future.

This thinking resulted in an article in the February 15, 1969 issue of Disc Magazine that said that Manfred Mann would not play live again in England. Also, Mike d'Abo signed up with the Immediate record label and released a solo single that same week - "(See The Little People) Gulliver's Travels." This double-barrel attack hit fans hard, but even the most casual Manfred Mann observer could see the final curtain ahead.

Fontana tried to cover up the situation by successfully having the d'Abo single recalled, claiming that d'Abo was still exclusively signed to Fontana as a recording member of Manfred Mann. This move and the release of what was to be the Manfreds' last single, "Ragamuffin Man," were only temporary fixes and fans were not fooled.

 When "Ragamuffin Man" made it into UK shops on April 18, 1969, the band was over, although the official announcement would not appear until June. "Ragamuffin Man" was another fine pop song from the pens of noted hitmakers Mitch Murray and Peter Callander, and successfully closed the Manfred Mann UK hit book with a #8 peak position.[53]

"Ragamuffin Man" was the band's last use of their successful formula: potent multiple vocals and a powerful keyboard punch. It was unfortunate that the band was not crazy at all about the song, but their fans were very satisfied.

Manfred reveals the reasoning behind the band's choice of "Ragamuffin Man" as their swansong: "It was me, again to my discredit, rather than credit, saying that 'Gee, this is going to be a hit record,' but really it was just a little, cute, silly song. It was the last record we had. We decided after that, Mike and I, before we formed Chapter Three, that this was not what our musical life was about, and it really was boring. The public was bored with us, but they liked the records and people were buying them, but there was no sense of excitement any longer. I think that all of us were more capable in all different ways. Again, we weren't playing live anymore and we just decided to quit."

The single's bottom side, appropriately named "A 'B' Side," was a 5+ minute Mike Hugg-vocalized smoky blues with strong note runs and solos by Tom and Manfred. Even a backwards organ tape was used - a precursor to Manfred's backwards tape use on later Manfred Mann's Earth Band records. Further exposure for "A 'B' Side" took place when it became the theme for a Mannikin Cigars commercial on TV, providing Mann and Hugg an excellent segue into their next ventures.

End of an Era

When Manfred Mann broke up, they accomplished something that very few bands accomplish at the end of their lifetimes - they ended with a big hit. They were on top, and that is how they wanted to be remembered. By going out in this way, the name Manfred Mann has remained in high esteem by '60s music fans everywhere.

Unlike their British contemporaries, Manfred Mann was not pure pop or guitar-oriented; they were instrumentally proficient and vocally balanced, thanks to their jazz leanings. One thing that they noticed very early in their career was that jazz was always in style, but jazz had to be carefully handled. Manfred gives his feelings on this issue: "On listening back, I feel that the jazz influence was very good when it was mixed with R&B. But when it was played as 'jazz' on its own, I think it was second rate or tenth rate."

In the Jones era, the gentle friction between the jazz and R&B factions within the band drove their inventiveness. Unlike the Jones-led HMV recordings, Manfred can be heard counting off nearly every Fontana session take. Still, during the Fontana period, Manfred and Mike Hugg had a greater sense of the band's musical direction than their band mates. No one agrees with this more than Manfred: "There never was any serious friction, blues versus jazz, that I can remember. Both groups had a huge respect for each other, and we learnt from each other. I never had any control of the '60s groups; any influence I had was by general consensus and consent. The consensus was also that I would be the catalyst and motivator."

To sum it up, the Manfred Mann group took a unique musical path and succeeded by fusing their topnotch arrangement and playing skills to ignite mainly outside material. In fact, the songs they made famous have seldomly been covered successfully by other artists, and the same also applies to covers of original Manfreds material.[54] Unquestionably, Manfred Mann's recordings, whether original or not, have distinguished themselves in their own ways.

Mike Hugg expresses the success of Manfred Mann in this way: "It wasn't an individual thing. We found a formula which you can't write down and put into words, but when the musicians involved got together on one side, we managed to have a hit come out the other end. We all came into the business as musicians, either from the jazz side or the blues side. We never did it to make a killing. Where we ended up was a surprise to all of us! It wasn't where we originally aimed our careers at all. We never considered copying anything. If we couldn't do something our way, we wouldn't contemplate doing it."

Manfred agrees heartily with Hugg on his point: "The blues influence came from the other guys, but the jazz thing came from Mike and I. I gradually turned into a pop musician, but that was the way of surviving. I think some of the first album is very good for the time . . . and the other records do stand up."

In addition, Manfred felt that it was the playing atmosphere that was responsible for the band's production of such consistently high quality records: "The main difference between '60s and '70s music was technology. In the '60s, everybody had to play at the same time - there was no way around it, and the spirit in the music came from that, if you could play your instrument and all play together. So, whatever came out on tape was a collective event. When you get to the '70s, you all played together but you could replace whatever you wanted, and so the concept of live playing was still there but you could overdub. Something went with that, even though something else came. Nowadays, people think playing live is playing your instrument - the rest of it is using machines."

Still, with more hits than most groups could dream of, Manfred himself was not happy. Manfred's unhappiness was not due to his attitude, as he has tried to put his realism and the working conditions that existed in the sixties in focus: "A lot of the time, the music scene hadn't grown up and concert promoters didn't know what they were doing. Musicians were treated as cattle, as commodities, by record companies and promoters. I personally found that around about the '70s, it finally seemed like a proper business. A musician was treated as an artist, both in the way he was being paid and the way he was treated by people. I didn't personally enjoy the '60s period very much, that not in any way to denigrate it musically in any sense, or that it had a great impact on a lot of people in the way they thought, and the kind of music they listened to and developed into, and the influence it had. It's just that I personally wasn't that happy at that time. In the '70s, when I toured the States, all the guys in radio were the people that loved rock 'n' roll. It was a totally different kind of scene. To me, it was much nicer than the people I used to meet in the '60s."

"I was away from home a lot. I was touring around a lot in situations that weren't as good as they were later. Everyone looks back to the 'good old days,' and I think to myself, 'Perhaps, there's something wrong with me because I'm so realistic that I don't look at it with rose colored spectacles at all. I look at exactly what happened. Perhaps it's that, that I don't look back in that sense. I don't look back at school days as the best days of my life or anything like that. I find today is a pretty good day and I'm enjoying myself. I don't always look back with nostalgia, so it may be that as much as anything."

One could ask if the group could have turned out any other way. Probably not, unless Mann and Hugg started from scratch, and wasting the abundance of talent already in their ranks would have been foolish. Tom McGuinness always proved to be a strong asset in all aspects of the band's output, and Klaus Voorman was very adept on bass and recorder, and was extremely adaptable.

In a time when "far-out" was in, '60s music had to stretch boundaries to compete in the marketplace. Within the pop spectrum, Manfred Mann skillfully succeeded on this level by creating music that required the listener's full attention. When further recordings were required from the band, they took these opportunities to exorcize whatever jazz demons they had inside them. Besides, they did their best to avoid the whole drug-influenced arena, so they were fully aware of their limitations, musical and otherwise.

Fast, aggressive R&B was not Mike d'Abo's strong suit, but he shined on slower cuts. In McGuinness, Manfred Mann had a guitar player who basked in '60s blues and jazz contexts. This attitude was unlike that of flashy guitarists like The Yardbirds' triumvirate: Eric Clapton, Jeff Beck and Jimmy Page. Flashes of McGuinness' brilliance are evident from time to time, especially on the 1968-1969 recordings. Another example is the unreleased fifth version of "Up The Junction," on which Tom's Eric Clapton-inspired fuzz tones clearly marked his tremendous growth from December 1963. McGuinness' playing today encompasses all these talents and much more.

Therefore, as a result, Manfred Mann could not go completely psychedelic or hard rock. By carefully touching on (but not converting to) these '60s musical trends, which would have been very difficult for a band who had already accomplished jazz to blues to pop crossovers, Manfred Mann was able to survive from 1962 to 1969.

Another thing that affected the band was their total attitude. By examining the HMV and Fontana session tapes, the prevailing atmosphere on the Fontana recordings is clearly more relaxed. On selected tracks, Mann and Hugg can be found playing Les Paul and Mary Ford's hit "How High The Moon" and a certain member who shall remain nameless can be heard belching just before serious takes! What was the output of these relaxed Fontana sessions? On the whole, the released Fontana performances are not as precise or clean sounding, and more editing was needed to make the songs work. Examining the raw Fontana multi-track tapes, the sound was almost equal to the HMV period. From this evidence, it appears that the band was done an injustice from an audio perspective. However, since their records were made for radio play, which had no great audio demands at the time, such sound quality concerns were not as important as they are today.

The Recording Process

During the EMI years, John Burgess would follow standard EMI operating procedures in recording the band: if the recording artist could not successfully complete an entire recording, a composite version of two compatible takes would be created. In Manfred Mann's case, five of the most popular album tracks from "The Five Faces Of Manfred Mann" were put together in this way: "Sack O' Woe" (an edit of takes 5 and 2), "Smokestack Lightning" (takes 3 and 1), "It's Gonna Work Out Fine" (18 and 20), "Bring It To Jerome" (5 and 11), and "I'm Your Kingpin" (takes 2 and 7). To the uninitiated, these recordings sound like complete performances, but they are edited so well that only upon very close listening do the edits become apparent.

The original Manfred Mann lineup was so tight that sometimes only one or two takes were required to record their material. "Did You Have To Do That" and "Can't Believe It" were recorded in just one take, while "Tennessee Waltz" and "You've Got To Take It" were laid down in just two passes.

In making recordings, Fontana did things much differently than EMI. The Fontana methodology for the recording artist of the mid to late '60s was to deliver mono mixes of recordings made on then standard 4- or 8-track recording and mixing equipment. Because of this process, few recordings mixed to stereo from any Fontana act of this period surfaced. Consequently, this had an adverse effect on the sound quality of their records, especially since the stereo mixes that have appeared usually bear little aural resemblance to their mono counterparts.

Until mid-1968, Manfred Mann recordings for the Fontana label were made on 4-track recording equipment. The problem was that since Manfred Mann's output and that of the entire music scene was getting more complicated, four tracks were not always enough. To get around this, Manfred Mann's producers (Gerry Bron, Shel Talmy, Tony Visconti, et al.) and recording engineers recorded the band's songs in <u>stages</u> by linking together 4-track machines like George Martin did with The Beatles. The remainder of their recordings was made with 8-track equipment.

As for the unreleased recordings made by the band for EMI and Fontana, they ranged from strong originals to more wild jazz instrumental cover versions. Quality was variable, but no one could deny the band's enthusiasm and dedication to their craft. The band's quality control mechanism was sound. Even on takes that seem perfect, the multi-track tapes always reveal a complaint or comment from Mann or Hugg.

Even today, the band feels that none of these songs should be released, but these opinions are based on remembrances that are over 25 years old. Perhaps the Manfreds can be proven wrong on this!

Reunions

Until recently, the '60s band members had no great animosity between them. Previously, Manfred's avoidance of recreating '60s material was the only thing that created some friction when reunions were discussed. However, the '60s touring group's use of the potentially misleading name The Manfreds has created some distance between them and Manfred, since Manfred is not (and will not be) involved in their activities. A planned reunion to be recorded and filmed at the Marquee on April 30, 1983 to celebrate the venue's 25th anniversary was canceled for this reason, but a get-together without Manfred called Manfred-X occurred at London's Dominion Theatre in 1984.

To be fair, Manfred's reasoning for not participating in reunions of the '60s group must be expressed: "My feeling is that I don't mind other people doing it. I just feel that you can't actually recreate what's gone before - the moment is gone and it had its strengths and weaknesses. I feel, for me anyway, and I don't imply criticism of people that do that - The Tremeloes or The Searchers - they're still doing what they did before, that I personally don't want to do that. I mean, there's really nothing wrong with that - people make fine music, jazz musicians do what they do all their lives, classical musicians do what they do. They don't feel that they have to do anything different.

"For example, with Tom McGuinness, The Blues Band is really, really good and I've seen them and they're great at what they do. And, I've heard a radio recording of the reunion '60s Manfreds, and I thought it was very good and very musical. But for some reason or other, I'm cursed with this thing of wanting to do something different and changing. Perhaps through this innate sense of doing things differently, one is capable of doing other things through one's life. For me, to get together and do it, and I hesitate to say it, there's a slight embarrassment factor in 'What are these people doing?' I'm in my fifties. Doing what you <u>were</u> doing . . . I wouldn't want to be doing that. I feel it's mainly a nostalgia trip."

To celebrate Tom McGuinness' 50th birthday in December 1991, a party was held in his honor at the Town & Country Club in the London area. It was a star-studded night for Manfred Mann fans, as the musical performers included former Manfred Mann members Mike Hugg on keyboards, Paul Jones and Mike d'Abo on vocals, Mike Vickers on sax, and Tom McGuinness himself on lead guitar. Noted musicians Tom Robinson (bass) and former Jimi Hendrix Experience bassist Noel Redding were also on hand, as well as The Blues Band and Gallagher And Lyle. The band performed very well, considering that rehearsal time was short. The one person missing was Manfred, touring Germany with his Earth Band on that night.

Re-Releases

The endurance of Manfred Mann's sixties output has made it possible for a consistent flow of reissues and compilations. For the EMI material, the more budget-oriented packages "The Greatest Hits Of Manfred Mann" and "The Best Of Manfred Mann" (and its accompanying EP) made way for the most successful Manfreds reissue of all, the TV-advertised album "Semi-Detached Suburban (20 Great Hits Of The Sixties)." "Semi-Detached" also included the major Fontana hits, and earned a gold record for its potent sales. Surprisingly, when the album was released in August 1979, it performed miserably. It was not until a secondary promotional push took place in early 1980 that the album finally went up to #9 during its complete 14-week run. Other interesting Manfred Mann reissues include See For Miles' "The R & B Years" and "The EP Collection," and EMI's "The Singles Album" (retitled "The Singles Plus" for CD).

With all these compilations floating around, it was unusual that no previously unreleased tracks were being introduced to the public. This occurred although a multitude of unreleased material was available. The first album that broke through and presented unreleased material was the US CD "The Best Of Manfred Mann - A Definitive Collection." On this package, the Jack Bruce era track "Come Home Baby" was presented with many other rarities, including the Canada-only versions of "5-4-3-2-1" and "Do Wah Diddy Diddy," and the very humorous US promotional album group interview. Quite a lot of this album's material was reused on UK EMI's "The Best Of The EMI Years" disc. The main selling point for this collection was the aforementioned unissued cut "Sticks And Stones."

Singles fans could rely on a steady diet of reissues from EMI (singles and albums) and the singles-slanted Old Gold label, and sales of these records were carefully monitored. Even so, it must be stressed that EMI got the better end of the deal over the years, as the members of the HMV lineup collectively earn only 4p (or about 6 cents US) for each CD sold. In 1992, EMI around the world finally took notice of the sizable sales and interest in their Manfred Mann catalog and limited licensing of the recordings to present their own compilations. Until the early '90s, the inferior compilations available in the States have driven US fans to the sheer quantity and quality of British reissues. Even US singles reissues have proven to be rare, resulting in a longer unavailability of "Mighty Quinn" than in Britain.

On the other hand, Fontana and parent company PolyGram have not given the same level of attention to Manfred Mann material, since very few Fontana era compilations have appeared over the years. The first of this select group was "This Is . . . Manfred Mann," not necessarily a hits collection but a cross-section of the band's singles, EPs and album tracks. The first of two Manfreds albums in Germany's "Attention!" series was more hit-oriented and more successful, while the second album dealt more with revelatory album tracks. The Philips LP "Mannerisms" was by far the most successful example of PolyGram's hits collections, presenting the band's hits in chronological order and offered rare B-sides, including "By Request - Edwin Garvey" (its only album appearance). An EP with three tracks from "Mannerisms" and "A 'B' Side" was released a year after the album. The 1986 Fontana album "Hit Records 1966-1969" (including the first LP listing of "A 'B' Side") was the last opportunity that fans had to purchase d'Abo era hits for a while, since all the members of Manfred Mann sued PolyGram for underpayment of royalties.

During the seventies and eighties, many compilation albums of Manfred Mann material on Fontana were issued outside England, mainly in Germany, Holland and Spain. Some of these albums sported covers with recent photos of Manfred Mann's Earth Band, even though the entire album contents were from 1966 to 1969. The band was neither notified nor paid for sales of these albums, and the misrepresentation of the Earth Band was the final straw as far as Manfred was concerned. Litigation resulted and lasted until 1992. PolyGram offered a monetary settlement to the entire Manfred Mann group under the agreement that all future use of their material would compensate the group properly. With legal matters out of the way, the gates were now open for the re-release of the Fontana hits.

The "Ages Of Mann" album was the first offspring of this new agreement, but it was not without some problems. The album took various shapes during its formulation, including the possible inclusion of the Manfred Mann's Earth Band hits "Joybringer" and "Blinded By The Light." These ideas were nixed by Manfred, who controls the rights to Earth Band and Chapter Three material outside of North America. With a track selection combining EMI and Fontana hits and EP and album tracks, the collection was originally set for release on the new television-promoted PolyGram TV label in November 1992. However, the label could not meet this deadline, since extra time was required to line up promotion and distribution of the album. What <u>was</u> ready was a very rare promotional CD with six hits from the album. Even so, "Ages Of Mann" was presented as a quick cash-in package with inexpensive packaging and dull sound quality.

In different ways, the US "Chapter Two: The Best Of The Fontana Years" and the Australian "Mann Made Hits And Other Delicacies" CDs attempted to redress the balance, but they were not comprehensive enough and lacked in the sound quality department.

The Return Of The Manfreds

After the d'Abo lineup settled the Fontana case and Paul Jones provided input on the album's track selection, the combined HMV and Fontana lineups (Jones, McGuinness, Vickers, Hugg and d'Abo, minus Manfred and Klaus Voorman) decided to go out on tour under the clever name The Manfreds to promote "Ages Of Mann." Augmenting this lineup was Blues Band drummer Rob Townsend and bassist Benny Gallagher (of Gallagher And Lyle). Another problem for the band was that since the album was finally set for release on January 11, 1993, The Manfreds' short tour was coming to a close. They were essentially promoting an album that was not in the shops. Since fans had nothing to purchase after seeing the band, some sales were inevitably lost. Still, the tour did have its positive effects, since "Ages Of Mann" crashed onto the charts at #23 upon release. The album's sales declined rapidly afterward, but sixties compilations have rarely appeared at all on recent sales charts, let alone at #23!

To further promote the album, all the main HMV and Fontana group members except Klaus Voorman did live interviews on British radio. The Manfreds did an acoustic set on Radio One, and d'Abo appeared on Radio 5 and on television. Even Manfred participated! On the "Rave" program for Radio 5, Manfred, Tom McGuinness, Mike Vickers and Mike d'Abo stood at the ready to answer the usual questions!

The 1992 Manfreds tour was so successful that further touring took place in 1993, and 1994 gigs have taken place. Paul Jones tells us how the first tour went: "It was wonderful. To hear Mike Vickers and Mike Hugg, for instance . . . the improvised solo strength in that band is phenomenal. To hear these guys playing better than they ever played back in the '60s was really thrilling . . . " Mike d'Abo's continues Jones' thought: ". . . and genuine warmth and love, I mean we actually give each other a hug, what I would call a "mann-hugg!" It is a bad pun, isn't it?

Their set included all of the hits by the Jones and d'Abo lineups (except "Hubble Bubble") plus some bonuses. A jazz medley featuring "Watermelon Man" and Jones' solo "I've Been A Bad Bad Boy" worked very well and the blues favorites "I'm Your Kingpin" and "Smokestack Lightning" did the business. The solo side of the band was also expressed, with Benny Gallagher singing one of the hits he had with Graham Lyle ("Heart On My Sleeve") and d'Abo vocalized two of his songwriting hits, "Build Me Up Buttercup" and "Handbags And Gladrags."

A small tour of the US also took place in 1993, but it failed miserably since the promoter promised quite a lot of money for The Manfreds but delivered nothing. Most of The Manfreds then retreated to the UK, while Tom McGuinness, for one, had a holiday in California.

In between their tours, The Manfreds have done some studio work for a possible record release, but only basic tracks have been laid down. In addition, Mike Hugg and Mike Vickers have finished recording an instrumental album, a potential candidate for release soon.

The Commercials Period, Emanon and Manfred Mann Chapter Three

The image of a commercial singles band was not what Mann and Hugg desired. To get their minds off the pop grind, Mann and Hugg got into the jingle industry for TV commercials in the fall of 1967. In September of that year, Manfred wrote the music for a German TV commercial for British European Airways. Many other jingles were written by the pair, including one for Hovis. At one point, Mann and Hugg were writing two or three jingles per week. On the Hovis commercial, Klaus Voorman provided his inimitable "Feeling So Good" low voice! The 1968 BBC-1 TV production "The Gorge" featured music written by Mann and Hugg, and it was rebroadcast on the same station in October 1993.

In January 1969, Manfred and Mike were commissioned to compose music for a filmed documentary about the making of the major ocean liner, the Queen Elizabeth II (better known as the QE2). And, as mentioned previously, "A 'B' Side" was the Mannikin Cigars theme for an extended run starting in 1969. Another Mann/Hugg composition, "House In The Country," was recorded by the studio group Perfect People for single release and use as a Dulux house paint TV commercial in the spring of 1969.

In September 1969, Mann and Hugg announced their formation of a new company, Together Sounds. This company, though short-lived, handled their jingle-writing endeavors. However, the pair's most notorious musical contribution of the period was for the soft-core pornographic film "Venus In Furs," released in 1970.

The "Venus In Furs" Disaster

Mann and Hugg were asked to write the music for "Venus In Furs" in September 1968, but there were a few problems, as Manfred explains: "I had a bit part in a soft-core porn movie called 'Venus In Furs' in which I was playing the piano. Mike and I did the music for the film (which has not been released) and they edited the piano part in this ridiculous scene. I didn't even know it was in the scene! That was enough for me."

Regarding the same scene, Hugg remembers: "There was a jazz sequence in a club and Manfred and I were both supposed to appear in it. The only reason I didn't make it, and I thank my lucky stars, was that I was getting divorced at the time! I actually had to go and make an appearance in court, and so I didn't get to film that sequence. So Manfred did it, and I was very relieved!"

Mike Hugg's recollection of the entire "Venus In Furs" project sounds like a Monty Python routine! "Well, that film was funny actually, because we'd been coaxed into doing it and it was supposed to be an 'art' movie and they wanted some off-the-wall music for it. There's two funny stories about it, actually. One is when we were overdubbing the music - three funny stories - four funny stories - I thought of another! First of all, we flew to Madrid to meet the guys making the film and they wouldn't let Manfred in because he had a South African passport! We had to spend the whole day at the airport in the bar. The second one was that there was a girl in the film (Barbara McNair) who was going to sing a couple of songs in it. She was in cabaret in Las Vegas, so they flew Manfred and I to Las Vegas for three or four days to sit and meet her and sort out the keys to the songs. We had a good time over there, and we spent about five minutes going through the songs and wrote the keys down on a bit of paper, which we lost along the way! So we thought we'd remembered what keys they were in, so we went into the studio to record them and out of the three songs, we got two songs in the wrong key. So, she came to the airport at 12 o'clock one night to sing these songs, and we had to ring up musicians in the middle of the night and get them to come back and re-record the backing tracks in the right key! And then, very early in the morning when it was dubbed to the film, it was six o'clock at Olympic Studios in Barnes, and we were all tired. The film was on and there was some bondage bit. It was very soft-core porn, and this old lady came into the studio pushing this broom. On the screen was this sort of scene, a dungeon going on, and she was sweeping away. Suddenly, she turned around in sweat and looked up at the wall! And the engineer was a Catholic, and we had to really coax him - he was refusing to do it at one point! So it was quite an eventful film!"

Manfred's recollection of this story is much shorter, but it summarizes the desperation of trying to save an already disastrous project: "As I remember it, Mike lost the piece of paper, and we only realized it in London as we got ready to do the backing tracks. I still have an image of Mike looking through his pockets!"

The film was truly awful and fell in the "so bad it's good" category. It starred James Darren and Barbara McNair, and both are embarrassed by the movie. As for the music, Mann and Hugg offered a diverse and interesting score, and perfectly captured the carnival time atmosphere of

Rio De Janeiro. Manfred appears in two jazz scenes in the film, one of which includes a pre-Chapter Three performance of "Jump Before You Think."

Emanon

The seeds for Manfred Mann and Mike Hugg's next musical move were being sown during their commercial work in 1968. Manfred and Mike finally actualized their wishes of creating a more satisfying musical unit by creating Emanon, which is "no name" spelled in reverse. After some abortive rehearsals with drummer Hughie Flint, the core members of Emanon became Mann, Hugg, drummer Craig Collinge, Steve York on bass, and alto sax and flute player Bernie Living. Notably absent was a full-time guitar player, and this omission was completely intentional. Mann and Hugg wanted a different sounding group with a musical punch, and a guitar did not fit into their plans.

Just after the 1968 session for "Fox On The Run," Mike Hugg produced most of an album for the Australian band Procession, featuring guitarist/vocalist Mick Rogers and future Chapter Three drummer Craig Collinge. Hugg recognized Mick's talent through these sessions, and two important connections took place. Manfred was first exposed to Mick Rogers, and Procession's manager, David Joseph, ended up managing Mann and Hugg's band affairs. Though his new band was fully set, Manfred made a mental note of Mick Rogers for the future.

Eight days after "Ragamuffin Man" was released on Fontana, Emanon made their first appearance at London's Institute of Contemporary Arts (ICA) on Saturday, April 26, 1969 at 8PM. For live appearances, a five-piece sax and wind section was added to Emanon's ranks: Gerald Drewett (trombone), David Coxhill (baritone), Sonny Corbett (trumpet), Clive Stevens (tenor sax), and Carl Griffith (flute). Different permutations of these and other musicians formed the group for about the next year and a half. The group also scored an important date at the Marquee on the 13th of May, so they were on their way. The Manfred Mann pop group's official disbanding in June 1969 enabled Mann and Hugg to devote their full energies to this new band.

To finance Emanon, Mann and Hugg kept their hands in composing TV jingles. One of these, "The Michelin Theme (Go Radial, Go Michelin)," was recorded with the Emanon lineup and was privately pressed and released as a very rare one-sided single. Manfred had a spoken intro on the track, a brassy jazz instrumental with a strong melodic sense. This record, as well as their other two released commercial jingles, was shown as by Manfred Mann and Mike Hug (one "g" - his original name).

Manfred Mann
Chapter Three

As the months went by, a more applicable name was required for this massive ten-piece group. Since Manfred had already completed two chapters of his musical life, the band was named Manfred Mann Chapter Three to reflect Manfred's past and present. As Manfred Mann Chapter Three, the group made its first stage appearance in Newcastle on Friday, October 16, 1969. On occasion, the "Three" in the band name was shown in Roman numerals, as Manfred Mann Chapter III.

The intent of Manfred Mann Chapter Three was to play mainly jazz-oriented original material with freeform elements. In this way, Mann and Hugg were not necessarily sticking to the rigid chord patterns and song structures that, in their opinion, hampered their pop output. Manfred Mann Chapter Three signed up with the new, progressive-oriented Vertigo Records label, home of the "swirl" record label design and deluxe gatefold album packaging. In North America, the band appeared on the Polydor label.

"Manfred Mann Chapter Three" - The Album

Appearing in November 1969, Manfred Mann Chapter Three's self-titled LP was Vertigo's third album release, and it certainly shocked those expecting more pop records from Manfred. In fact,

Mike Hugg was the vocalist, pianist and principal songwriter for the group, and Manfred took more of a "behind the scenes" role, playing organ and arranging the album's contents. Brass arrangements were handled mainly by Mann and Hugg, and Derek Wadsworth took care of the rest. "Manfred Mann Chapter Three" was Manfred's longest album, clocking in at 51:27, but for most music fans, it was 51:27 of music they didn't want. The album did not sell well, but the newness of this group attracted a sector of the audience looking for something different and more progressive. From the five-piece adjunct horn section, Sonny Corbett and David "Dozy" Corbett contributed to the LP, as well as Harold Becket and Ian Fenby (remember him from the 1962 lineup?).

The debut album, produced by Dave Hadfield, was full of heartily arranged tunes with sinister vocals by Mike Hugg. The main problem that can be cited with the LP is the overbearing sax playing of Bernie Living, and its other problem was the mixing of the tracks, mainly the drum positioning on one channel. In some places on the album, the sheer power of the horn sections obscured the drums. Compared to some of the mixes Manfred suffered with during his pop period like "So Long, Dad," this album was a sonic improvement. Still, the album's production did not bring the full talents of the group into the best possible light.

However, there were many things to recommend on the "Manfred Mann Chapter Three" album. The album's highlight was "Snakeskin Garter," combining an eerie Hugg vocal, Manfred's keyboard and fine horn punctuation. Adding to that an excellent Steve York bass solo at the song's end, "Snakeskin Garter" was an all-around winner. "Travelling Lady," the Mann/Hugg composition formerly known as "A 'B' Side," was interestingly rearranged with different lyrics. [55] "Time," a live favorite, worked the same way as "Travelling Lady," in that Hugg's vocal navigated well around the song's carefully constructed instrumental sections.

There were chances taken on the LP, such as the Mann-penned instrumentals "Konekuf" and "A Study In Inaccuracy." The first was a nice horn-based melody, but the second was exactly what the title implied: an intentionally dissonant piece with wild mood changes. A choir singing "How Great Thou Art" is even audible in one section! The song that Mike and Brian Hugg gave to The Yardbirds, "You're A Better Man Than I," was retitled with a "Mister" in front of it, and played as a song of mourning. "Devil Woman" combined a vile-sounding Hugg vocal and Madeline Bell's convincing backing vocal contributions with a horn chart to match.

Argentine single

Manfred even sang on another of his melodically balanced songs, "One Way Glass," on which Steve York supplied his usual powerful bass line.[56] The quieter side of the group was tastefully expressed by the wistful "Sometimes" (assisted by Brian Hugg's guitar), "Ain't It Sad" and "Where Am I Going."

In the midst of this adventurous jazz-squeezed in the recording of another salsa number "The Maxwell House on a one-sided flexidisc, this very loose sung by session musicians (encouraged Maxwell House coffee ad.  slanted material, Mann and Hugg TV commercial they wrote - the spicy Shake." Appearing in February 1970 but energetically performed tune was by Mann and Hugg) and used as a

Eschewing the recorded arrangements of their songs for the most part, live Chapter Three gigs revealed only snatches of their original song formats. The band's material would be vastly rearranged in front of audiences, and they played at least three unreleased songs: "So Long" (previously recorded by the d'Abo lineup for a BBC session), "Breakdown" and "Bluesy Susie" (a dedication to Manfred's wife).

The band toured extensively to promote their first album, even playing in the States - Manfred's first US concerts since 1964. Their stint in America was capped by their appearance at the Fillmore East in New York's East Village, on May 5th and 6th, 1970. Also appearing on the same bill was The Jefferson Airplane.

At these concerts, a new Chapter Three showed up. Sax player Bernie Living departed and was not replaced, and Conrad Isidore became Chapter Three's new drummer. Isidore remained in place for the last three months of Manfred Mann Chapter Three's existence.

Later that month, Chapter Three was back in the UK, playing at the Woods of Dartmouth Festival in North Dartmouth, Manchester. At this festival, the band previewed a new arrangement of "Mighty Quinn" (sung by Hugg), "Saturn, Lord Of The Ring" (not performed again until the days of Manfred Mann's Earth Band) and the group's next record, the single "Happy Being Me." Adding to their already populous lineup, Chapter Three was joined by two female backing singers (Linda Lewis and Liza Strike) on live versions of "Mighty Quinn" and "Happy Being Me."

From this point on, Manfred's continual reevaluation of his recordings for live consumption has exhibited two separate personalities: 1) Manfred Mann, the live performer; and 2) Manfred Mann, the recording artist. While his character in a live setting has always been very spontaneous and experimental, Manfred has been inhibited by studio surroundings and the lack of fresh audience feedback.

The Next Sessions

By the time "Happy Being Me" was finally released at the end of August 1970, Manfred Mann Chapter Three was nonexistent, collapsing under the weight of their tremendous lineup and unrealized goals. However, for the single here, "Happy Being Me" was an upbeat pop tune with a memorable chorus, and in its second part, it repeated that chorus instrumentally in a shuffle tempo. This second half was a different take than the one that would soon appear on the "Manfred Mann Chapter Three Volume Two" LP about two months later. In fact, the song had the backing of the British trade publication Record Retailer, who predicted it to hit the British Top 50!

Still, the band completed a second album ("Manfred Mann Chapter Three Volume Two") and started a third ("Manfred Mann Chapter Three Volume Three") before being laid to rest. Midway through the second album's sessions, Craig Collinge left the band, and session drummers Conrad Isidore (on "Happy Being Me") and Andy McCulloch ("It's Good To Be Alive") filled in.

The "Volume Two" album (incorrectly shown in Record Retailer magazine with the title "December Fourth") was mostly written by Mike Hugg, and was more successfully executed than its predecessor. This time, production was handled by the triumvirate of Hugg, Mann and Dave Hadfield, and Manfred got to play more on the album. Live sidemen Sonny Corbett and David Coxhill also contributed, in addition to sax players Dave Brooks (tenor), Clive Stevens (soprano/tenor) and trumpet player Harold Becket.  Unfortunately, US fans weren't able to obtain it easily, since Polydor did not want a repeat of the first LP's poor sales and passed on releasing it Stateside.

The best examples of what Chapter Three wanted to accomplish are exhibited by the tracks "Lady Ace," "Jump Before You Think" and "Virginia." Even though each of these songs had its own personality, they all featured another Mann arrangement aspect that would appear frequently in the following decades: seamless, overlapping solos. "Lady Ace" displayed a keyboard motif with vocals that worked impressively around its horn arrangement and solos. The multiple musical transitions of "Jump Before You Think" illustrated Manfred's movement from the main horn theme to a bass solo, through an organ solo and back into the main theme. With this exhibition of talent, "Jump Before You Think" was justifiably a very successful live number.

Mann's own "Virginia" was an excellent foreshadowing of his Earth Band playing style. The song worked by trading a simple Hugg-sung melody off with powerfully dissonant horn runs. After this section, Manfred's organ solo midway through the song burst into a nasty, distorted sequence of 32nd notes (similar to his later Moog solos) before settling into a soft piano conclusion that drifted away. From tracks like "Virginia," Manfred became fond of incorporating keyboard playing extremes within the same song.

Surprisingly, German Vertigo had such faith in "Virginia" that they released it as an edited stereo single, backed with the tuneful "I Ain't Laughing," ably assisted by Brian Hugg's acoustic guitar and backing vocals.

The album version of "Happy Being Me," which at 15:54 was the longest song Manfred has ever released, was a cornucopia of smoothly flowing piano, sax, organ and bass solos, before a segue into another quiet piano ending. "Happy Being Me" was yet another live smash, even in its revised live form.

The album was not without its controversial moments either. "It's Good To Be Alive" was the complete opposite of its title - a depressing but compellingly melodic song with a spooky piano and vocal to match its "gloom and doom" motif. The song "Poor Sad Sue" was another case, however. It started nicely as a bass and organ-driven tune with slightly dissonant horn punctuation and hot piano and violin solos (the latter by Jerry Field). Unfortunately, it soon disintegrated into over one full minute of squeaking sax and violin bow scraping before it came back to its main theme. Not only was this section completely unnecessary, it lasted forever! It was this kind of musical torture that finally turned fans away from the band.

John Arkle, a Platform End contributor and devoted Manfredian since 1964, has provided an eyewitness account of Chapter Three's effect on two different British audiences in Newcastle: "First of all, the Newcastle Mayfair was a ballroom, where many top acts have played. I also saw Derek And The Dominoes there. One of the other unusual features about it was that it had a revolving stage. The support act played while the main act set up. There was a balcony above the stage, and this allowed you to see all this going on. I remember thinking Chapter Three wouldn't quite fit - but they did! Manfred was stage left, Craig Collinge was adjacent with Hugg in the center on electric piano. The horn section was in front. They opened up with "Time," that is, everyone except Manfred, because his organ was silent! The roadies had one hell of a time trying to fix it - on - off - on. You could imagine how Manfred must have felt. It then became obvious that the young audience were finding this "new style Manfred Mann" hard to cope with, with Bernie Living and Clive Stevens blowing hard!

"After about four numbers, the crowd were chanting for 'Mighty Quinn' and 'Fox On The Run' amongst others! Things were turning hostile, and it wasn't long before many started to walk out. I would think Manfred played for no more than 45 minutes to an hour. Then, seeing what the reaction was, he suddenly took the band off stage! That is, all except Mike Hugg, who didn't seem to believe it - he realized he was left on his own, and eventually departed! I think I was shell-shocked and worried - what was Manfred doing? This was one hell of a turnaround. That said, Chapter Three were brilliantly tight!

"When I saw them for the second time at a club gig in the same area, Conrad Isidore was on drums, Bernie Living had left, Linda Lewis and Liza Strike were on backing vocals and they went down well!"

Breakdown

When asked why his Chapter Three didn't work, Mann stated: "Well, it didn't succeed because people didn't like the albums enough to buy them. I mean it's no more or less than that. There were a lot of people in that band, you couldn't carry on. It also ran out of creative steam. Actually, I got tired of it.

"It (Chapter Three) was an overreaction. I think the problem we had was that we had these rules: weren't going to have a guitar, we weren't going to do any songs we hadn't written. In the end, the rules became a strait jacket. It wasn't freedom; it was just the exact opposite. That's why I didn't want to do it anymore, apart from the fact that it had failed, which is a powerful incentive to give something up! But it's also the sense of 'Well, I'd like to do that, but no, no, that's not our kind of thing' and then to bring a guitar into that somehow and do it. I was like I landed up producing Mike Hugg - he was singing and writing most of the stuff, and I was saying, 'Yeah Mike, that's good, but you can do it better.' I figured that I didn't want to do that. That was just as restrictive as before."

Mike Hugg's opinion on Chapter Three's failure was along the same lines: "Initially, it was too big and unwieldy. It didn't work I suppose because Manfred and I had already started going in different directions and it might have been different if we got a singer. Honestly, I never felt I was a singer. I was never happy singing, actually. I didn't know how I ended up singing, and I never felt at ease with it. That might have been another factor. The first tour was good fun, actually, for about six months - it was very enjoyable. Within six months of that happening, we already weren't seeing eye to eye on musical concepts, and that was obviously another large factor. I don't think we thought it through properly. Chapter Three came out of the frustration of the previous few years, and maybe we just went over the top."

Going over the top could certainly be attributed to Bernie Living, the band member that strayed the most from their musical format. Living's prior background was with jazz groups, so it was perplexing to people in the know as to why he played this way and why Mann and Hugg allowed his clearly off-key playing to mar Chapter Three's records. The other group members managed in their own ways to be melodically jazzy with avant garde touches, but Living went overboard in his sax playing within Chapter Three. The vast majority of Living's playing was not subtle, mainly squealing pyrotechnic solos that were out of context with the musical backing. To paraphrase a line from a Woody Allen film, Living was "just blowing into it!" Living was also not able to display instrument control and to effect the necessary volume-changing transitions within each song that were to become important and exciting parts of Manfred's post-pop group repertoire.

Furthermore, Manfred Mann Chapter Three played a modified version of freeform jazz, an extreme style of jazz that was never popular in jazz circles. In addition, not enough of a pop element entered into Chapter Three's mix to make their music palatable to fans. It was a shame that Steve York's outstanding bass playing and Craig Collinge's solid drumming were obscured by the restrictiveness of the band's rules.

The Last Sessions

Mann and Hugg's last released production and composition together, the Ski yogurt commercial "Ski 'Full Of Fitness' Theme" b/w "Sweet Baby Jane" came out in January 1971. Recorded after Chapter Three's breakup, session musicians played on both recordings. The A-side was like the straight pop from the Fontana days, including overlapping harmony vocals. Manfred can be heard on the song's choruses, and the drumming and guitar work, especially on the end solo, are exceptional. "Sweet Baby Jane" was a short country flavored tune with soulful backing vocals and a simple organ solo from Manfred.

"Manfred Mann Chapter Three Volume Three" was to include the first version of Hugg's composition "Messin'" (later to be an early Manfred Mann's Earth Band live favorite) and other tracks. Chris Slade, a session drummer most known for his 6-year stint with Tom Jones, did one session for the "Volume Three" album. When this album was scrapped, Manfred took about four months off and then called up Chris Slade to find out if he would be interested in a new group that he was forming - the band that would become Manfred Mann's Earth Band.

Manfred Mann's Earth Band

As a reaction against the fleeting psychedelia of 1966-67, the British progressive movement came into being throughout 1968 and 1969. Its main proponents included Emerson, Lake & Palmer, Yes, Jethro Tull, and many others. Most of these artists relied on keyboard and guitar wizardry, with Jethro Tull relying on flute and guitar. No matter what instruments were used, the approach was the same: longer songs were in, and expressing playing ability and heavy musical statements with meaningful lyrics was a necessity.

To compete in this new and musically demanding environment, Manfred formed a new band, again called Manfred Mann. Manfred's goal was advance past the outdated "hit record" methods of the '60s by creating music that stimulated the minds and ears of listeners without falling into the trap of self-indulgence. As many progressive groups soon found out, protracted soloing and cryptic song lyrics had their downsides. While losing an audience, a band could also destroy their reputation in the process.

Manfred explains why he formed a new band: "I was trapped in a pop band and then I was trapped in a kind of jazz thing - I told myself that I had to be jazzy, and that's why the band started. The principle here is to not be trapped, it is to do what you feel is right, so that you don't put yourself within any parameters."

After Manfred called up Chris Slade, Chris recommended seasoned bassist Colin Pattenden for the group. Among others, Pattenden played with Engelbert Humperdinck when he was known as Gerry Dorsey. With Slade and Pattenden already in, Manfred called his next card - Mick Rogers. Through former Chapter Three manager David Joseph, Manfred invited Mick to come to England to create this new group. Rogers (born Michael Oldroyd - another vocalist name change!) was doing sessions in Australia when he got the call. On December 30, 1970, he arrived in England to meet the rest of his bandmates.

During January 1971 the band's direction was finalized and everyone felt comfortable. Soon after, Manfred Mann signed up with Phonogram's Philips subsidiary (Polydor in the US and Canada). Their first public appearance was at the Piper Club in Rome in March 1971. Approximately two months later, the band performed in Australia as Manfred Mann Chapter Three. At this concert, their third, "Virginia" (the Chapter Three favorite), "Mighty Quinn" and others were played to an overwhelming response. On its next Australian appearance, the band was rewarded with headlining status (still as Chapter Three) over the enomously popular Deep Purple.

The band's first output on the Philips label was the pop single "Living Without You," a cover of the Randy Newman tune. This song, "So Long, Dad" and four other Newman songs originally appeared on Alan Price's 1967 album "A Price On His Head." "Living Without You" was Manfred's first recorded use of a synthesizer, his latest acquisition. Featured prominently in the mix, Manfred's synthesizer fills and solo functioned well as the song's commercial hooks.

The record's B-side was "Tribute," a Mann-written instrumental in which clockwork keyboards floated around a strong mesmerizing theme and guitar solo. An ad in Record Retailer magazine said that the band's debut album was coming soon, but this did not materialize.

With both sides of this single Manfred Mann completed other tracks release - "Stepping Sideways." This unreleased songs "Ned Kelly," the Wind," "It Ain't No Crime" and "Holy ("California Coastline," "Captain "Sloth") were also planned for the Bobby Stout" and "Prayer" worked retained the last five tracks. The other was canceled. Manfred Mann then considered more satisfactory, and the until 1972.

available for inclusion on the album, for their first LP slated for August album was to include the still original take of "Ashes To The Holy." In addition, five other tracks Bobby Stout," "Prayer," "Tribute" and album. Since songs like "Captain better with audiences, the band tracks were rejected and the album went back to record material that they resulting album would not appear

The band's broadcast television debut from Paris took place in August 1971, followed soon after by their second single, "Mrs. Henry" b/w "Prayer." This simultaneous release included the US and Canada, which previously bypassed "Living Without You." Known as "Please Mrs. Henry" on US and Canadian copies, "Mrs. Henry" was a Bob Dylan "Basement Tapes" song recorded with The Band. Again, Manfred's treatment of the song was on

the commercial side, using strong vocals between heavy note runs. "Prayer" was credited solely to Manfred Mann, but it actually evolved from the "As Is" LP track "Dealer Dealer." When played live, this song was called "Dealer" (singular) with its 1966 lyrics and the solo-lined arrangement of "Prayer." Whatever the band wanted to call the song, it was a very powerful live number through its movements from very loud to very soft sections. Different versions of the "Please Mrs. Henry" single were made available around the world, but the single enjoyed only minor success in one country - a #108 chart appearance in the US.[57]

The Name Change

With their increasing concert success, the band wanted a more distinctive name. Manfred thought that since "Mann" almost rhymed with "band," a word was necessary between them to define what they played. Names like "arm band," "elastic band" and "head band" were offered and rejected. The latter was rejected the quickest, especially since Manfred felt it was more suited for hippies! After playing a concert in Ireland, the band came upon their name while waiting for a plane at Dublin Airport in October 1971. With an ecological movement going on, the idea of an "earth band" was suggested by Chris Slade and this did the trick.

At an important show called "Implosion" at London's Roundhouse on October 17, 1971, the band gave an overwhelming performance. This concert was covered in great detail the following week in The Observer Review. At this show, the band reported to columnist Tony Palmer that they would soon be using Manfred Mann's Earth Band as their new name. That same month, the BBC's "Sounds Of The 70's" became their first radio broadcast.

The band's first Manfred Mann's (MMEB) took Wales in early Another gig was Bumpers on their first major their December 7, at the Marquee (featuring Elkie Palmer).

engagement as Earth Band place in South November. at the London club November 14, but gig as MMEB was 1971 appearance with Vinegar Joe Brooks and Robert

Based on the somewhat encouraging reaction in the US to "Please Mrs. Henry," the band's first album "Manfred Mann's Earth Band" was released Stateside near the end of January 1972. This was almost one month earlier than

canceling their first LP try, the themselves more time to create However, the complete album was a real letdown. environment, the album suffered low fidelity and high tape hiss the LP was not representative of produced live. Nothing more sound than Manfred's primitive when compared to his 1971, Manfred made his Moog Uriah Heep's "Look At its British counterpart! By Earth Band wanted to give a more satisfactory album. production of the released Produced in a controlled studio from poor sound quality. The also could not mask one thing: the excitement that the band exemplified the album's poor synthesizer, which sounded contemporaries. In the fall of album debut on two tracks from Yourself" LP: "Tears In My Eyes" and the 10-minute extravaganza "July Morning." These tracks were recorded extremely well· by comparison, and fully reflect the interesting and exciting sounds that could be obtained from that instrument.

Containing both sides of their first two Philips singles, the "Manfred Mann's Earth Band" album was mostly produced by David Mackay. Production chores for the remainder were handled by Manfred and Dave Hadfield. Beyond the singles, the other songs within the album fell into two categories: obscure outside tunes and humorous originals.

On the obscure side, Walt Meskell and Timothy Martin provided the clever song "California Coastline" and Lane Tietgen did the honors on "Captain Bobby Stout." "Stout" was a powerfully sung blues tune that figured strongly in live performances until 1978. It was originally combined with an instrumental section that soon became known as "Glorified Magnified."

Though relatively unknown outside New Orleans, Dr. John (known early on as Dr. John Creaux) was the source for a spicy bit of Cajun R&B - "Jump Sturdy." Manfred spotted this song on the good doctor's 1968 "Gris-Gris" album. By using a strong chorus and a lovely cascading jazz piano solo at its end, Manfred added another taste of originality to the song. A snatch of Manfred's solo was reused in 1973 on the track "Earth The Circle Part 1."

Manfred and a writer friend David Sadler wrote two songs that could not be taken seriously in their recorded forms: "Part Time Man" and "I'm Up And I'm Leaving." Both featured intentionally scratchy Manfred Mann vocals and told subtle but humorous stories. In particular, the keyboard arrangement of "I'm Up And I'm Leaving" complemented the overall feel of the track. Still, the appearance of both songs was beyond the context of the album. Rounding out the album was "Sloth," a synthesizer instrumental with guitar which functioned well as a lead-in track to "Living Without You."

Just after the US release of the album, Polydor finally decided to release "Living Without You" as a single. Unlike European releases, this single was credited to Manfred Mann's Earth Band. Polydor's decision to wait actually paid off, giving the group a #69 charting single in March 1972.[58]

Whatever the track lineup, MMEB's debut album was not received well at all in the UK. In the US, the album received a desirable four-star rating (out of five) from Rolling Stone magazine. In addition, the album performed well Stateside, making #138 on Billboard Top 200 Albums chart. The UK album chart position might have been that high if their chart had as many positions as in the US, which of course it doesn't!

To capitalize on Manfred's newly found recognition, Polydor decided to dip into the album further by issuing the two humorous Mann/Sadler songs back-to-back as a single in July: "I'm Up And I'm Leaving" b/w "Part Time Man." This mono single made #112 upon release.

The Necessity of Touring

The Earth Band was receiving quite a lot of airplay, but record sales were not proportional to airplay. This problem in particular has consistently dogged Manfred Mann throughout his post-'60s career. Luckily for Manfred, he figured out early on why this was happening: the live factor. Since the US record market is touring sensitive, a concentrated touring effort is required to sustain sales there for a long period. The sales that MMEB did experience were based only on radio play, without the benefit of touring. As a result, MMEB was not able to pick up any additional fans who were curious of their talents in a live atmosphere. In Manfred's case, this atmosphere was a different world entirely. Manfred's live world provided listeners with aspects of the band's interactive playing, but most of this personality was not presented on their recorded output to date.

Manfred immediately remedied this situation by taking the Earth Band out on the road on their first official tour. Outside the US, they were packaged in a tour with Free and Deep Purple. While in the States, MMEB made three cross-country trips with British bluesmeisters Savoy Brown. By making a concerted touring effort (no pun intended), the band gradually became known throughout major countries as a strong live act. With a series of warm receptions on their resume, the Earth Band came back to England to lay down tracks for their second album, "Glorified Magnified."

"Glorified Magnified" was released in September 1972 with production by Manfred and Dave Hadfield.[59] In terms of musical importance, "Glorified Magnified" started five traits that Manfred would return to repeatedly: riffs, parallel fourths, polyrhythms, crossfades and overlays.

Riffs

Concerning content, the album was much closer to the Earth Band's energetically played live shows. As such, "Glorified Magnified" exhibited MMEB's musical trademark: exciting vocal passages surrounded by a combination of pyrotechnic yet melodic instrumental sections, and repeated musical phrases on keyboard and guitar known as <u>riffs</u>. When these riffs were played in unison, Mick and Manfred provided a very heavy sound. In the Earth Band's case, riffs weren't excuses for songs; a strong sense of melody, tension and excitement was built around them. "Look Around," for one, used the band's live riff-based arrangement of "Black Betty." This was the same Leadbelly blues that Manfred recorded as "Big Betty" for the "Mighty Garvey!" ("The Mighty Quinn") album.

Parallel Fourths

"Look Around," and many others in the future, also involved the use of <u>parallel fourths</u>. In musical terms, if Mick Rogers plays a riff in a certain scale (say, A minor), Manfred plays the same riff using the fourth tone of the same scale (namely, D) that Mick is playing in. By using parallel fourths, Manfred created a multi-level instrumental sound scheme. This was a natural extension of the multi-tiered harmony vocals used on the Fontana recordings, which also employed fourths.

Polyrhythms

In addition, Manfred's personal, improvised Moog synthesizer sounds could turn funky on occasion, exhibiting a polyrhythmic motion that served two purposes: 1) it served as a brilliant aural backdrop on which Rogers could decorate, and 2) it generated listener interaction. Nothing demonstrated this sound better than the album's title track. Manfred's scampering synthesizer solo took the listener from the grooved rhythm track through the main riff to Slade's drumming showcase at the end. With a choir backing Slade's continuous drum rolls, the song personified rhythm in motion.

Group efforts like "Glorified Magnified" scored heavily with audiences. On top of the solid rock platform laid down by Chris Slade and Colin Pattenden, Manfred and Mick Rogers were able to leap into the perilous world of improvisation. It was this sense of danger that fans wanted and that Manfred and Mick thrived on.

Crossfades

Yet another Manfred Mann studio technique was exhibited on the album: the crossfade. This technique was most known by Mike Oldfield through his album "Tubular Bells," but "Glorified Magnified" was issued about nine months earlier. By crossfading, one instrument is faded out of the mix and another instrument is introduced into the mix by fading it in. For Manfred, his instrument of choice for fading out is drums, and he favors fading in keyboards. After the new section is introduced, Manfred brings the drums back, either at full force or in stages, depending on the mood of the song. On two other Manfred compositions ("I'm Gonna Have You All" and "Our Friend George"), crossfades take the drums out at tense points and return them for powerful conclusions. Both songs had heavy riffs, and this helped Manfred's use of crossfading to alter volume for maximum effect.

Overlays

The layering of keyboards and guitars used on many "Glorified Magnified" songs was yet another evident aspect of Manfred's recorded output that he would use continually. Originating from the Chapter Three days, "One Way Glass" was re-recorded with Mick on vocals. This time, the song was softer, with smooth multi-tracked guitar work. Manfred finished it off with a deliciously bent Moog solo and double-tracked keyboard overlays. This overlay feature on MMEB recordings is another one that pops up quite frequently. Also on the soft side were the short multi-tracked synthesizer instrumental "Wind" and its lead-in track, the obscure cover version "Ashes To The Wind."

For those craving levity, humor was exhibited in the form of "Meat" and "Down Home." The former was Manfred's heavy riff-based tune about Chris Slade's vegetarian lifestyle with a Zappaesque touch thrown in here and there for good measure. "Down Home" was a Mick Rogers composition following in the same humorous vein as the previous album's "Part Time Man."

Bob Dylan's song catalog made another appearance on a Mann record through MMEB's take of "It's All Over Now Baby Blue." The song was obtained from Zimmy's "Bringing It All Back Home" LP, and was Mick's favorite among the band's Dylan covers. The band kept a tight arrangement throughout, thanks to the production by Manfred, Dave Hadfield and former partner in crime Tom McGuinness.

Promoting the Band

In England, "Meat" was issued as a single, but it did not sell well. One reason for its low sales figures was certainly that it was incorrectly credited to "Earth Band." US Polydor passed on this single by releasing "It's All Over Now Baby Blue" b/w "Ashes" instead. This single also failed, though the single was the first instance of Manfred's retitling of an album track appearing as a B-side of a single ("Ashes" is the same as "Ashes To The Wind").

Mann expressed why he changes titles of album tracks for use on singles: "The titles are always different to the album versions. You would find the titles of almost all of the B-sides that occur on an album over the years are all different. This is because I have a system going where everybody I work with shares in the royalties on a B-side, even though I have written the track, and in most cases, I have. It's just one of those things I got into in the late '60s when we found out that if somebody wrote the B-side of a hit record, he was earning a lot of money, while the other guys who had all put in the same work would earn very little because maybe they were on a B-side of a record that wasn't a success. That always struck me as unfair. I think that we are the only band that does this. It doesn't matter whether anybody wrote a note, we all share the B-side. It's quite a nice thing, and it's a good thing to be a member of the band for."

Unfortunately, "Glorified Magnified" did not sell well in the UK or the US, as it missed both album charts. The Earth Band certainly had their work cut out for them at this point, especially since they issued two albums that year.

Club Successes

One thing that is true about Manfred's work is the stream of consciousness running through it, similar to Frank Zappa's "conceptual continuity." Old material is shaped, adapted and referred to in Manfred's reworkings to create new songs with vastly different results. Manfred's continual reevaluation of his song catalog helped the Earth Band score two major successes on the tour supporting "Glorified Magnified": a club appearance at Sundown, and a live John Peel session. The Sundown appearance on October 26 featured a blistering performance by the band. At Sundown, they blasted through "Dealer," "Messin'," "Buddah," "Captain Bobby Stout" (incorporating "Glorified Magnified"), and "Mighty Quinn." The John Peel session broadcast on the 10th of November was equally impressive, incorporating just three songs: "Ashes To The Wind," "Black Betty," and "Happy Being Me." By mixing exciting reworkings of current and otherwise unavailable songs, these performances first put MMEB on the map.

"Dealer" and "Black Betty" were interestingly played in their intermediate forms, instead of their recently released versions - "Prayer" and "Look Around," respectively. Even the arrangement of "Ashes To The Wind" followed the unreleased first album version instead of the take that appeared on "Glorified Magnified." Also worth noting is the inclusion of "Messin'" and "Buddah," both held for their third album "Messin'." While the reworking of "Mighty Quinn" started back in the Chapter Three days, it has taken a place during every MMEB show since. On the other hand, the fascinating and well-appreciated BBC version of Chapter Three's "Happy Being Me" quickly disappeared from their set.

Exclusively recorded studio sessions for the BBC also helped the band bring attention to themselves and their latest releases. These tracks are also listed in the discography.

More Outside Projects

Manfred was very busy with side projects during 1972. Within the same year, Mann produced Coulson, Dean, McGuinness and Flint's "Lo And Behold" LP, played on two tracks on Mike Hugg's "Somewhere" album, and produced the US-only soundtrack for the film "Swedish Fly Girls." "Lo And Behold" was a collection of Bob Dylan songs that had not been officially released by Dylan. As such, it was an extension of Manfred's interests. The "Swedish Fly Girls" album was mainly standard soundtrack fare, but included a song contribution from Melanie and an uncredited Sandy Denny on four vocal tracks. The song "One Way Glass" turned up with different lyrics on the album and was called "Broken-Glass Lives." For some reason, Manfred and co-writer Peter Thomas received no writer credit for the song on the LP.[60]

"Messin'"

Closing out 1972, MMEB played the United States without a warmup act for the entire month of December. In early 1973, the band hit Europe, either headlining or supporting The Electric Light Orchestra, ZZ Top, The Climax Blues Band and Uriah Heep. After this stint, Manfred and the gang were back in the US. Between March and April 1973, they played with Savoy Brown. These events prepared fans well for the next Earth Band

album project. Entitled "Messin'," this album marked Manfred's return to the Vertigo label.[61]

To preview this album in April, the single "Get Your Rocks Off" was issued. In the US and Canada, the top side was bypassed for "Mardi Gras Day" b/w "Sadjoy." Both singles were ignored.

Another preview came through the song unfortunately named Vertigo 2LP Rogers sang Manfred's lyrics describing notable religious figures, while rising chord progressions to great been played live for over six months, with audiences. 'Buddah," first appearing on the sampler "Suck It And See." Mick latter-day meetings of Buddah and other powerful riffs and solos took turns with effect. Since "Buddah" had already this arrangement was a proven winner

The "Messin'" album was produced by Manfred himself, and was issued in June 1973. The nearly 10-minute title track was the "Chapter Three Volume Three" leftover, and its ecological message and sound effects tapes played well at the time. Mick took advantage of a good opportunity to solo before a crossfade carried the song through Manfred's lead and the song's conclusion.

The Mann-written instrumentals "Cloudy Eyes" and "Sadjoy" provided beautiful melodies, a marked contrast to the heavier messages of "Buddah" and "Messin'." "Cloudy Eyes" featured sterling interaction between Manfred and Mick until another crossfade took the song down then up with a Moog piece. Through repetition of its guitar melody, "Sadjoy" expressed both emotions in its title by transforming itself from a "sad" feeling to "joy." This good feeling was also translated into the Earth Band's purposely inexact reading of Dr. John's "Mardi Gras Day." Manfred's three-minute take trimmed over five minutes from the original Dr. John track appearing on his 1970 album "Remedies."

Bob Dylan poked his way in again, as his "Basement Tapes" entry "Get Your Rocks Off" made it onto the album as a straightforward rocker - a rarity! The song was first released by Coulson, Dean, McGuinness, Flint on their Manfred Mann-produced "Lo And Behold" album. It was McGuinness, in fact, who located the song in the first place.

Mick's exposure to Australian music led him to discover "Black And Blue," a slow burning prison blues written by the group Chain. Most important about this song was its use of a "1-flatted third-4" ($1\ 3^b\ 4$) chord progression. This chord progression and its inversions became yet another important feature of Manfred's recordings and live act. For example, in the key of C, this progression would be C-E flat-F, the first note, a flattened third and the fourth note of the C scale. This chord configuration proved to be very successful with audiences, as performances of "Black And Blue" from the previous year illustrated.

"Black And Blue" was not considered suitable for North American albums, which had a different cover and the new title "Get Your Rocks Off." Instead, a cover of John Prine's aptly titled energetic blues "Pretty Good" replaced "Black And Blue" on the album. This song originally came from Prine's self-titled 1971 debut LP. Unfortunately, sales for "Messin'" and "Get Your Rocks Off" (#196) were not up to par, and the later US 45 release of "Get Your Rocks Off" did not revive sales.

Shortly after the US release of "Get Your Rocks Off," interview segments with Manfred appeared on a US religious radio program produced for the Presbyterian Church - "What's It All About?". As a promotionally released single, this record is quite a rare item. On the program, Manfred's agnosticism and downplaying of religion's role in society seems to be humorously at odds with the program's intention!

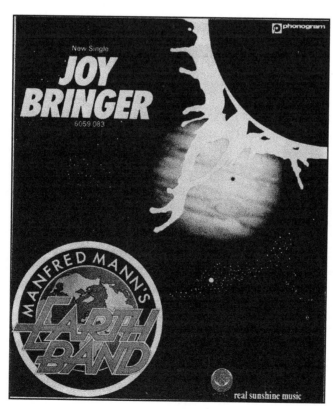

"Joybringer" and Holst's "The Planets"

Manfred's next musical presentation was the single "Joybringer." The song's title and musical form was an adaptation of the *allegro giocoso* movement from "Jupiter, The Bringer Of Jollity," a section of Gustav Holst's suite "The Planets." After hearing "The Planets," Manfred got the idea to incorporate some of the work in his next creations. This was the initial inspiration for the MMEB single "Joybringer." However, it was not clear to Manfred how to put it together until he asked Mick Rogers for input, as Manfred explains: "It ('Joybringer') was Mick's idea. He had a song called 'Make Your Stash.' It was an Australian sort of drug song! I suggested to him, with the greatest of respect, I didn't think that was the best title. 'What's wrong with "Make Your Stash"?,' said Mick. I said, 'Mick, I don't think it's right. What's the Holst original called?' Mick said, '"Joybringer"' (sic). I said, "How about 'I bring joy?'. I was kind of being obvious and simple, but it was Mick's idea and it came from a song he was doing in the band. I just picked up the middle piece from 'The Planets' suite."

Manfred, in fact, had done things backwards by recording the song first and seeking permission afterwards. For our benefit, Manfred has laid out the dilemma he faced: "We'd made the record and I hadn't had a hit record for many years. I then found out that I had to get Imogen Holst's permission. Somebody played her our record, and to her credit, she said 'yes' because it was a good record and it was done nicely. But it was actually up to her to do it and I had absolute panic about that. It was in copyright and you couldn't just do it."

MMEB became the first permission by Gustav as the executor of his Ltd., to perform his "Joybringer" was finally by Manfred with writer Rogers and Chris Slade. In hit #9 in the UK, marking that Manfred had a Top 10

rock group to be given Holst's daughter Imogen, estate, G. And I. Holst compositions.[62] When released, it was produced credits to Holst, Mann, the fall of 1973, the single the first time since 1969 single. Still, the US single

did not even come close to charting.[63] As far as B-sides were concerned, the British issue used "Can't Eat Meat" (a retitling of "Meat"), and the US utilized an edit of "Cloudy Eyes."

Even with this singles success, Manfred was never comfortable with playing "Joybringer" live. Thanks to frequent requests, the song was finally played to delighted audiences during warmup gigs in 1991. Still, Mick and Manfred were not happy with the way the song was presented live. They decided to shelve it until 1993 gigs, using it as an instrumental bridge to their first full song on stage, Bob Dylan's "Shelter From The Storm."

"Joybringer" marked the end of their Phonogram contract, and in September 1973 the band moved over to the up-and-coming Bronze Records label, headed by Manfred's sixties manager/producer, Gerry Bron.

"Solar Fire" and the Bronze Age

Still inspired by Holst, Manfred and the Earth Band continued with "Solar Fire" [64] - an album project that relied on the spiritual and celestial influence of the Holst work without being derivative from it. The release of the self-produced "Solar Fire" in late November 1973 marked the Earth Band's fourth LP, and it was their first widely-regarded masterpiece. This was Manfred's first album recorded at his new studio, The Workhouse. Sales picked up again, with a #96 US placing in the spring of 1974. In the UK, "Solar Fire" was a steady seller over a long period, reaching gold status without ever charting. Starting with "Solar Fire" and continuing throughout their Bronze tenure, MMEB was extremely popular in Germany, frequently achieving Top 10 LPs and gold and platinum sales awards.

The centerpiece of the "Solar Fire" project was another Bob Dylan song, "Father Of Day, Father Of Night." It was a mere 1:28 track shown as "Father Of Night" on Bob Dylan's "New Morning" album, but on "Solar Fire" Manfred expanded it into a 10-minute tour de force. Emotional extremes from the introductory solitude of The Grove Singers choir to explosive interplay between Mann and Mick Rogers were powerfully expressed. Inspired by sections from Holst's *adagio* movement of "Saturn, The Bringer Of Old Age," the song remains a live MMEB staple today.

Group compositions like "In The Beginning, Darkness," "Solar Fire," and the instrumental "Pluto The Dog" expanded the time limits of Holst's suite. The first two tracks looked at the time before the creation of the world as we know it, and then the assumed solar fire that set life into motion. The latter cut dealt with the most recent and distant planetary discovery - Pluto. "In The Beginning, Darkness" was formed around a hot guitar riff and after moving into a shuffle tempo, Mick's "call-and-response" guitar solos brought the song to its conclusion. "Solar Fire" used alternating vocals between Mick Rogers and session singer Doreen Chanter to counter ripping guitar work and keyboards. "Pluto The Dog" was a fluid Moog solo over Colin Pattenden's insistent bass riff and Chris Slade's percolating rhythm. With "Pluto The Dog," Manfred communicated both Pluto's distance and unassuming behavior.

Unlike Holst, Manfred used "Saturn" and "Mercury" as instrumental opposites. Contained within the same track, "Saturn, Lord Of The Ring" (a renamed version of Holst's movement) and "Mercury, The Winged Messenger" provided an exciting contrast between old age and the speed of youth. The Earth Band's slow pace on "Saturn" matched the *adaggio* movement of Holst's "Saturn" section before it rose to a peak. Guitar and synthesizer lines were sensitively combined with an original Mick Rogers melody to carefully preserve Holst's feeling of old age. After "Saturn"'s final sustained guitar chord, synthesizer effects and backwards piano on "Mercury"'s introduction took the listener on an exciting ride of alternating guitar and synthesizer solos and dual riffs. By using an upward and downward chord progression on its finale, MMEB's re-invention of "Mercury" equaled the darting speed inspired by Holst's *vivace* movement of the piece.

Completing the album was Manfred's two-part composition on Earth, "Earth The Circle." It was certainly unusual, as only Manfred would put "Part 2" of this piece <u>before</u> "Part 1" on the album! Sung by Mick, the second part was another riff-heavy song with sped-up piano and synthesizer. As another contrast, the Manfred-vocalized first part was quiet with quick bursts of synthesizer energy and jazz touches.

In the spring of 1974, "Father Of Day, Father Of Night" was finally released as a single from the album. In a practice that dated back to Chapter Three's "Happy Being Me," the A-side of this single was vastly different from its album counterpart.[65] Though released too late to make an impact, the single spotlighted what album fans already knew: Manfred Mann's Earth Band did commanding versions of Dylan.

What really put the band over the top with fans was their latest BBC concert in 1973, taped at the Paris Theatre. The performance of just five lengthy numbers ("Mercury, The Winged Messenger," "Buddah," "Messin'," "Father Of Day, Father Of Night" and "Mighty Quinn") sealed their reputation as an electrifying live attraction. At this show, bits of "Captain Bobby Stout" and "Glorified Magnified" were worked into "Father Of Day, Father Of Night," creating an ingenious, 16+ minute production.

Touring to promote "Solar Fire," the Earth Band played the US for 15 weeks, between May 4 and August 18, 1974. For the first three weeks of the tour, the Earth Band was paired with Blue Öyster Cult. Later in this American tour, Manfred and the gang were joined by Uriah Heep. Heep and the Earth Band shared billing on the following comprehensive European tour.

"The Good Earth"

With critical acclaim and robust sales for their last album, the band produced its follow-up in October 1974 - "The Good Earth." This album was the Earth Band's first release for their new American label, Warner Brothers. The album's unique selling strategy involved the distribution of a square foot of earth (get it?) in Wales. For UK fans, all they had to do was redeem the coupon located in the top left-hand corner of the album's inner sleeve. US MMEB fans had to cut the entire corner of the <u>album cover</u> to get the same deal. Ouch! Sales for the album proved to be a major letdown when compared to "Solar Fire," with only a US #157 placement to reward the band's efforts.

The crowing rooster of "Give Me The Good Earth" got the album started on an arousing note. This cover of Gary Wright's "Footprint" LP track was more guitar-oriented than past efforts, but contained the same amount of instrumental prowess that Earth Band fans expected. "I'll Be Gone" and "Launching Place Part II" were the respective top and bottom sides of a Top 10 hit single by another group from Oz, Spectrum. Manfred retained the pop feel of "I'll Be Gone" while ending it with a crossfade into Chris Slade's drum track. On "Launching Place," Manfred employed the opposite technique. After a slow one-minute fade-in, the song moved into a nice synthesizer riff that slid into a fluid Mick Rogers solo.

Bookending side two of the album were two radically different versions of Mann and Slade's "Earth Hymn." The first take transformed bells, backwards keyboard tapes and treated vocals into a multitude of exciting guitar and synthesizer interplay. This was capped off by backwards tapes of the entire band - a thoroughly exhilarating performance. The other version used more tape effects and deep Moog notes into a reprise of the first version, providing continuity to the album in the process. The rapidly moving instrumental "Sky High" was a Mann/Rogers piece that took drums and an excellent bass line into more electrifying tradeoff solos between Manfred and Mick.

The intelligent "Be Not Too Hard" was certainly the most commercial song of the lot. Mick Rogers took a poem by Christopher Logue entitled "Be Not Too Hard For Life Is Short" and created a very melodic tune with good keyboard and guitar interludes. Again, Manfred's effective volume shifts within the song were the main reasons the song worked so well. It was no wonder then that an edited version of "Be Not Too Hard" became the single from the album. However, it was very curious that the single received very little interest or airplay. It was backed by the confusingly named "Earth Hymn Part 2A" (just ignore the "A" please!).

Despite their mediocre record sales, the band's live turnout grew rapidly thanks to their extensive touring. In November, MMEB was back in the US on its first headlining tour with Uriah Heep and future Canadian superstars Rush. On some dates, the Earth Band was supported by The Sensational Alex Harvey Band and Hudson Ford. Before the band's arrival in the States, it was announced in New Musical Express that their concerts in Chicago, Atlanta and Cleveland were already sold out. The Earth Band returned to England two days before Christmas 1974, and they quickly went to back to work on European audiences and their next album project.

Record sales were still not commensurate with the extremely positive feedback that the Earth Band was getting. It then became clear to Manfred that instead of purchasing MMEB records, fans preferred to see and hear the group in a live setting. This was their natural habitat, figuratively speaking.

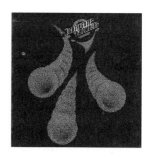

"The Boss" and "Nightingales And Bombers"

During one of his US tours, Manfred had obtained a copy of the debut LP by still relatively unknown Bruce Springsteen, called "Greetings From Asbury Park, N.J.". From this album, Manfred covered "Spirits In The Night" (also shown as "Spirit In The Night") and an edited version appeared as a single in July 1975. The live track "As Above So Below Part Two" (another retitling!) was the single's B-side. The record did the business in Europe, but British sales success was elusive. On top of this, the unnecessarily negative press that Manfred received in covering Springsteen compositions before and after Bruce became famous with "Born To Run" in 1975 have haunted Mann to this day. Manfred was certainly not the first artist to cover Springsteen, but he was the first to gain a notable degree of success with "The Boss"'s material.

"Spirits In The Night" was a more direct reworking, using volume shifting by slowly building verses into loud choruses. On the instrumental sections, Mick's wah-wah effected guitar solo segued well into one of Manfred's unique Moog solos. A crossfade at the tumultuous end of the song removed all the backing except a fast synthesizer run and the chorus vocals, both of which came to an effective abrupt ending.

1st US issue

2nd US issue

Nearly a month later, MMEB's sixth album appeared: "Nightingales And Bombers." First released in August 1975, this band production reached #120 on the US album chart. Its title came from a recording of nightingales made by a World War II-era ornithologist that, by accident, also included the sound of passing wartime aircraft. This incident was sonically described at the end of the B-side "As Above So Below," on which choir, birds and plane sounds concluded a synthesizer instrumental with a fuzzy 1 3^b 4 guitar riff. Also using this motif was the instrumental title track, navigating between interweaved guitar and synthesizer parts. As with "Spirits In The Night," "Nightingales And Bombers" crossfaded all the instruments out, leaving just the concluding synthesizer solo.

Another pair of instrumentals ("Countdown" and "Crossfade") used trading synthesizer and guitar solos into new improvisational territory. "Crossfade," in particular, took a funky sounding Moog piece into a mesmerizing guitar riff with searing Rogers solos.

Up-and-coming songwriter Joan Armatrading was the source for "Visionary Mountains." Written with original writing partner Pam Nestor for Joan's first LP "Whatever's For Us," MMEB's take on the song featured even more interaction between Manfred and Mick. The most notable interaction in this well-building song is Manfred's Moog solo, which seamlessly moves into a guitar solo. When Mick Rogers returned to the band in the '80s, "Visionary Mountains" was a strong live piece that lost none of its impact.

Manfred went back to his past to create "Time Is Right." A close comparison to "Driva Man" from

Manfred's "As Was" EP will reveal that "Time Is Right" is a direct descendent of the Oscar Brown Jr./Max Roach tune. In fact, "Driva Man" was played live with its new arrangement and original lyrics during the 1974 tour. With a lyric rewrite, the song became "Time Is Right." As with "Driva Man," "Time Is Right" used the $1\ 3^{b}\ 4$ chorded riff to create an exciting song with a driving groove. Surrounding its varying tempos, Mick's long guitar solo and Manfred's keyboard fills took flight. This treatment also decorated the Manfred/Peter Thomas composition "Fat Nelly." Again, close examination of the keyboard playing on "Fat Nelly" will reveal a similar rhythm to the upcoming "Blinded By The Light."

A bonus for North American fans was the added inclusion of another straightforward, guitar-powered Bob Dylan cover: "Quit Your Low Down Ways."[66] Fans outside North America have long sought out "Nightingales And Bombers" with this cut since it has not appeared elsewhere.

In the US, "Spirits In The Night" received a belated single release in a different edit, and "As Above So Below" was not retitled. It still did not sell, although after Bruce Springsteen's breakthrough it was re-released using the original British edited version. This release reached only #97 in the US.[67]

Changing Of The Guard

"Nightingales And Bombers" turned out to be an extremely difficult album to produce for two reasons: it contained loads of audible tape splices and Mick Rogers' musical direction was heading back toward Procession-like experimental jazz/rock (i.e., Weather Report and The Mahavishnu Orchestra). After the album was finally completed, Mick left the group and formed the band Eclipse in Australia. Still, Mick remained friendly with Manfred, appearing on the later Earth Band albums "The Roaring Silence," "Chance" and "Somewhere In Afrika." On these, Mick's exact contributions were not made clear on the albums themselves. One thing that is for sure is that Mick started working on "Blinded By The Light" before leaving the group. Mick's other musical activities after his departure are listed in his solo section.

Manfred expresses what happened during "Nightingales And Bombers": "We really were reaching the end of where we knew where we were going. Towards the end of the album, we were thrashing around in the dark. I thought some of it was good, and some it was a bit schizophrenic. It was just very, very hard to put together."

Despite the wide range of music that MMEB created, Mick Rogers felt trapped during "Nightingales And Bombers," as he describes: "It was the parting of the waves between myself and that band. I wasn't getting through a situation where I wanted to stretch out a bit. Being a guitarist, I was very fortunate when I was in America to play with Frank Zappa, playing bass and not guitar. I had a feeling for the John McLaughlin sort of thing and a lot of guitarists were influenced by that at the time. It just wasn't happening in the Earth Band frame. I was becoming such a pest that Manfred called a band meeting and said, 'Well, I'm sorry Mick, but you will just have to go, because you obviously want to do something else."

Fans of the Earth Band have had difficulty putting their finger on why the band was so effective. To put it into words, the original Earth Band worked so well because the members had a chemistry that enabled them to anticipate each other's musical directions. With this innate sense, they excelled on stage. Except Colin Pattenden, the Earth Band was interested in jazz, with Ornette Coleman, Miles Davis, and Dave Brubeck being the main overlaps. Even the masterful work of Frank Zappa was another common thread among the band members, and an important one at that. While Zappa's influence on MMEB was not obvious, touches of his musical approach, namely of conceptual continuity and humor, appeared from time to time.

Mick has also described the original MMEB magic: "I think it was the pure energy of Chris Slade and Colin Pattenden to get a great rhythm section - a lot of energy, really tight, like the early Free rhythm section but looser, and this enabled Manfred and myself to have a lot of freedom on top of that, and it used to fly. One of our first major tours was in Australia. We opened up for a local band, there was us, then Free, then Deep Purple and we went down so well that they tried to shove us up the order. On the strength of that tour, we did our own shows.

"It was amazing. Manfred and myself, taking nothing away from this band (the '90s MMEB lineup) or the band Chris Thompson was in, but we have an affection for that band. At that time we didn't have any hit records until 'Joybringer.' We simply built it up out of the live performances, and when we toured America supporting people like Uriah Heep, we used to go down a storm. We even got our own gig at the Philadelphia Spectrum simply because we had a huge following but no albums were selling - peculiar . . . all paving the way for 'Blinded By The Light.' We weren't selling records because we simply didn't do the right records then or then it all started to happen when Manfred found it. In fact, I learned 'Blinded By The Light' then went on my way and did other things."

To replace Rogers, Manfred located vocalist/rhythm guitarist Chris Thompson and lead guitarist Dave Flett. Thompson was in the New Zealand backup band Hillberry Walker and had released two singles as one half of the duo Central Park Reunion. Before these activities, Thompson auditioned in 1969 for Rod Argent's new band, Argent. Because he was overweight and bald, he did not get the job even though he was the best vocalist that auditioned. Of course, Thompson lost a lot of weight and got numerous hair transplants after that experience! Dave Flett was from Scotland, and he had previously played with many bands in Aberdeen. When Manfred discovered him, Dave was driving a laundry van!

After some quick rehearsals, the "Mark II" MMEB lineup hit the road to maintain their momentum. In December 1975, the band hit the small New York nightclub My Father's Place and gained a lot of exposure through its live broadcast on the late WLIR-FM. From this moment onward, US audiences were turning out in increasing numbers to catch Manfred and his associates. In Europe, MMEB toured again with American heavy metallers Blue Öyster Cult.

Before his departure, Manfred pitched in a distinctive Moog solo to the Sergei Prokofiev-written "Peter's Theme" on the concept album "Peter And The Wolf." Vivian Stanshall of The Bonzo Dog (Doo Dah) Band narrated the children's story on the English language version, and German, Italian, Spanish and French album editions were also released.

Just a thought: When Mick Rogers was in the band, group shots appeared in nearly every album. After Mick left in 1975, only three regular albums have sported photos of Manfred or the Earth Band: "Watch," "Angel Station" and "Budapest." Presumably, the band only wanted you to see them live!

"Blinded By The Light" and "The Roaring Silence"

The Earth Band's first single with Thompson and Flett was a remake of Bruce Springsteen's "Blinded By The Light," an edited preview of the cut appearing on their album "The Roaring Silence."[68] Backed with "Starbird No. 2," the single packed a powerful 1-2 punch. "Starbird" (its title on the resulting album) was an unusual song with two personalities. After an operatic voice traded vocal lines with Chris Thompson, this crossfaded into a blistering "call-and-response" solo extravaganza. Between Pattenden's hot bass run and solos by Manfred, Dave Flett and Chris Thompson, a crossfade led to a restatement of the first operatic theme. With all of its high quality musicianship, "Starbird" was an unforgettable performance.

As with "Spirits In The Night," "Blinded By The Light" came from Bruce Springsteen's debut LP "Greetings From Asbury Park, N.J." Springsteen's writing style on his first album involved telling stories in a personal, indirect way. Bruce's songwriting became more direct with each successive album, and with this directness came an equal increase in fans.

Manfred soon discovered that his respect of Springsteen was mutual. Springsteen had been listening to Manfred over the years, and Bruce has been spotted playing "Pretty Flamingo" during many of his marathon live sets over the years.

As for Manfred's fans, they were overwhelmed by the outstanding quality of this record. "Blinded By The Light" immediately received a lot of airplay in the UK and reached #6. It was Manfred's first hit since "Joybringer." In the US, airplay was not as immediate, but the result was even more amazing: a #1 record!

When I asked Manfred if he was trying to improve upon Springsteen's "Spirits In The Night" and "Blinded By The Light," Manfred simply stated: No, Springsteen's record was irrelevant. I was just making a record. I wasn't trying to improve on them. I don't think there was any way they could be improved upon, really. It was just good material to work with. It's like getting a piece of stone if you're a sculptor."

Manfred's most successful records have been difficult to assemble, and Manfred certainly had to sculpt this one: "The first time I heard the Bruce Springsteen album, I liked 'Spirits In The Night,' and as I listened to it more and more, I liked 'Blinded By The Light.' I thought perhaps that something could be done with 'Blinded.' But I worked on it a <u>lot</u>, and there were a lot of problems

in doing it. Even the original because it builds up through the build before you get to (sings) back down to the pianos. I didn't then, but I knew it had to reach a spent so long trying to find out could never find it in the song playing it louder and screaming, synthesizer bit because I couldn't wanted to do successfully. So I which built to sort of a screaming main problem with that. It didn't imagined, as I actually imagined

arrangement was quite hard, verses. I knew it needed a strong 'Blinded By The Light' and cut know that I would use pianos peak before it cut back, and I how to build up to that peak. I itself. It seemed we ended up so I eventually had to do that actually achieve what I originally had to kind of fake a section pitch and cut back. That was the come out quite how I originally the verses like 'Madman...' (sings

lyrics) much more like 'Spirits In The Night,' much more relaxed. It would have been very relaxed with an empty backing and then building up and up and up and then screaming and then cutting back. I never achieved that very gentle, relaxed thing, but something else came out of the band's arrangement. This is where the band will alter an arrangement or an idea that I have, and another arrangement came out of it. But, for a while, I was unhappy with that. That was not how I heard it, and it would have been nicer if I <u>had</u> heard it."

UK promo 12"

As Manfred described, putting together "Blinded By The Light" was a chore, but as a cover version it still contained some of Manfred's favorite ingredients. These included rearranging and resequencing the song using most, but not all, of Springsteen's lyrics. "Blinded By The Light" had a lot of things going on at once, and Dave Flett's blistering guitar solo could definitely be categorized as a career performance! Manfred even shared a dual vocal with Chris Thompson at the exciting ending build of the song. It is funny that Manfred is most associated with this song in his later period, and Manfred didn't even get a solo in it - unless you count "Chopsticks!" No one can deny, however, that Manfred's arrangement skills formed the reason for its massive success.

The enormous acclaim that Manfred Mann's Earth Band received with "Blinded By The Light" was matched by the album "The Roaring Silence." The album reached #10 in both the UK and US. Manfred and the Earth Band produced themselves again, with help from Mick Rogers on backing vocals and horn arrangements by Derek Wadsworth (remember Chapter Three?). Starting with this album, Manfred's atmospheric synthesizer backing joined his usual pyrotechnics to become a frequent part of his song makeup. This backing functioned as a bed on which the rest of the arrangement rested.

The whole album was awash in keyboard tracks, but none of these tracks sunk the fully developed song arrangements. The most striking of these were "Singing The Dolphin Through" and "The Road To Babylon." Mike Heron's 1975 album "Mike Heron's Reputation" supplied the former (as "Singing The Dolphin"), and Chris Thompson handled lead guitar chores on this one. Noted backing vocalists Doreen and Irene Chanter helped tremendously with uniquely arranged vocals, and well-known sax player Barbara Thompson kicked in a solo that rivaled Bernie Living in notes played, but with more control! The overlapping choir on the intro to "The Road To Babylon" sang an adaptation of lyrics from Psalm 137 from the Bible. This adaptation was called "Babylon" nearly two thousand years later, and its most notable appearance was on Don McLean's landmark 1971 album "American Pie." The choir section segued into a straight ahead rocker with stinging synthesizer and guitar fills. The smooth rhythmic changes of the song highlighted another blistering Flett solo before a choir crossfade took the

Turn a good ear to the Earth...
Manfred Mann's Earth Band
Listen close to the sound of success.
THE ROARING SILENCE is shaping up to be the biggest MM LP ever: with heavy FM play, the single "Blinded By the Light" spreading fast, and strong sales accompanying the band's strongest tour to date.

song to its abrupt and surprising end. During 1975 live shows, this song was performed as a work in progress with different lyrics, entitled "Well, Well, Well."

With "Waiter, There's A Yawn In My Ear" and "This Side Of Paradise," Manfred firmly took center stage. Despite "Waiter"'s heavy studio overdubbing, the 1976/1977 concert opener's live feel was retained from Manfred's slowly building synthesizer solo to its exciting climax. "This Side Of Paradise" was one of the last songs in Manfred's riff phase, and its heavy riff interludes provided a nice contrast to Thompson's intentionally passive vocals. Manfred's multi-tone synthesizer solos whipped through the proceedings and featured lots of bent notes, as did Dave Flett's playing.

The album ended on a reflective note with "Questions." Alternating between soft keyboards, an effective Thompson vocal and an uplifting guitar line, "Questions" closed the book on a perfect album. As a UK follow-up single, "Questions" b/w "Waiter, There's A Yawn In My Ear Part 2" was released, but it was inexplicably ignored.

US promo with
incorrect title

The band then did a quick, even more commercial re-recording of "Spirits In The Night" with Thompson on vocals. The recording featured the identical but remixed Mick Rogers era backing track with Thompson's vocal. This single was also ignored in the UK, but American fans brought the single up to #40 on the heels of "Blinded By The Light." The UK flip side was "The Road To Babylon," while North American copies used the previous British A-side "Questions" as its coupling.

As "Blinded By The Light" was falling off the US singles chart, US fans were unaware that the common flesh-colored edition of the album quickly went out of print. As a result, the album took a nosedive off the album chart due to its unavailability. Even so, the LP remained on the album chart for 37 weeks. A modified version of the album was soon issued, featuring a blue cover and a banner at the top stating the inclusion of the re-recorded "Spirits In The Night."[69] Cashing in on the Earth Band's tremendous success, their old label Vertigo issued the compilation album "Manfred Mann's Earth Band 1971-1973" with liner notes by Mick Rogers.[70]

2nd US issue

Meanwhile, the exposure that Chris Thompson received as the vocalist for the band got the attention of Jeff Wayne, who offered Chris an opportunity to appear on his concept album "The War Of The

Worlds." Thompson appeared on the song "Thunderchild," starting a long string of session appearances that are described in his solo section.

Manfred was recognized in another way: in 1977 he was co-opted as Fellow to the University of London's Goldsmith College. At this college, Manfred lectured on teaching music theory to young musicians.

MMEB was on the road in the US and in Europe for most of 1977. The highlight of the European leg was their Pink Pop Festival co-headlining gig with The Kinks in Holland. This tour also featured a song that was recorded at the time but remains unreleased: "Love In The Sun." After the tour for the album was completed, original bass player Colin Pattenden decided he had enough. He was replaced by Pat King.

"Watch"

Closing out the year, the Earth Band issued the single "California" in November 1977. This song signaled a link to the past of sorts, as its writer was Mike Vickers' wife Sue. Despite reaching the top of Radio One's playlist, the single did not make a chart dent in the UK. Softer than much of the band's recent output, "California" also sported stunning overlapped Flett solos and an equally amazing one by "Moogmann" himself. Since the single version was an edited remix of the forthcoming "Watch" LP version, some of this impact was lost.[71] However, for the singles market, the record was very suitable. The flip was called "Chicago," but its real title ("Chicago Institute") appeared on the album "Watch."

This was another strong B-side, using backwards vocal echo and exciting guitar runs (including another overlap). The US single, issued after the LP, was a direct edit from the album. It was backed by "Bouillabaisse," a French retitling of the album track "Fish Soup."

The group-produced "Watch" February 1978, but it proved to keyboard-heavy "Watch" was mainly a collection of different mental conditions dictated their strangeness, but Institute," "Circles," "Martha's Dry Land/Fish Soup" can all be "Circles" was an unusual one for builds reinforced this tale of an unconventional "Martha's Tietgen ("Captain Bobby Stout") a heavy riff, many tight solos part of "Drowning On Dry synthesizer and acoustic flavored did not appear until late be well worth the wait. The included both single titles and strangely themed songs. The described in the songs essentially also their charm. "Chicago Madman," and "Drowning On cited as examples of this nature. sure, and the exciting volume unsure person. The equally Madman" was another Lane composition from 1972 that used and volume changes. The first Land/Fish Soup" used a swirling tune. It soon turned into the exciting Chris Slade instrumental "Fish Soup" with another first-rate guitar run before returning to the song's first theme.

More customary fare was presented on the album by two songs that became MMEB's next two singles: "Mighty Quinn" and "Davy's On The Road Again." Both cuts were European live recordings enhanced by many overdubs, but this is not how both were presented on 45. The completely rearranged and rocking version of Manfred's sixties #1, "Mighty Quinn," received yet another overhaul for the single, and was released to remind fans of its first release nearly ten years before. The MMEB single of "Mighty Quinn" used about 15 seconds of the live "Watch" version before a new studio take unfolded right in front of the listener! Both versions used the now-familiar 1 3^b 4 riff employed so effectively in live shows. Although this arrangement had been used since Chapter Three, it really didn't come alive until Chris Thompson sang it. More B-side confusion was caused by the single's flip "Tiny," which was nothing more than the edited second half of the live LP version! Despite all of the publicity centering on the song's tenth anniversary, sales were poor and the record was not released in the US.

This was quickly rectified by "Davy's On The Road Again," a 1970 composition by The Band's Robbie Robertson with John Simon that was copyrighted in 1976. Simon was known to Manfred Mann fans as the writer of Manfred's sixties hit "My Name Is Jack." This record was another stroke of luck for MMEB in the summer of 1978, hitting #6 in the UK. But, this was to be their last Top 10 British hit. The single of "Davy's On

The Road Again" was a very different animal, using a patented Mann vocal crossfade in the middle of the song. This section of the single made the song even more commercial than it was originally, and the brilliant Flett and Mann solos present on the LP ended up on the cutting room floor. "Bouillabaisse" was the other side of the single, this time receiving a US release without chart success.

Recording "Davy's On The Road Again" had been on Manfred's mind for many years, and it was finally time to make it happen. Manfred reveals the song's source and his reasoning for re-recording parts of it for its single release: "I had a tape of John Simon's songs and I don't know whether it came from that period (the late '60s), but I had it for years and I'd often tried to record it. I've still got the

tape and there's other songs on there I've been thinking of doing - very nice tunes and 'Davy's On The Road Again' was one. I had been mucking around for ages with it at home, and then we did it live for a while - everyone said, 'You better make that a record, or else that's going to be it' and I said, 'No it ain't, it ain't.' Anyway, we recorded it off a live recording and I still thought 'No it ain't,' because it started off with the 'Davy's On The Road Again' vocal piece. A lot of the charm of the record is the way it starts as a ballad and picks up, this kind of rock 'n' roll shuffle. I knew it couldn't be a hit record unless you could start again, so I did this rather silly thing in the middle on the single. The whole thing on that was to try to get back to the beginning and bring the bass in again. So I had to do these elaborate crossfades to just get back to the beginning. Otherwise, you were just left doing Moog solos, which weren't going to be right for a single. We re-recorded some other singles because it was the only way we could make sensible singles out of them."

As for "Watch" itself, it proved that sales were very deceiving. Despite the success of "Davy's On The Road Again" in the UK, the lack of US hits resulted in only six US chart weeks and a peak of #83. Strangely, the British album charted <u>three months</u> after it did in the US, cresting at #33. However, German sales were immediate and tremendous. By this point, once an MMEB album got into the German Top 10, it would stay for months at a time, even without the aid of a large hit single. Despite its uncertain chart activity, "Watch" has proven to be the most enduring album for the band, since three "Watch" tracks are still in their live repertoire: "Davy's On The Road Again," "Martha's Madman," and the revised arrangement of "Mighty Quinn."[72]

The Earth Band's fortunes ended completely opposite of what they predicted with "Davy's On The Road Again," as it <u>was</u> it when Manfred broke up the Earth Band in late 1978 after touring the US for the last time.[73] After "Watch," another ending was marked as Manfred was divorced from his wife Susan.

Davy's On The Road Again

Words & Music by JOHN SMITH & J. ROBBIE ROBERTSON

Recorded by
MANFRED MANN'S EARTH BAND
on BRONZE Records

ISLAND MUSIC LTD/EARTHLY MUSIC LTD/MUSIC SALES LTD
78 Newman Street • London W1

35p

"Angel Station"

Even though MMEB disbanded in late 1978, Manfred had already started recording the next album "Angel Station" that August. The recording was finished in January 1979 with a revised lineup: Mann, Thompson, King, and new associates Steve Waller (guitar/vocals) and Geoff Britton (drums). Waller was a well-known South London pub musician and was previously with the group Gonzalez, who scored the Waller-recorded UK/US hit "Haven't Stopped Dancing Yet" after he left. Geoff Britton was yet another seasoned musician, with Gun, East Of Eden, The Wild Angels, and a successful stint as a member of Paul McCartney's Wings on his resume.

Still, a troubling note from Manfred was found on the album's back cover, stating that "Angel Station" would be Chris Thompson's last Earth Band album. These fears proved to be premature, as Thompson was always accessible. Amid his MMEB and Jeff Wayne sessions in 1978, Thompson had formed Filthy McNasty with Stevie Lange. Including Robbie McIntosh, Nicky Hopkins and Rick Marrotta, this band quickly evolved into Night, who had two Top 20 hits in the US: "Hot Summer Nights" and "If You Remember Me (Theme From 'The Champ')." Thompson's later activities have been documented in great detail in his solo section.

Preceding the album was Manfred's take on the Bob Dylan "Planet Waves" album track "You Angel You."[74] Manfred used some of Dylan's country flavoring and spiced it up with assorted keyboard solos and fills. Combining his artistry with triple lead vocals from Thompson, Waller and session singer extraordinaire Stevie Lange, Mann came up with an intelligent and delicious confection. The flip, "Out In The Distance" (correctly titled "'Belle' Of The Earth" on US copies) had a beautiful melody and vocals and fast, prepared synthesizer effects created by a sequencer. "You Angel You" managed to reach #54 in the UK and #58 Stateside.

For "Angel Station," Manfred made a clear break with the past by bringing outsiders in for assistance with the album. Anthony Moore produced this time with Manfred as deputy, and Moore also contributed on guitar, synthesizer and sequencer. Jimme O'Neill from the group Fingerprintz helped on arrangements and guitar tracks, and the popular session singer Dyan Birch also decorated the album with her backing vocals. Using this method, Manfred Mann's Earth Band was rewarded with a #30 British chart peak, but only a #144 US best.

In many respects, the songs on "Angel Station" were as strange as its predecessor, but they managed to be hauntingly beautiful on many occasions. Nothing more personified this feeling than three of the album's tracks: "Hollywood Town," "You Are - I Am" and "Don't Kill It Carol." "Hollywood Town" was written by songwriter Harriet Schock, who recorded it on her album of the same name in 1973. Manfred and Waller guided this instantly memorable pop song through a multitude of sensations, including a naughty synthesizer solo that sent chills down one's spine. "You Are - I Am" was unusual in that it used the same synthesizer line and arrangement from "Hollywood Town" with beautifully poetic lyrics to create a different, riveting track. The female vocal on this song was provided by Ann Kelly, and Manfred's spooky use of backwards spoken word tapes cast their spell.

Mann tapped into the Mike Heron songbook again with "Don't Kill It Carol," originally appearing on Heron's "Diamond Of Dreams" collection. Steve Waller's guitar effect riff and unique vocals on the song's verses were convincing lead-ins to the intensity of Chris Thompson's chorus parts. A beautiful bridge with Manfred's vocal took the listener through a creative, extended multi-keyboard solo. Complete with backwards echo on its ending chorus, the song was an underground winner. An edited version of the song, backed with the full "Blinded By The Light," soon became MMEB's next single (a #45 hit).[75] "Don't Kill It Carol" hit the Top 25 in Germany, but it was not a US single.

UK picture disc

German 12"

The angels motif was presented on the tracks "Angels At My Gate" and "Platform End." The former track, misspelled "Angelz . . . " on the US issue, was another Waller showcase. Steve Waller's vocals were as mysterious as Manfred's synthesizer accompaniment, and Steve's guitar voice box solo flowed well into a straight guitar run. "Platform End" was a short (1:31) twin guitar instrumental with keyboard flourishes and a vocal tag. In order to share publishing royalties on this improvised piece, its six participants were listed as writers of the track.

The final two "Angel Station" tracks couldn't have been more different. "Waiting For The Rain" was an extremely beautiful song, both in its melody and arrangement. New York songwriter Billy Falcon (real name: Falcone) wrote the song and performed it on his 1978 album "Billy Falcon's Burning Rose." In Manfred's arrangement, a dynamic Thompson vocal and Mann's piano and synthesizer bed were the perfect match. In addition, Graham Preskett's violin solos were something to cheer about.

For this ad, note the extra hair drawn to cover the woman's breasts - only in America!

If there was any source of controversy on "Angel Station," Manfred's song "Resurrection" was certainly it. The incorrect (but unfortunately common) opinion of the song was that it was making fun of the second coming of Jesus Christ. This is definitely not the case, as "Resurrection" is in fact about how an unscrupulous business agent would make money off Christ's return. An analogy to this excessive and immoral merchandising would be the wide assortment of unauthorized T-shirts and paraphernalia sold in countries that the Pope has visited around the world in recent decades. Reflecting the reality of the T-shirt "pirate," the business agent that Manfred portrays vocally in "Resurrection" treats the second coming of Christ, which for many people is a very serious event of great religious consequence, very lightly. Similarly, the humor of Manfred's recitations and the John Potter Choral Arrangements underscore the callousness that people display for others when personal gain is paramount. Without question, the song was not meant to be taken seriously, as it contains musical errors that Manfred acknowledges at its end. (Manfred's humorous statement, "a few mistakes on that one" is only audible on the original LP.) Misconceptions about the lyrical content of "Resurrection" led to Warner Brothers in the US omitting its lyrics from the album's inner packaging.

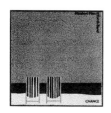

"Chance" - The Manfred Mann Project!

When it came time to tour for "Angel Station," Geoff Britton's recurring glandular fever prevented him from carrying on. Unfortunately, Britton had to be replaced and John Lingwood met this requirement. Like Britton, John Lingwood had a lot of session and group drumming experience.

Unlike previous tours, cartoon film footage was projected behind the band to provide a visual complement to the music that the Earth Band was performing. German television presented how this concept worked by airing part of an Earth Band concert interspersed with Manfred Mann interview segments.

Unusually, John Lingwood's first appearance on record with members of the Earth Band was not with a MMEB album. Rather, it was on an LP by Jimmy Hibbert called "Jimmy Hibbert's Heavy Duty." Hibbert was formerly with the UK cult group Alberto Y Lost Trios Paranoias. On "Heavy Duty," Lingwood, Steve Waller and Pat King provided the rhythm section on most of the album, and Manfred played synthesizer on four cuts.

With Thompson out of the picture (or so everyone thought), Manfred decided to hold a vocalist audition to replace him. This time, a long list of vocalists tried out, including: Paul Young, Huey Lewis (!), Graham Bonnet (ex-Rainbow vocalist), Pete French (Atomic Rooster's former singer) and Brian Johnson (ex-Geordie). The thought of Brian Johnson singing with the Earth Band is humorous enough, as is the fact that Johnson is currently with original MMEB drummer Chris Slade in AC/DC!

As it turned out, these auditions were held in vain. Even in a limited recording and performing capability, Chris Thompson was able to return to MMEB. However, once Thompson decided to split his time between Night and the Earth Band, the latter lost its strong group identity. The Earth Band essentially became an Alan Parsons Project-type unit with Manfred playing with what felt like a bunch of session men.

Nothing more exemplified this feeling than the tenth MMEB album, "Chance." Issued in October 1980, "Chance" is considered by some as a Manfred Mann solo album since it lacks a singular purpose or sound. Using six lead vocalists and five guitarists (Mick Rogers, Trevor Rabin, Steve Waller, Geoff Whitehorn and Robbie McIntosh), a wide assortment of songs and styles was presented. Of these players, future Yes star Trevor Rabin held the project together as associate producer to Manfred.

The album was preceded by the single "Lies (Through The 80's)," a clever song written by Denny Newman. Newman just happened to be a friend of a MMEB roadie! "Lies" managed to squeeze in snatches of Joni Mitchell's "Taxi" and The Who's "My Generation" while accurately describing how we would rely heavily in the future on cash machines and the like! Both sides of the single were edited from the versions prepared for the album, and Dyan Birch's second lead vocal played important parts on both cuts. The A-side was loaded with heavy Manfred riffing, guitar chords and another potent Thompson vocal. This led into another brilliant instrumental sequence with a lightning-fast synthesizer solo and a dual riff with guitar. This riff segued seamlessly into a guitar solo. After an abrupt stop, Manfred's unique ending section with vocals, synthesizer and soft guitar chords closed the book on the song.

The record's bottom side "You're Not My" was called "Adolescent Dream" on the album "Chance." Manfred wrote and sang the tune, and used sequenced synthesizer and drum backing to complement the unusual and eerie arrangement.[76]

In many ways, the aptly named "Chance" can be viewed as a collection of snapshots taken over a long period, May 1979 to July 1980. The "band"'s frustrations at The Workhouse and in a Portuguese studio led to many takes for which only fragments were usable. Rabin and Mann had to literally edit the best fragments together to make the best and most coherent song composites. Combined with the depressing tone of most of the songs, the overall effect was unsettling despite the many exciting musical moments that the album provided. Still, some levity was provided by the humorous liner notes and quotes presented on the album's back cover. The album did not sell well in the UK, but it did reach #87 in the US a few months later.

Chris Thompson was represented on lead vocals on the first three tracks: the aforementioned "Lies (Through The 80's)," "On The Run" and "For You." Manfred collaborated with Tony Ashton (former Family and Ashton, Gardner And Dyke member) and Florrie Palmer to create "On The Run." Unfortunately, the song's arrangement proved to be a tough nut to crack. Chance intervened when Manfred's frustration led him to experiment with sequenced keyboard and mechanical drum effects. This sequencing was what the song needed to hold it together, and Barbara Thompson's ending sax solo was icing on the cake.

"For You" came from the same well that produced "Spirits In The Night" and "Blinded By The Light" - Bruce Springsteen's first LP. Drawing from this powerful source, Manfred's final result of "For You" is nothing short of stunning. Chris Thompson's vocal rode the wave of heartfelt emotions communicated in Springsteen's unique style, and the band's arrangement was right on the money by alternating between playing it soft and hitting hard. Manfred's piano on the verses and synthesizer solo was powerful, and his segue into a guitar solo was very effective. "For You" then concluded with an ending that rivaled "Lies" for unconventionality.

"For You" was released as the second single from these sessions, but again it displayed a completely different personality on 7".[77] The odd yet amusing "A Fool I Am" was the other side of this record.

118

Like its A-side, it has not yet appeared on an album. Interestingly, the US received this single first and then "Lies," since "Chance" was released three months later than its UK counterpart. Some interest on US radio was generated, leading to a #106 chart entry in March 1981.

A few other songs on "Chance" underwent many transformations before their final resting place on the album. "Fritz The Blank" was an aborted vocal track that became a melodic synthesizer instrumental. "No Guarantee" had a danceable rhythm track but Manfred had to take words from a guarantee form to replace the lyrics on the rejected version! The Dyan Birch-sung "No Guarantee" also featured intermittent operatic choruses and a majestic sounding synthesizer ending. Manfred's problems on Mike Heron's melodic "Stranded" predated this album. "Stranded" was attempted with Chris Thompson for the "Watch" album, but Manfred felt that it was not good enough for release. The song originally appeared on Heron's "Diamond Of Dreams" LP as "Stranded In Iowa." By effectively rewriting the song and having relative unknown Peter Marsh sing it with Thompson, Manfred was finally able to piece together a satisfactory version.

Two obscure songs finished out the album. Dennis Linde's 1973 country flavored song "Hello, I Am Your Heart" was retitled "Hello, This Is Your Heart" for Manfred's version. Steve Waller's growl was a nice contrast to the spare backing, including bits of backwards piano, synthesizer riffs and hard guitar chording. Manfred then topped the tune off with a jazzy piano riff. The Tom Gray song "Heart On The Street" was another nicely performed tune sung by British pub favorite Willy Finlayson and Dyan Birch. This song used much of the previous song's effects, and included Manfred's patented fade-away piano trick at its end!

Manfred did his part by fully promoting  this album in concert, but fans did not exactly know where he was going. Another unreleased song from these sessions, "Hello Hello," opened concerts during the "Chance" tour. Manfred also did an interview with the German magazine Rennbahn Express, and interview segments and "Chance" song fragments appeared on an exclusive (and tantalizingly rare) flexidisc.

As a gesture of thanks to Trevor Rabin, Manfred and Chris Thompson made valuable contributions to Rabin's UK-only "Wolf" album. "Wolf" was produced by Kinks leader Ray Davies, and completely contained heavy guitar-powered rock. Manfred's searing solos appeared on two cuts, and Chris Thompson and Night co-vocalist Stevie Lange fired up the entire album. This appearance became Manfred's last outside session, as he started to spend increasing amounts of time at The Workhouse. This intensive studio time led to the vast amount of recordings that would eventually surface over the next 2 1/2 years.

Manfred has always found frustration when trying to determine the material he plans to release on albums. In 1981, he expressed it this way: "I've listened to tracks that I've done, and think, Jesus, that sounds like me in 1977! I don't like some of the things I find that eventually come out on a particular album. I listen to somebody else and I say, 'I like that more.' It's such a direct, personal thing of me, that it's my life on the record. I listen to some things I've done, and I feel it's out of date - it feels wrong to my own ears. So the next year, it will be different!"

Manfred's constant reevaluation of his studio and live work is understandably frustrating to long-suffering fans, who have to wait longer and longer for each new release. Even in concert, fan favorites undergo new arrangements each tour. Manfred definitely keeps his fans on their toes! In the studio, Manfred literally records and/or mixes hundreds of versions of his songs. When recently asked about how he selects versions and songs for release, he replied: "With extreme difficulty and immense confusion!"

Personnel changes have always been part of Manfred's history, but one wonders what their creative effects would be over the long run. Manfred gives his opinion on this issue: "Well, maybe personnel changes stop one from being less creative. The changes seemed necessary at the time. They're not the thing I enjoy doing, I don't like making personnel changes, but often it's necessary to keep a creative flow going."

The Singles Period

After the 1981 "Chance" tour, Pat King decided to leave the band. Original Babys member Matt Irving took his place. Chris Thompson was busy with Night's activities, so the new MMEB lineup was a four-piece again: Mann, Waller, Irving and Lingwood.

In November 1981, the first MMEB record with this personnel combination was "I (Who Have Nothing)" b/w "Man In Jam." The top side was a British hit for both Shirley Bassey and Tom Jones, and a US hit for the latter. The band's eerie arrangement of "I (Who Have Nothing)" worked extremely well, and the B-side was an excellent instrumental with marvelous jazz touches. Vocals on the A-side were by Steve Waller and Shona Laing, a strong vocalist in her own right.[78] Both tracks have not appeared on any album, and the A-side is one of Steve Waller's favorite MMEB tracks. This single and the next few were non-US releases, since Manfred's contract with Warner Brothers expired with the release of "Chance."

"I (Who Have Nothing)" was another happy accident, as Manfred relates: "It was very unusual. I liked it because it was such a strange way of doing the song. I quite like the song. It's almost worth redoing again one day! It was just that Shona Laing and then Steve Waller sang. I tried them both singing the song to see who would work best, and then suddenly, when you put them both together, they kinda worked. Anybody who listens to it thinks, 'Isn't Manfred clever of thinking how to do it,' but I didn't, you know, I spotted something that had happened."

In February 1982, the same lineup with Shona Laing produced their second 7" (and first 12"): "Eyes Of Nostradamus" b/w "Holiday's End."[79] Another completely non-album single, the top side was a haunting and retitled version of the Al Stewart epic "Nostradamus" from his "Past, Present And Future" album. "Eyes Of Nostradamus" is very different from the Al Stewart original, since Manfred and the Earth Band wrote original lyrics and only retained Stewart's chorus to create an entirely refreshing and different feel to the track. With some free time at his disposal, Chris Thompson chipped in vocally on the choruses. "Holiday's End" was one of Manfred's quirky songs with his own vocals, and its funky, rhythmic keyboards and percussion hinted at the African feel that would permeate future MMEB releases.

The third non-album 45 made its appearance that June: "Redemption Song" b/w "Wardream." The A-side was Bob Marley's "song of freedom" and originally appeared on his 1980 "Uprising" album. In covering the song, Manfred made sure to retain its serious nature. Manfred Mann's use of African chants ("No Kwazulu, No Bophuthatswana") over Marley's lyrics packed a powerful message. This message was Manfred's presentation of the disastrous apartheid situation destroying South Africa (his birthplace) at the time. The unconventional African-sung vocals were literally cries for help, so MMEB's version of "Redemption Song" was nowhere near as commercial as Bob Marley. Interestingly, Manfred did not use Marley's first verse as he picked the song up from the second verse to its end, but both versions were equally riveting in their own ways. "Wardream" also used African chants within another unusual Manfred Mann composition. Manfred and Shona Laing did the vocal honors this time. While it contained some musical errors, "Wardream" honestly expressed South Africa's problems.

"Somewhere In Afrika"

Being formerly from South Africa, Manfred was incensed with the effects of that country's apartheid system. On the other hand, he was inspired by the impact of his single "Redemption Song." This duality led Manfred to continue in the same vein by producing an album centering on South Africa's apartheid system, from the viewpoint of those affected by the system. This album was "Somewhere In Afrika," and it was first released October 1982 in Germany before its British release four months later. The album was a tremendous seller in Germany, selling well over 150,000 units upon release. Despite being way ahead of Third World concerns and African music trends popularized by Paul Simon and Peter Gabriel, Manfred's album sales in the UK proved to be disappointing. The LP had only a lone chart week at #87 to its credit.

It was then appropriate that the A-side of the Earth Band's next single release in November 1982 would be written by a South African, Andy Qunta. Sung by the returning Chris Thompson, Qunta's driving pop song "Tribal Statistics" was a politically-driven song of deception. "Tribal Statistics" powerfully expressed how people are treated as statistics. Reflecting shades of the past, the song featured a crossfade that took the drums out before the band returned to end the song.[80]

The record's other side, "Where Do They Send Them," was equally potent. On this Mann-written song (retitled "To Bantustan?" on the upcoming LP), Steve Waller sang about how the South African government broke up African families. By keeping black fathers in city-based work camps and forcing their families to live hundreds of miles away in homelands called Bantustans, fathers would not be allowed to see or communicate with their families for months. The song was backed up by heavy guitar riffs and drums, using the same "No Kwazulu" chants found on "Redemption Song."

Manfred's current, politically charged output was being scrutinized very carefully by the South African government. Contrary to popular belief, Manfred was not forbidden to see his family in Johannesburg and Matt Irving did not make the South African field recordings described in the liner notes. Manfred describes what actually took place: "I was never prevented from visiting South Africa. The 8-track Matt Irving recordings didn't exist, and the sleeve note was written so the South African government wouldn't realize that the (main) recordings were done in South Africa."

The album was titled "Somewhere In Afrika" for a couple of reasons. The first was that the sensitive nature of the African chant recording locations could not be revealed, as the South African participants could have been arrested for using some of the words and chants in public. One example, the chant "Amandla, Awethu," which translates as "power is ours," was one of the motifs used on the album ("No Kwazulu, No Bophuthatswana" is the other) and was frequently chanted during protests. The spelling of Africa with a "k" occurred because the Earth Band's biggest market was (and still is) Germany, and <u>Afrika</u> is how Germans spell the country's name.

Back cover from the South African issue

A lot of thought went into the preparation of the album "Somewhere In Afrika," and Manfred describes how the album came together: "In recording the album, the idea of an African concept came up at some time, and we pursued it fully. When we came to finish the album to look at all the tracks we had finished, we'd found that we'd really followed two lines - we'd had some tracks that we certainly wanted to use that didn't fit that concept. And I've never been one for thinking that a concept should be more important than a piece of music, so if we had some tracks we liked and wanted to keep - we didn't want to say, 'This idea has to control the music, it has to be a total African-oriented album.' In running orders, in fact, we were mixing the tracks up, trying to make a coherent album. In the end, we just decided, 'Let's put the African stuff on one side and the other stuff on the other side, and let's see what happens.' And that's what we stayed with."

"Somewhere In Afrika" was a distinctive mixture of rock, recent electronic techniques and African music. The African-influenced part of the album featured Zulu chants first heard on the preceding singles. Though the overall tone of the album was very serious, Manfred's intention was to keep it interesting to the listener, as he related: "I really do want to make it absolutely clear that the album can be enjoyed and listened to without necessarily having to be serious or concerned, etc., etc. At all times during the recording I was conscious of the fact that music must first and foremost be enjoyed on its own level. Zulu words and the sounds of the choir sound extremely powerful in their own right, irrespective of any so-called 'deeper meaning.'"

Besides the South African recordings that Manfred described, other sections of "Somewhere In Afrika" were recorded at The Workhouse II and Underhill Studios in London and Mastersounds in Sweden. Helping out again on guitar were Robbie McIntosh, Mick Rogers and Geoff Whitehorn. This time, Stevie Lange and Vicki Brown helped on backing vocals, and the album featured re-recordings of "Eyes Of Nostradamus" and "Redemption Song." These incorporated some of the basic tracks from their single versions, but the resulting LP takes were unfortunately inferior.[81]

"Third World Service" and "Demolition Man" also forcefully brought the African motif home. The former track was written and released as the single "World Service" in June 1982 by "Angel Station" producer Anthony Moore (spelled "More" on the record). Manfred's "Third World Service" used a synthesizer line with good guitar and percussion work to further Moore's vision of the song. "Demolition Man" was a funky reworking of the Sting song first recorded with his group The Police (on the LP "Ghost In The Machine") and later re-recorded solo for the Sylvester Stallone film "Demolition Man." Manfred's treatment used a solid beat and twin vocals from Steve Waller and Shona Laing to complete a guitar-based rocker with a rapid, synthesizer ending. An edited version of "Demolition Man" was the final single from the album's sessions, backed with "It's Still The Same" (aka "Brothers And Sisters Of Azania"). Unfortunately, this record and its accompanying video (MMEB's first) did not gain enough exposure to sell records.

Manfred sang on his own "Brothers And Sisters Of Azania," using a sequenced synthesizer pattern and percussion to peel off a funky synthesizer solo before moving into an African vocal sequence. This theme was restated as "Brothers And Sisters Of Africa," the first segment of the four-part "Africa Suite" that kicked off side two. This revised theme used the "No Kwazulu" chant and a Chris Thompson vocal to take the listener into the second part, "To Bantustan?" The third, the Shona Laing-sung "Koze Kobenini? (How Long Must We Wait?)," was a short African-vocalized song about the plight of the Bantustan family. "Lalela" concluded the suite as an enjoyable synthesizer romp with African chants and galloping drums. The title track (spelled "Africa") was a Lingwood/Mann arrangement of a traditional African melody sung by Africans with synthesizer backing, and completed the album on an up note.

MMEB hit the road for a comprehensive 3-month tour in Europe, and the most notable of these dates were the three "sold out" nights they played in Budapest, Hungary in April 1983. The overwhelmingly received concerts from this tour opened with an instrumental overture of "Pretty Flamingo," and two otherwise unavailable songs were performed: "Hobo Bill (Eastbound Train)" and "Step By Step." After the tour was completed, Steve Waller left the band. To everyone's delight, Mick Rogers returned to the Earth Band full-time to replace Waller.

For those curious if Manfred would actually play "Somewhere In Afrika" material in South Africa, Manfred made his opinions very clear: "It has never come up, and I wouldn't do it, mainly because it's interpreted as being support for the system. That's how it's interpreted over there. It doesn't matter what logic you use. That's how people see it. For example, if you talk about Sun City, it's basically taking place in South Africa. There's a pretense that it's not actually in South Africa, but that's really a sham. It takes place within South Africa, and it's interpreted by white and black South Africans as being a kind of acceptance and support of South Africa. So, generally speaking in that sense, I'm against it, because I don't feel there should be that support."

In 1983, Manfred signed a record deal with Arista Records in the US. However, it was agreed that the "Somewhere In Afrika" album would have to be modified to make it more appropriate (read: commercial) to the American audience. This was accomplished by substituting edited and/or remixed versions of "Eyes Of Nostradamus," "Third World Service," "Demolition Man" and "Redemption Song." In addition, two brand new recordings featuring Mick Rogers were added: "Runner" and "Rebel." These two songs were Matt Irving's last with the band.

The decision to modify the album for November 1983 release in the US proved to be exactly right, as it reached #40 during its 21 weeks on the album chart. This was MMEB's best-selling US album since "The Roaring Silence," but it was unfortunately their last US LP.

US promo 12"

US promo 12"

Throughout the life of Manfred Mann's Earth Band, album-oriented radio (AOR) stations in the US were fully responsible for exposing the band's music to the public. After an unsuccessful try with "Demolition Man," it was therefore appropriate that AOR stations took hold of "Runner" and made it #3 on Billboard's Rock Album Tracks chart in 1984 before its ultimate success at Top 40 stations. "Runner" was written by Canadian singer/songwriter Ian Thomas, and an edit of it became the band's first Top 40 single (#22) since 1977's "Spirits In The Night." The Earth Band's arrangement of the song featured slicing guitar from Mick Rogers, Chris Thompson's emotive lead vocal and Manfred's use of trumpeton (a keyboard simulation of a trumpet). The ending chorus employed Manfred's specialty: overlapped vocals from Thompson and Rogers before two crossfades (drums and then vocals) led to an ending trumpeton piece. The single was backed by "To Bantustan?"'s alter ego, "Where Do They Send Them."[82]

Arista president Clive Davis suggested that Manfred record "Runner" and "Rebel." By coincidence, "Runner" was timed perfectly with the preparations for the upcoming 1984 Summer Olympic Games. Shortly after the US single release of "Runner" in January 1984, its accompanying video appeared on MTV and other American television programs. This exposure helped the band sell records in a market that had not previously existed in the '70s. Manfred has always shown his displeasure with the video medium, although he welcomes the extra sales that it generates! Since Matt Irving left the band after recording "Runner," he is not in the video. Just for fun, look for Chris Thompson's hairpiece!

Reg Laws' song "Rebel" showed another commercial facet of the band's abilities by tapping into a Police-type sound. A superior remix of "Rebel" with vast overdubbing was issued after "Runner" ran its course, but airplay was minimal at best. Manfred describes how these songs came about: "'Runner' and "Rebel" came

US promo 12"

from Clive Davis at Arista Records, who suggested, 'These are good songs - record these.' Being a flexible chap, I was prepared to listen. It was a coincidence that we were playing onto the Olympics to a certain extent. I like the fact that it's coincidental, and in making the video, we tried to use some Olympic shots to enhance that tie-up. With 'Rebel,' I tried very hard to make a credible record out of it, but it just didn't quite work. Yet in its own way, it's quite a charming song." "Figures On A Page" ("Tribal Statistics" in its single guise) was the other side of the "Rebel" single.[83]

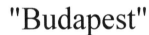

"Budapest"

In England, the success that "Runner" scored in the US did not make it a priority for UK release. Instead, the live single "Davy's On The Road Again" and live LP "Budapest" were released that February. "Davy's On The Road Again" was backed by the new "Budapest" version of "Mighty Quinn," and the 12" featured another live track - "Don't Kill It Carol."[84] "Runner" then appeared the next month, backed by a live version of "No Transkei," yet another retitling of "To Bantustan?" (are

126

you following this?). A 12" version of "Runner" also included a third track, a live version of "Lies (Through The 80's)."

The tapes from the April 6 and 7, 1983 Budapest gigs were supposed to been the ones compiled, mixed and produced by Chris Thompson and John Lingwood for the live album "Budapest." Mann did not participate, as he opposed the idea of a live album. In actuality, most of the album's tracks were taken from a concert at London's Dominion. Manfred expressed his distaste for releasing a live album when I first spoke to him in May 1982, almost two years before "Budapest" was released: "A lot of people say that because the band is very good live, we should do a live album. But, I've always found that the band is good live when you're at the show watching it. I think from what I've heard, the tapes we've done aren't that good when you just listen to what we're doing. We really change the songs a lot, unlike say Supertramp, who play just like the record. Then, that works because you listen to it and you say, 'Hey, this has got a bit of live atmosphere, but I can relate to it'. We change the songs so much for dramatic effect. I think if you just listen to a record, without being there and seeing the lights, and the way the whole thing is done, then the dynamics are destroyed. We use enormous changes of volume - very quiet and very loud, and it just doesn't come across on record. A live album would probably sell quite well incidentally, and there's a great pressure financially to do it, but I don't want to do it."

"Budapest" was not released in the US, as the band's deal with Arista soured. However, the LP contained all three Springsteen covers, "Lies," "Demolition Man," "Davy's On The Road Again," "Redemption Song" and "Mighty Quinn." Many of these appeared in completely different arrangements, especially "Blinded By The Light" and "Redemption Song." "Blinded" had a jazzy piano introduction with an ending similar to Springsteen's original, while "Redemption Song" was similar to Bob Marley's acoustic single version. The "Budapest" cassette featured all these tunes plus three bonus tracks: a live version of "Brothers And Sisters Of Africa," the live B-side "Don't Kill It Carol" and a longer version of "No Transkei" called (you guessed it) "Where Do They Send Them." Later in Germany in 1984, "Budapest" became Manfred's first album release on the new compact disc format. Over the next few years, the entire MMEB catalog would follow on CD in Germany and then England.

Lingwood and Thompson's overproduction on "Budapest" made the recordings sound as if they were studio recordings with dubbed applause. In addition, each song faded out, so the "live" feeling of being at the concerts was replaced by edited highlights. These edits were most noticeable on "Don't Kill It Carol," whose Manfred Mann-sung bridge section was edited out. This inevitably reduced the impact of the song.

"Criminal Tango"

The Earth Band went into the studio for their next album, but they did not have a home for it since apparent mismanagement at Bronze Records led to its bankruptcy. In its 11-year association with Manfred Mann's Earth Band, Bronze had served the band well. Securing a recording contract became the next priority, and Manfred soon settled on Virgin's 10 Records label. Even with a record contract in place, Manfred still took a long time to put together the material for the soon-to-be released album "Criminal Tango."

The first fruit from these sessions appeared in March 1986 on the single "Do Anything You Wanna Do." In 1977 Eddie And The Hot Rods collected a Top 10 hit with this pop song, but Manfred's version received little notice at all. On the Earth Band take, Manfred used his guitar, synthesizer and volume change formula to fashion another view of the song. Again, overlapped vocals by Thompson and Rogers on the last verse formed a strong bond, but it was unclear to everyone how this song could become a hit again just nine years after its first appearance. After all, it's not "The Locomotion!" The B-side "Crossfire" was the latest in a long line of strong band instrumentals, comprising bass, guitar and keyboard solos before a crossfade into Manfred's drifting piano finish. The 12" single release of this single also included the 7" edit of the A-side.

Three months later, another hit cover was released as a single - "Going Underground." The Jam had hit #1 in 1980 with the song, so it became even more unlikely for Manfred to hit with it as well. "Going Underground" used vast volume changes well within its pop format, but it worked better in the more unrestrained live arena. Manfred and Mick's brilliant song "Rescue" (entitled "I Shall Be Rescued" on the single) was this record's superior side and featured many classic MMEB elements. Mick's uplifting vocal and the joint playing of Mann and Rogers elevated the band to new heights. The synthesizer lead, which bursts into a guitar solo, is an absolute delight, and the entire tone of the song leaves the listener feeling better about themselves. "Rescue" was even more exciting live, as audiences were rewarded with even more guitar and keyboard interplay during its solo. Again, the 12" of this single also included the 7" edit of the top side.

When "Criminal Tango" was made available to UK fans in the middle of June 1986, the album's contents unfolded snappy pop songs with crackling keyboards and drums, and fluid guitar work. Even by today's standards, "Criminal Tango" still sounds modern and fresh. Still, its relative failure in extremely loyal Germany was very surprising. Beyond the previous single tracks, the album contained some surprises, musical and otherwise. In the "otherwise" department, the album and the previous singles were billed as "Manfred Mann's Earth Band with Chris Thompson." In 1985, journeyman Steve Kinch was selected mid-album as the band's permanent bass player, but Kinch, Durban Betancourt-Laverde and John Giblin all appeared on the album in this capacity.

The nature of the songs on the album was not geared toward British audiences, so "Criminal Tango" had no chance of succeeding in that country. "Criminal Tango" was the band's most American-sounding album to date but it did not receive an American release. On top of this, the Jam and Eddie And The Hot Rods singles were complete failures in the States. US Virgin had no interest of releasing it Stateside, and that was that.

Further musical surprises on this Manfred Mann/Steve Forward produced album were in store for fans with the covers of "Banquet" and "Bulldog." Joni Mitchell's "Banquet" originally appeared on her "For The Roses" album in 1972, and Manfred's keyboard sequences and riffs flowed well with the song's volume builds. The song also became an exciting concert opener in 1986, 1991 and 1992 shows when combined with or rearranged as a synthesizer solo. Undoubtedly, one of the strangest song choices that Manfred has made was redoing the Beatles "Yellow Submarine"-era song "Hey Bulldog" as simply "Bulldog." Manfred used more of a group vocal sound in his rearrangement, and stinging guitars and overlapped vocals made an interesting if not off-center take on the song. One can only presume that the song was retitled "Bulldog" because the song's title was not mentioned until a vocal overlap hidden in the background near the song's end!

The other three songs were derived from mainly obscure sources. Garland Jeffreys, a US songwriter who enjoyed a cult following in the late '70s/early '80s, teamed up with Manfred to write "Who Are The Mystery Kids?" Powerfully chorded with excellent keyboard and guitar runs, this song was the essence of '80s rock. Denny Newman, writer of "Lies (Through The 80's)," contributed "Killer On The Loose" to the album. Like "Lies," the tune was a hard-edged pop song with pointed synthesizer and guitar runs. "You Got Me Right Through The Heart" was a new song written by unknown Robert Byrne. This song also used the same riff-based arrangement used on "Killer On The Loose," and it developed well in a live setting during the handful of shows at which it was performed.

While all of the album's tracks were rehearsed, only "Bulldog" and "Killer On The Loose" did not make the final cut for the "Criminal Tango" tour set list. This tour sparked renewed MMEB interest and excitement within the band was immediately revived, especially since the live arrangements of "Criminal Tango" tracks allowed the band to stretch out and create far superior performances. The tour also introduced surprising live versions of The Spencer Davis Group classic "Gimme Some Lovin'" and the blues song "Automobile." For this tour, Steve Kinch was brought in on bass. In any event, the tour schedule was not as long as everyone had hoped. MMEB made their final appearance in England at the Woking Old School House on the 19th of August, 1986. The European leg of the tour reached Germany and other locations that September. Further surprises awaited those audiences, who were treated to a different arrangement of "Runner" and a medley of "3rd Man Theme" (the 1965 Herb Alpert classic) and "Flying Home" (the Lionel Hampton Orchestra staple).

Manfred had a difficult decision to make. He had to maintain the band's well-being while still producing high quality music, but the Chris Thompson situation had to be resolved immediately. Mann decided to keep recording with the Earth Band, but without Chris Thompson. Since 1986, Chris has developed both his solo career and his highly successful session work.

"Masque" - Songs and Planets

This extended break enabled Manfred to focus all of his energies toward the album that would function as a sequel to "Solar Fire" - "Masque," released in England in November 1987. Unlike "Solar Fire," the complex "Masque" directly used many themes from Holst's "The Planets" within a modern framework. This approach was combined with non-planetary songs, leading to "Masque"'s unofficial album subtitle "Songs And Planets."

With Chris Thompson now gone, the core members (Mann, Rogers and Lingwood) had to be augmented by outside help to complete the album. This assistance was provided on bass (Durban Betancourt and Andy Pask), horns (Guy Barker on trumpet, Frank Mead on saxophones), and vocals (Maggie Ryder and Denny Newman). In many ways, "Masque" was another Alan Parsons Project-type album. On this occasion, it was very coherent sounding and consistently produced. This consistency was an impressive surprise, especially since four differently produced sessions were required to complete it.

The Mann/Hard Times Production session that created "Sister Billie's Bounce" and "Billie's Orno Bounce" was definitely the most adventurous. Both tracks used a combination of jazz and a danceable yet hardhitting rhythm track, anticipating the prevalent sampling of jazz classics within the bass and drum heavy rhythm tracks found in '90s rap music. The most successful example of this marriage of jazz and rap occurred in 1994 with Us3's use of Herbie Hancock's "Cantaloupe Island" for its own "Cantaloop (Flip Fantasia)." While Manfred's readings of "Sister Sadie" and "Billie's Bounce" were not rap by any stretch of the imagination, the scat vocals used on the MMEB versions produce a cadence that would not be out of place in recent rap crossover recordings. Maggie Ryder and Manfred wrote the scat lyrics superimposed on top of these rhythm tracks, and piano and trumpet solos were incorporated into the mix of "Billie's Orno Bounce."

As for the jazz content of Manfred's creations, "Sister Billie's Bounce" used elements of the jazz classics "Sister Sadie" and "Billie's Bounce," while "Billie's Orno Bounce" used the "Billie's Bounce" portion. (The "Orno" part of the title refers to "Ornithology," another classic Parker performance.) Jazz pianist Horace Silver recorded "Sister Sadie" in August 1959 for his album "Blowin' The Blues Away," and Charlie Parker's "Billie's Bounce" dated from November 1945.

Mann and Steve Forward produced four mainly planet-related tracks for the album, with Denny Newman's "Telegram To Monica" being the only exception. "Telegram To Monica" was an excellent, melodic song with a pained Denny Newman vocal. Excellent overlapped backing vocals by Mick Rogers and Maggie Ryder matched the accompaniment, and solo turns on synthesizer and guitar completed the picture. A remake of their 1973 Holst-based hit "Joybringer" was also included on the album, as was "Hymn (from Jupiter)" (originally titled "The Hymn"). "Hymn" was a band-backed trumpeton solo based on the *andante maestoso* movement of Holst's "Jupiter." The final track from this session, "Hymn (Reprise)," was a short instrumental restatement of "Hymn." However, the reprise did not make the final track listing as it may have been possibly considered too similar to the major "Hymn," though in actuality this is not so.

In fact, Manfred pulled the original LP and its running order just before release and the LP cover was pasted over with a sticker revealing its new contents. Since CD booklets were prepared after the LP covers, they were not pasted over. The final album version was edited and resequenced with three songs added ("Neptune [Icebringer]," "Rivers Run Dry" and "We're Going Wrong") and one removed - "Hymn (Reprise)." Although Mick Rogers was not fairly represented, the entire first version of this album was superior in every way.[85]

The three new songs added to the album were the result of a Mann/Rogers-produced collaboration. Mick, Manfred and Denny Newman created the 1-minute "Neptune (Icebringer)" by adapting the *andante* section of Holst's "Neptune, The Mystic" with overlapped vocalizations of new lyrics. "Rivers Run Dry" and "We're Going Wrong" came from a slew of solo demos that Mick made at home, and both were edited and remixed with minor touch-ups by Manfred and the band. "Rivers Run Dry" (originally called "Rivers") was a Mick Rogers-written song that he had previously released as a solo single for Mooncrest Records. The "Masque" version was missing its introduction, bridge and ending, but the song remained powerfully vital. Cream's "Disraeli Gears" album track "We're Going Wrong" also had the Rogers magic touch. What may have seemed another odd song choice for the band was quickly forgotten by its mesmerizing ambience, arguably making it superior to the original. Two other songs that Rogers originally attempted ("Stay Young" and "Man Against Machine") were re-recorded by the Earth Band but remain unreleased. The popular '70s Gallagher And Lyle pop tune "Stay Young" was nicely done by the Earth Band, and included another copyrighted Mann piano fadeaway at its end! "Man Against Machine" was a strong Rogers original, and its non-release has stumped all who have heard it.

The session that Manfred produced himself proved equally frustrating to fans, as its contents suffered more from last-minute tampering than the rest of the album's sessions. A cover of another #1 Jam hit, "Start," was more successfully reworked as "What You Give Is What You Get (Start)." Again, its original unedited (and unissued) version reigned supreme. Related to "Start" was "Planets Schmanets," a jazzy piece that used the former's theme on trumpeton.[86] "A Couple Of Mates (From Mars and Jupiter)" (misidentified as "Mars and Saturn" on the original album) was taken from the *allegro* movement of Holst's "Mars" and the *allegro giocoso* section of "Jupiter." With smooth vocal backing and a jazzy backdrop, Manfred's trumpeton gracefully alternated with Frank Mead's sax. Completing this session was the song coupling that made up the unsuccessful single preceding the album, "Geronimo's Cadillac" and "Two Friends (From Mars & Saturn)."

"Geronimo's Cadillac" tackled the Murphey) US Top 40 number from rhythmic way. What was most released album and singles opposite its unused version.[87] Airplay question, since its "retro" nature was Radio in England.

Michael Murphey (later Michael Martin 1972 in a most unconventional and frustrating to fans was this song's presentations, as these were completely for any of these records was out of the forbidden on Radio One and Capitol

Movements from "Mars" (*allegro*) and "Saturn" (*adagio*) formed the basis for the other side of this single, "Two Friends (From Mars & Saturn)." A hard drum track backed a blistering keyboard instrumental, and a funky end section revealed a bass solo and concluding synthesizer riff that perfectly encapsulated what made the Earth Band so enjoyable. Conclusively, "Two Friends" marked the perfect ending to the Earth Band's first go-around.

Through "Criminal Tango" and "Masque," Manfred made a strong case for the proper use of synthesizers in rock music. Throughout the '80s and '90s, synthesizers have been used either for mechanical dance rhythms or as wallpaper, so their usage within the formats contained on "Masque" and "Criminal Tango" was welcome indeed.

For all these reasons, "Masque" was definitely a case of Manfred being a little ahead of his time. The album sold a little better than its predecessor, but the sales dropoff in Germany and its non-release in the US were very noticeable. "Masque" did take the band into exciting new directions, and they might have worked well for the Earth Band today if they had developed them. Instead, no tour for "Masque" was planned, and the Earth Band was officially disbanded.

The period following "Masque" was one of frustration and failure. Manfred tried forming a trio with Greg Lake (of Emerson, Lake & Palmer) and a drummer, but very quickly things ground to a halt at The Workhouse. Still, after two poor selling albums, Manfred had the option to record singles for 10/Virgin. At this point, a fire occurred at The Workhouse. Since nearly all of the multi-track tapes recorded by Chapter Three and the Earth Band were stored there, they were destroyed. So, Manfred relocated to a studio in Milton Keynes (in England's Midlands) for nine months while The Workhouse was being refurbished. Looking solely at the singles market, Manfred tried in vain to come up with something commercial. Some of his failed attempts included The Lovin' Spoonful hit

"Summer In The City" and yet another version of Dr. John's "Mardi Gras Day" (originally on "Messin'"). Manfred also tried Cyndi Lauper and Mick Rogers songs, but Manfred became even more frustrated and discarded all these recordings.

In an attempt to try something different, Manfred played the tune to what developed into "Medicine Song." Finally, he had something to focus on: the American Indian-related music project "Plains Music."

Manfred Mann's Plain Music

German/US cover

Manfred's recent attempts at pop music left him despondent, but his ongoing interest in investigating the obscure has been the bridge leading Manfred to new creative directions. Such was the case with "Medicine Song." The original structure of this song and many others was contained in Nathalie Curtis' "The Indians Book," a 70+ year old song book of American Indian tribal chants. By tentatively trying some of these songs in 1988, Manfred gradually gained the confidence to use this book as the framework for a different kind of album - "Plains Music." That same year, backing tracks took shape in South Africa except for the Workhouse tracks "Sikelele I" and "Sikelele II."

Manfred clearly describes how his interest in American Indian music began and how his experience with it developed into "Plains Music: "I bought a book several years ago and I recorded a song about Geronimo. I was trying to find a book which gave me some historical background information, and I had a look at this book and it was full of music. It was quite expensive and I realized it had nothing about Geronimo in it, but I bought it anyway, and at the time I was doing some straight commercial pop music and I suddenly felt that actually it was something that I didn't want to be doing any longer, and I started playing these melodies, just playing around on the piano. I started off with a song called 'Medicine Song' - [I felt,] 'God, this is a really nice melody, just playing it simply.'

UK cover

"Increasingly disenchanted with the recordings I was doing, I was more and more attracted to these melodies. It wasn't so much North American music as such, it was just the melodies. I don't know anything about North American Indian culture, I am pretty ignorant, so it was really the melodies. And some time after that I was going to visit my family in South Africa and I took a tape with me because somebody had sent me a tape of a guy called Smiles Makama, who played African hunting bows and stuff, and I thought, 'Well, maybe we will just do something.' Slowly the idea came together very casually in Johannesburg, and the album came together in four weeks. I spent two years fiddling around trying to improve it and change it, adding choirs on and things, throwing most of that away, leaving what's on the 'Plains Music' album, and it (the album) was very similar to what I recorded just in four weeks. A lot of it was mixed quite quickly, even though it took me a long time to fiddle."

Being a different type of music, a different collection of musicians was required. Enter Manfred Mann's Plain Music, a racially mixed studio group of musicians mainly based in South Africa. This entity consisted of Manfred, vocalist Noel McCalla, Peter Sklair on bass, drummer Ian Hermann and MMEB session veteran Barbara Thompson on sax. A friend of Manfred's helped him to locate the extremely suitable McCalla in London, while Thompson took time off from her successful European jazz outfit Paraphernalia to participate in this project.

Additional assistance on "Plains Music" came from Kelly Petlane on pennywhistle, the aforementioned Smiles Makama on African hunting bows and a trio of backing vocalists: Doren

Thobeki, Walter Sanza and Chief Dawethi. The interaction of these racially integrated performers naturally created a cross-cultural environment, effectively enabling them to produce this album containing the melodies of five tribes: four North American Red-Indian (Kiowa, Apache, Dakota and Laguna), and one African (Xhosa). The latter theme, "Sikelele," was the only African tribal melody on the album, with lyrics supplied by Mike Heron.

Due to Manfred's South African background, the inspiration of "Sikelele" may seem obvious on the surface. However, Manfred stressed that the song's development and outcome were based more on the band's own surroundings: "Well, I was in South Africa, so there's a natural influence, and for the musicians I was playing with, they themselves would have an African influence. If I was playing in England with different musicians it would have been different, but I don't particularly look for influences. Whatever is happening at the time, whatever seems to work, I go with that. In the end you are looking for the same feeling in all music you do. It's a kind of emotional content that you're looking for. I don't particularly look for influences, but there have been influences."

South African front cover

South African back cover

With an entirely different band and distinctive material to work with, a new work process was also required to record it. Using the recording method of the '60s, Manfred and this band cut about 80% of "Plains Music" as live studio takes. Again, "Sikelele" was the only exception to this rule. However, Manfred relates that he also had commercial considerations when creating that song: "That is the only non-Indian song and it was my realization halfway through that in the real world, I wanted to sell this album. The record companies are going to want to hear something that they believe could be a single or successful, and so it was quite calculated to find a song that had more obvious communicative powers, you might say accessible, although I think the whole album is very accessible. 'Sikelele' I did with samplers and machines and stuff in England. That took more time than the rest of the album."

The African Xhosa stick fighting theme "Sikelele" appeared on the album in two different ways, a

mainly vocal version ("Sikelele I") and an instrumentally-based piece ("Sikelele II"). Noel McCalla's mellifluous lead vocal on the first take matched the picturesque quality of the lyrics, and mixed well with Doren Thobeki. The chorus worked as a fugue, in which one vocal stated the chorus melody and then backing vocals developed as counterpoints to that first vocal. This chorus became an extension to the vocal overlapping that Manfred has employed throughout his recorded career. As with

his other projects, Manfred's proper use of volume switches worked well with "Sikelele I." Soon, it was released on many different single formats for the German Intuition label.[88]

Hunting bow, piano and vocal chants led off "Sikelele II," moving into unique vocals by Doren Thobeki and Manfred's piano melody. Not merely a reprise of the first version, "Sikelele II" was a creative entity unto itself.

The Kiowa tribe was represented by the wind song "Kiowa" and two versions of a war song, "Hunting Bow" and "Hunting Bow (Reprise)." "Kiowa," as the album's first track, was a subtle instrumental with Barbara Thompson's sax leading the way over piano and hunting bow accompaniment.[89] This placid feeling was contrasted by "Hunting Bow," on which the warlike sounds of the title instrument led into a piano and an equally powerful sax run. "Hunting Bow (Reprise)" was mainly a showcase for Thompson's proficient sax abilities, and it was played slower than the first take.

The medicinal methods of the Apache films and television, but none of these "Medicine Song." The Manfred Mann's medicine song included lyrics from lead vocal from Noel McCalla. Equally pennywhistle, and its melodic nature led single.[90] Though not as successful as Song" received accolades when Indians have long been documented in presentations was as honest as that of Plain Music treatment of the Apache Anthony Moore and another brilliant emotive was Kelly Petlane's wistful to its release as "Plains Music"'s second "Sikelele I" in singles sales, "Medicine presented live by MMEB in 1991.

On the instrumental side, this melody was also presented on the album by "Instrumedicine Song." Manfred used his atmospheric synthesizer backing to great effect here, and the track's full arrangement of horns, vocals, piano and hunting bow were soothing and tremendously satisfying. Apaches also had a song to celebrate their fishing expeditions - the atmospheric and free-flowing "Salmon Fishing." Manfred's keyboards alternated between an airy feeling and warm bursts of energy with Barbara Thompson's saxophone.

The Dakota ghost dance "Wounded Knee" built Manfred's music box-style piano into a sax and pennywhistle transition. Sporadic backing vocals worked their charm here, evoking the feeling of an apparition within the song.[91]

The meticulous process of grinding corn, a staple of the Indian diet, was expressed in the Laguna tribal melody "Laguna." The slow burning nature of "Laguna" was Manfred's musical analogy of this process, with Peter Sklair's bass standing out. As another fully arranged track, horns, piano and percussion worked their wonders here, until another trademark Mann ending piano slide.

Longer versions of the album's songs do exist, but unlike "Masque," the essence of each was retained by carefully measuring each musical ingredient. For the most part, sections that Manfred considered repetitious were deleted from the final versions, as he remarks: "Most of the songs have got a pop song format - they are very short with a jazz element. Everybody likes jazz for eight bars, but they don't like it for 20 minutes. That includes me, so I kept all the solos really short. I just did it to what seemed natural to me." By doing this, "Plains Music" was finely crafted with a genuinely ethnic atmosphere.

Manfred wrote the liner notes for "Plains Music" in February 1991 when it was ready for release, and the album was first issued in Germany that May on the Intuition label. In South Africa, the album did quite well on local charts.[92] Later in the year, the album was released by Rhythm Safari in the US with the track "Salmon Fishing" replacing "Hunting Bow (Reprise)" from the foreign editions. The US album received a small amount of airplay on alternative stations and hit #25 on the Adult Alternative album chart in early 1992.

"Plains Music" was not released in England until August 1992 on the Kaz label, but it was comprehensive, containing both "Hunting Bow (Reprise)" and "Salmon Fishing." Unfortunately, promotion for the UK release of the album was minimal. Manfred was featured just once on national British radio promoting the album, at the inconvenient weekday time of 2:30PM on Radio Two.

Concurrent with the final preparations of the album's release, Manfred reformed Manfred Mann's Earth Band in the spring of 1991. That May, the band played their first warmup gigs in England. The warm British reception they received has been overshadowed by the success that they have experienced in Europe and Scandinavia over the past few years.

With the musical success of "Plains Music" now behind him, Manfred has left the possibility open that more "plain music" projects can be produced in the future.

The Return of Manfred Mann's Earth Band

To reform the Earth Band in early 1991, Manfred called upon the most instrumental players in the projects he had worked on over the last five years. Mick Rogers and bassist Steve Kinch were vital during the end of the first Earth Band stint, and Noel McCalla's impressive performance on "Plains Music" gave Manfred the idea of stretching Noel's vocal boundaries by having him sing lead with the Earth Band. Although Noel was not very familiar with MMEB, Manfred's feeling that Noel could sing on material outside the scope of his previous work was unerring. A drummer of the highest degree, Clive Bunker, was selected after a short time. In true Manfred fashion, this decision was based on connections that a band member provided. Bunker was in the original Jethro Tull lineup that shot to fame in 1968, and just over a decade later Clive was playing with Mick Rogers in the group Aviator. Through Mick's recommendation, Clive was brought in and he has proved to be a fine addition to the band.

By reforming MMEB, Manfred's intentions were to develop the band's repertoire by touring first and then recording an album. Warm-up gigs in England in the late spring of 1991 led to tremendously successful tours of Germany and Scandinavia, two areas that remained loyal to MMEB throughout the years. In November and December of that year, the group hit Holland, Germany and France by storm. "Banquet" opened each show, and Bob Dylan's influence was very evident with "Shelter From The Storm," "The Times They Are A-Changing," "Father Of Day, Father Of Night" and the final encore "Mighty Quinn." "Shelter From The Storm" was a Dylan "Blood On The Tracks" LP track, and Manfred's dramatic rearrangement of it and "The Times They Are A-Changing" caught many fans by surprise. "Shelter From The Storm" was typical in that Manfred did not use all of Dylan's lyrics. What was important was that Manfred successfully retained the song's impact within a different setting. Two other new songs entered their 1991 set ("Castles Burning" and "Nature Of The Beast") and old crowd favorites were appropriately redressed for the occasion. "Martha's Madman" made a stunning appearance, and "Automobile" prepared fans for the solo piano snatch of "Sister Sadie" which preceded "Blinded By The Light." The most surprising change was how smoothly "Medicine Song" segued into "Redemption Song." This tour was the band's last use of

"Gimme Some Lovin'," and "Davy's On The Road Again" provided the killer encore that sent delighted fans home. On some early warmups, "Spirits In The Night" preceded "Davy's On The Road Again," but the former was dropped as it was not as successful.

When the Earth Band was not performing or recording at The Workhouse, each band member had his own side projects to pursue. After doing some of his ongoing solo recordings, Mick Rogers joined Joan Armatrading's band for an American tour and some other dates. Clive Bunker moonlighted with former Tull guitarist Mick Abrahams and his reformed group Blodwyn Pig. Steve Kinch went back to session work and Noel McCalla was finalizing his band's cassette release "Noel McCalla's Contact."

The summer of 1991 proved to be very busy and successful for the Earth Band, as the band played a German summer festival with The Beach Boys and The Allman Brothers. British warmups for this festival were supposed to have the band perform under the name of The Jitterbugs, but they eventually settled on M.M.E.B. when performing in London pubs. Again, "Banquet" was used as a concert opener, and the set followed along the same lines of the previous year's journey. More new live material like the Cyril Shuman-written "Miss You" was developing, and playing a novelty blues number like "Automobile" became unnecessary. During 1992, the Earth Band supported Status Quo in Denmark, while headlining numerous festivals in Germany and other countries.

The year 1993 was by far the most successful in the band's return. After some warm-up gigs in England, summer festivals and shows in Germany, Holland, Austria, Hungary, Switzerland, Sweden and Denmark kept the band visible and fresh. A more confident Earth Band emerged as their set became stronger, tighter and more enthusiastically received. All four Dylan songs were retained, and an instrumental version of "Joybringer" took the band forcefully into "Shelter From The Storm." Two other new songs made their first appearance, "Dirty City" and the first encore "Pleasure And Pain" (originally by Australian group The Divinyls). Also, "Demolition Man" reappeared in their set after a ten-year absence. Appearing as previously arranged were "Miss You," "Martha's Madman," "Blinded By The Light, "Medicine Song," "Redemption Song" and final encore "Davy's On The Road Again."

If you're wondering what happened to the album the Earth Band has been recording since 1991, it's been a long, painstaking process. Being the most important album of Manfred's career, the survival of the Earth Band depends on it. Manfred's indecision with this album mainly stems from his devotion to translating the excitement and drama of recent, successful live performances into a fresh album within the studio. Entrusted with this task in midstream was seasoned producer Richard Burgess, who has taken much of the pressure off Manfred.

At the time of this writing, the album's recording is almost complete but the track listing is constantly being modified. Its planned release date is in early 1996, with a widespread tour to follow. Let's hope all turns out well!

Manfred Mann's Earth Band in the CD Age

As with most groups of the '70s, the advent of the CD age did not do MMEB any favors! After finally gaining control of his Chapter Three and Earth Band catalogs, Manfred and business affairs manager Steve Fernie created Cohesion Records to get these albums back in the marketplace. Manfred Mann Chapter Three and Earth Band CD packaging has been disappointing, with original cover designs chopped up, distorted or eliminated altogether. The only exceptions are the Japanese versions (on "Blonze" Records), which give you obvious copies of front and back LP covers! In sound quality, compact discs of MMEB do not present the group fairly due to their muddy sound. Some discs have been transferred from record, and pieces of songs have been omitted due to engineering errors. In short, the entire MMEB catalog needs a complete overhaul, similar to the recent high quality remastering of the Led Zeppelin and Yes catalogs. In this way, both purists and casual fans will be impressed by the packaging, inside and out. If the MMEB catalog can be brought to the high quality level of the HMV recordings, everything will be for the better. At least the Chapter Three discs sound fine!

The following quick rundown of MMEB compact disc quality tells you which are the best value for your money, and which you should avoid altogether. The problem that we are now faced with is the location of the Bronze label's master tapes and artwork. After the label's closure, the whereabouts of their tapes became unknown. All current CDs originated from muddy and inconsistent sounding German tapes. Of course, the songs that I previously identified as non-album or non-UK tracks are the most affected here, and they will not appear on CD until some reliable tape source appears. Of course, US master tapes exist, but they do not cover the singles period between "I (Who Have Nothing)" and "Tribal Statistics." Don't worry - I'm working on it!

"Manfred Mann's Earth Band" - The sound on the German, Japanese and UK Cohesion discs is extremely muddy, especially since it has way too much bass and no highs to speak of. Your best bet is to seek the original British CD on Castle Communications, which was properly re-equalized with much more clarity. In addition, Castle has eliminated the excessive space between the tracks, so the album sounds more immediate.

"Glorified Magnified" - The original German CD was taken from a noisy record, but the Cohesion disc has cleaned up the sound somewhat through re-equalization. The disc is still very hissy, though.

"Messin'" - All CD reissues of this album, except the Japanese release, have redrawn album covers! (The Japanese CD cover was a photograph from a used LP cover.) With quality in mind, all but the UK Castle Communications CD have muddy sound. The only drawbacks for the Castle disc are its omission of the countoff on "Get Your Rocks Off" and an early fade on "Sadjoy." Again, Castle has less space between tracks, but you'll need a copy of the German or Cohesion CDs to get everything.

"Solar Fire" - This is where the troubles really begin! Although the German, Japanese and Cohesion CDs all sound fine, the ending of "Mercury, The Winged Messenger" fades down to its complete ending instead of remaining at the same volume. Only the UK Legacy CD presents the track properly, but don't rely on that disc for anything else, as it is a shambles! The tracks are in the wrong sequence for some unknown reason, the US single edit of "Joybringer" was included instead of "Earth The Circle Part 1," and "Earth The Circle Part 1" was misidentified as "Part 2." In addition, two other name changes took place on Legacy's CD: "Father Of Day, Father Of Night" was just listed as "Father Of Night," and "In The Beginning, Darkness" was shown as "In The Beginning." Other than those minor details, it's fine!

"The Good Earth" - No matter where you go, this album is taken from a record! The original bassy sounding German issue is missing the rooster introduction on "Give Me The Good Earth," and "I'll Be Gone" is edited for some reason. The Cohesion issue sounds a little better, but the first note of "Earth Hymn" is clipped. This album needs improvement more than any other.

"Nightingales And Bombers" - All issues except the UK Castle Communications CD have no high end, and Castle's crisp sound is impressive.

"The Roaring Silence" - For a major hit album like this, its presentation on CD is nothing short of disgusting. All CDs have switched the places of "Waiter, There's A Yawn In My Ear" and "Questions" on the album, and the sound is unremarkable. "Questions," "This Side Of Paradise" and even "Blinded By The Light" have clipped endings, and about 20 seconds are missing from the end of "Singing The Dolphin Through." Obviously, an engineer was trying to hide the fact that this album was taken from a record, but we Manfredians are too smart for him!

"Watch" - All CDs of this album sound great, although the original Legacy issue jumbled up the track order.

"Angel Station" - All CDs sound fine with one exception: Manfred's talking after the track "Resurrection" is entirely missing. Again, an engineer's lack of knowledge of the album must have caused the problem. The Legacy disc again has a mixed up track order, and they spelled "Resurrection" with two "s's" and one "r""! Try again!

"Chance" - For once, all of the CD issues sound fine. Hooray!

"Somewhere In Afrika" - All CDs have been taken from what seems to be a third or fourth generation analog tape, due to its hiss level. The album was originally processed digitally, so there is no reason this should have occurred. Unfortunately, every CD has mixed up song ordering, but the sound is uniform. Watch out for the German CD, which assigns separate track numbers to the "Africa Suite." These numbers are not listed properly on its cover.

"Budapest" - Every CD sounds about the same, but unfortunately none of the cassette bonus tracks have been included, though there is plenty of room for them.

The more recent original Manfred Mann albums, "Criminal Tango," "Masque" and "Plains Music" all sound fine.

Manfred (right) and business affairs manager Steve Fernie (left) enjoying
a gold record from the German release of "Blinded By The Light - The
Very Best Of Manfred Mann's Earth Band"

Compilations

So far in the US, the only proper representation of Manfred Mann's Earth Band on CD is the long version of "Blinded By The Light" that appears on the "Highs Of The Seventies" compilation (Warner Special Products). This situation is still uncertain, as plans have not yet been developed for US release of MMEB material. In

Of Manfred Mann's Earth Band 1971- disappointment on many accounts. The and the latest one ("Runner") was from stated by the album title). In addition, Light" was included instead of the quality of the collection was the single Again," which made its first album

England, the 1990 release of "20 Years 1991" on Cohesion Records was a earliest track was 1973's "Joybringer" 1983 (thus, not spanning the years the single edit of "Blinded By The album version. The only redeeming version of "Davy's On The Road appearance. "Joybringer" was faded

early and was also taken from a record, the "1971-1973" album alternate mix. To coincide with and to promote the album, "Davy's On The Road Again" was released on 7", 12" and CD singles with various track listings. These records made no impression on fans.

Cohesion Records also reissued 10 of the original 12 MMEB Bronze albums on CD across the Atlantic, but "Glorified Magnified" and "The Good Earth" were originally missing from the CD ranks due to Manfred's dissatisfaction with the albums themselves. After the uneventful compilation "Spotlight," the two missing MMEB albums and a Manfred Mann interview CD were included in a 12CD box set released in October 1992. "Glorified Magnified" and "The Good Earth" were reissued in late 1993, as was the entire catalog. In February 1994, both Chapter Three albums made their British CD debut.

The crowning achievement of Cohesion's existence so far is its licensing of MMEB recordings to the German TV label Arcade. Through its powerful advertising, Arcade took the December 1992 album, "Blinded By The Light - The Best Of Manfred Mann's Earth Band" for a 10-week ride in the German Top 20. Peaking at #10, the album has sold over 300,000 copies in Germany, enough to earn Manfred a gold record. Concurrent with its German release, the album appeared in Holland (resequenced with slight track modifications) and Denmark. Since the Earth Band went over to these countries a few months later during their 1993 summer tour, the band reinforced their dominance there. The success of this album sparked the release of a second (though less successful) volume from Arcade and a limited edition 2CD package containing both volumes. The first Arcade "best of" album was also released in Norway in early 1994 and amazingly hit #1 on that country's chart in March. A British volume was released in August 1994 and spent just one week at #69.

UK promo CD single

Conclusion - The Art of Being Unique

Playing Style

What has made Manfred's playing style so different? It is his unique way of dealing with the most unreliable of instruments, the Moog synthesizer, by turning its shortcomings into an advantage. It is best expressed in Manfred's words: "I am the only one who effectually found it a defective instrument! There's no touch response on a mini-Moog, and I was used to playing piano. All the time, you're looking for the ability, really, in any keyboard or any instrument, to distinguish one note from the other, to provide accent, to provide power, to provide life. I mean, on a guitar or on any real instrument, you play each note differently. Now the problem with all synthesizers, really the early synthesizers, was that they had no touch response. The synthesizer is an awful instrument! So when I came across the mini-Moog, there was this wah-wah pedal effectively in the filter, which just gave me an option to change one note to the next. To me, the whole key is changing from one note to the next. Even though for long periods of time you might leave the note untouched, so that you might play a whole section without doing that, it's also the fact that within microseconds you can change the sound to what you hear or feel. You can make it soft, you can make it harsh within seconds. You know it's just there in front of you as an automatic thing.

"The ability to bend notes - and I bend notes down, which a lot of people don't do, that's because Miles Davis used to do that on trumpet - it was an influence from Miles Davis. I think I just gravitated to using that filter all the time, and nobody else ever did. So, the reason I sound different is there's this sort of "wah-wah" going on - it's nothing special, but it lands up sounding quite different, and it's this inherent ability to make anything sound miserable and mournful, which is to bend the notes downwards, rather than up.

"I do sound different to other people. I just wish that that was a thing you could succeed at in the real world, rather than it being a very side issue at what you're doing. Another depressing thing about mini-Moog playing, or my mini-Moog playing, it sounds best live - I mean, in the studio, it never seems to hang on . . . it doesn't seem to come through in quite the same way unless it's a live recording, and I've no idea why.

"What's happened now with keyboards is, you get more and more sounds, and no real control. You get phony control, where you can alter a lousy filter or whatever, but not real control. Keyboard players are now more the keepers of the sound, using sounds to imitate real instruments, and not the real players everyone admires. There is something quite fundamental that comes from the acoustic world which you can't get away from too much. It's what you hear with your ears and what is made with organic, natural instruments."

Right now, Manfred hooks up two mini-Moogs via a MIDI (musical instrument digital interface) to give him the necessary touch and rich sound control to compete in the modern music world.

The Final Analysis

Manfred Mann is still contributing to the music industry after more than 30 years in the business. Thanks to the vast quantity of his CDs available, music fans all over the world have been steadily discovering Manfred's underrated talent. In addition, recent Manfred Mann's Earth Band concerts have proven that Manfred is not ready to pack it up yet. Manfred expresses this best himself: "Manfred Mann's Earth Band is just a name, isn't it? It's not a band as such, it's a name for a group of people that are working together. I'll go on for as long as I feel like going on. As long as it's feasible. It's not a problem to go to a studio and make music. The problem is people may not buy it or like it. If it makes it, you might as well do it. There's no reason to stop now."

If you still think that Manfred's main aim is to shoot for hit singles, you're dead wrong. Manfred realistically and modestly feels that the success that he experiences with his records is not merely a function of his talents, but of the material he chooses to record and the collective pool of talent that goes into and comes out of the recording process: "Really, I just listen to every kind of songwriter, every kind of album, every kind of thing I can find - obscure people. I've just got in this habit of listening continually to other material, other songwriters and other songs. I don't really have a formula. If anyone comes along and says 'This is a good album' or there's a local band, I always listen to the songs. I always listen to anybody who's written a song. I've gotten into this habit of listening to the most weird, obscure, way-out stuff!

"I'm not really trying all the time to have hit records - I'm really trying to make hit albums, which in Europe do very well. And if hits come off the albums, that's a great bonus. Why there's longevity in my case I think is because I'm really using a lot of other people's abilities in the sense that I'm not a songwriter. So, I have the advantage, you might say, of recording some very, very good songs without having to have the genius of writing the great songs over a long period, which very few people do have. In my case, it's the fact that other people sing - I use very good singers, there's good people in the band, and it isn't all down to me. I'm not relying completely, one hundred per cent, on my own abilities."

Despite the input from his musical colleagues, the pressure is still on, but that's what drives Manfred: "It's such a challenge every year. There's so many good new people, there's so much talent around. It's quite an achievement simply to even be around! The thing that keeps me going now is simple - life and the force of life. Just a day-to-day thing - survival - and just be as happy as you can because you only live today."

Putting aside occasional frustration, Manfred's fans have been truly blessed with the opportunity of enjoying his work over such a long time. As our reward, Manfredians, let's take heart by adapting the line from "Martha's Madman": "Manfred, yes, we guess you'll have to stay around another thousand years!"

MANFRED MANN

COMPLETE DISCOGRAPHY
1963-1995

ARTIST CODE:
(1)   Manfred Mann
(2)   Manfred Mann & Mike Hug (sic)
(3)   Manfred Mann Chapter III (Manfred Mann Chapter Three)
(4)   Manfred Mann, prior to name change to Manfred Mann's Earth Band
(5)   Earth Band, instead of Manfred Mann's Earth Band
(6)   Manfred Mann's Earth Band
(7)   Manfred Mann's Earth Band with Chris Thompson
(8)   Manfred Mann's Plain Music

NOTES:

(a)   Non-UK records listed are those necessary to complete a Manfred Mann collection, plus others with unusual song couplings. Non-essential foreign EPs and albums with slight track variations have not been included.

(b)   Each release date shown is an <u>in-store date</u>, that is, the earliest date (reported to trade publications) that a record would be available for purchase in stores. If a record company did not meet its final targeted date on a particular record, it's not my fault!

(c)   Various artists albums are listed only if a Manfred Mann recording is otherwise unavailable, or the album marks the recording's first appearance.

(d)   German release dates of Manfred Mann's Earth Band singles and albums were usually a few weeks earlier than their UK counterparts. When known, exceptions are noted below.

SINGLES

(3) Virginia (edit)/I Ain't Laughing	German Vertigo 6059 028	2/12/71
(3) Espejo (One Way Glass)/¿No Es Triste? (Ain't It Sad) (33RPM single)	Argentine Vertigo 6059 030	2/12/71
(4) Living Without You/California Coastline	Australian Philips 6006 121	6/25/71
(4) Living Without You/Tribute	Philips 6006 122	6/25/71
(4) Mrs. Henry (AKA Please Mrs. Henry) (2:40 edited mono remix)/Prayer (stereo)	Philips 6006 159	9/10/71
(4) Mrs. Henry (AKA Please Mrs. Henry) (2:40 edited mono remix)/Prayer (mono - 4:09 edit)	German Philips 6006 159	9/10/71
(5) Meat/Glorified Magnified	Philips 6006 251	11/10/72
(5) Get Your Rocks Off/Sadjoy	Vertigo 6059 078	4/13/73
(6) Joybringer/Can't Eat Meat (AKA Meat)	Vertigo 6059 083	8/10/73
(6) Father Of Day, Father Of Night (edited remix)/ Solar Fire Two (AKA Solar Fire)	Bronze BRO 9	3/15/74
(6) Be Not Too Hard (edit)/Earth Hymn Part 2A (AKA Earth Hymn Part 2)	Bronze BRO 13	11/01/74
(6) Be Not Too Hard/I'll Be Gone	Australian Bronze 21-013	11/01/74
(6) Spirits In The Night (Version 1 - 3:11 edit)/As Above So Below Part 2 (AKA As Above So Below)	Bronze BRO 18	7/25/75
(6) Spirits In The Night (Version 1 - 3:11 edit)/ As Above So Below Part 2 (3:20 edit) (AKA As Above So Below)	Japanese Bronze P-1413B	10/**/75
(6) Blinded By The Light (edit)/Starbird No. 2 (AKA Starbird)	Bronze BRO 29	8/06/76
(6) Blinded By The Light - Questions - The Road To Babylon - Singing The Dolphin Through/ (one-sided promo 12" - 33RPM)	Bronze I-1 MM1	8/27/76
(6) Questions/Waiter, There's A Yawn In My Ear No. 2 (AKA Waiter, There's A Yawn In My Ear)	Bronze BRO 34	11/26/76
(6) Spirits In The Night (Version 2 - 3:15)/ The Road To Babylon	Bronze BRO 42	6/10/77
(1) Ha! Ha! Said The Clown - Mighty Quinn/ Semi-Detached Suburban Mr. James - A 'B' Side	Philips 6006 575	7/08/77
(1) Pretty Flamingo/The One In The Middle - Got My Mojo Working	EMI 2644	8/05/77
(6) California (3:40 edited remix)/Chicago (AKA Chicago Institute)	Bronze BRO 48	11/18/77
(6) Mighty Quinn (live/studio edited remix)/Tiny (AKA Mighty Quinn [edited LP version])	Bronze BRO 51	3/03/78
(6) Davy's On The Road Again (edited remix)/ Bouillabaisse (AKA Drowning On Dry Land/	Bronze BRO 52	4/28/78

Fish Soup - edit)

(6) You Angel You (edit)/Out In The Distance (AKA "Belle" Of The Earth)	Bronze BRO 68	2/02/79
(6) Don't Kill It Carol (edit)/You Are - I Am	German Bronze/ Ariola 600 047-100	2/**/79
(6) Don't Kill It Carol (LP version)/You Are - I Am (12")	German Bronze/ Ariola 600 047-213	2/**/79
(6) Don't Kill It Carol (edit)/You Are - I Am	Australian Bronze K7507	6/08/79
(6) Don't Kill It Carol (edit)/Blinded By The Light (long version)	Bronze BRO 77	6/08/79
(6) Don't Kill It Carol (edit)/Blinded By The Light (long version) (picture disc)	Bronze BROP 77	6/08/79
(6) Lies (Through The 80's) (edit)/You're Not My (AKA Adolescent Dream) (edited remix)	Bronze BRO 103	8/29/80
(6) For You (edited remix)/A Fool I Am	Bronze BRO 113	1/09/81
(6) Stranded - Interview mit (with) Manfred Mann - LP-Überblick (Chance) - On The Run/ (one-sided Rennbahn Express flexidisc)	German Bronze 202 970	2/**/81
(6) I (Who Have Nothing)/Man In Jam	Bronze BRO 137	11/13/81
(6) Eyes Of Nostradamus (edited single version)/ Holiday's End	Bronze BRO 141	3/12/82
(6) Eyes Of Nostradamus (full length re-mix)/ Holiday's End - Man In Jam (12")	Bronze BROX 141	3/12/82
(6) Redemption Song (single version)/Wardream	Bronze BRO 150	7/02/82

[NOTE: The above single was released in Germany in February 1982.]

(1) The Mighty Quinn/By Request - Edwin Garvey	Old Gold OG 9252	9/24/82
(1) Do Wah Diddy Diddy (edit)/What You Gonna Do?	HMV PMS 1003	10/01/82
(6) Tribal Statistics (single version)/ Where Do They Send Them (AKA To Bantustan?)	Bronze BRO 157	11/12/82
(6) Demolition Man (edit)/It's Still The Same (AKA Brothers And Sisters Of Azania)	Bronze BRO 161	1/21/83
(1) Do Wah Diddy Diddy (edit)/If You Gotta Go, Go Now	Old Gold OG 9369	10/14/83
(1) Pretty Flamingo/5-4-3-2-1	Old Gold OG 9376	10/14/83
(6) Davy's On The Road Again (live edit)/ Mighty Quinn (live)	Bronze BRO 177	2/17/84
(6) Davy's On The Road Again (live edit)/ Mighty Quinn (live) - Don't Kill It Carol (live) (12")	Bronze BROX 177	2/17/84
(6) Runner (edit)/No Transkei (AKA To Bantustan?) (live)	Bronze BRO 180	3/30/84
(6) Runner/No Transkei (AKA To Bantustan?) (live) - Lies (Through The 80's) (live) (12")	Bronze BROX 180	3/30/84
(1) 5-4-3-2-1/Pretty Flamingo	EMI G45 15	3/30/84
(7) Do Anything You Wanna Do (edit)/Crossfire	10/Virgin TEN 115	3/21/86

(7) Do Anything You Wanna Do/Do Anything You Wanna Do (edit) - Crossfire (12")	10/Virgin TENT 115	3/21/86
(7) Going Underground (edit)/I Shall Be Rescued (AKA Rescue)	10/Virgin TEN 121	6/13/86
(7) Going Underground/Going Underground (edit) - I Shall Be Rescued (AKA Rescue) (12")	10/Virgin TENT 121	6/13/86
(1) Pretty Flamingo/Come Tomorrow	Old Gold OG 9697	3/27/87
(6) Geronimo's Cadillac (edited remix)/ Geronimo's Cadillac (extended remix) - Two Friends (From Mars & Saturn) (12")	German 10/Virgin 609 443	9/**/87
(6) Geronimo's Cadillac (edited remix)/ Two Friends (From Mars & Saturn)	10/Virgin TEN 196	10/16/87
(6) Davy's On The Road Again (edited remix)/ Blinded By The Light (edit)	Cohesion COMMES 1	11/12/90
(6) Davy's On The Road Again (edited remix)/ Blinded By The Light (edit) - California (12")	Cohesion COMMEST 1	11/12/90
(6) Davy's On The Road Again (edited remix) - Blinded By The Light - California - Tribal Statistics (CD5)	Cohesion COMMESC 1	11/12/90
(8) Sikelele I/Wounded Knee	German Intuition 1103067	5/**/91
(8) Sikelele I (7" Remix) - Sikelele I (12" Remix) - Sikelele I - Wounded Knee (CD5)	German Intuition INT 3062 8 (master #: INT 30628)	5/**/91
(8) Sikelele I (7" Remix) - Sikelele I (12" Remix) - Sikelele II - Medicine Song (CD5)	German Intuition INT 3062 8 (master #: INT-30628)	5/**/91
(8) Sikelele I (Workhouse Remix) - Sikelele I - Wounded Knee - Sikelele I (12" Remix) (CD5)	German Intuition INT 3062 8/2 (master #: INT-30628-2)	5/**/91
(8) Medicine Song (Remix) - Medicine Song - Wounded Knee (CD5)	German Intuition INT 3062 9	7/**/91
(1) Do Wah Diddy Diddy (edit)/If You Gotta Go, Go Now	Old Gold OG 9991	12/09/91
(1) Pretty Flamingo - If You Gotta Go, Go Now - Come Tomorrow (CD5)	Old Gold OG 6178	9/07/92
(1) 5-4-3-2-1 - Do Wah Diddy Diddy (edit) - If You Gotta Go, Go Now - Pretty Flamingo - Fox On The Run - Mighty Quinn (promo CD5)	PolyGram TV MANN 1	12/07/92
(6) Blinded By The Light (edit) - Davy's On The Road Again (edited remix) - Mighty Quinn (live) - Joybringer (alternate mix) (promo CD5)	Arcade MMP001	8/22/94

US:

(1) 5-4-3-2-1/Without You	Prestige 45 - 312	3/02/64
(1) Hubble Bubble (Toil And Trouble)/	Ascot AS 2151	5/14/64
I'm Your Kingpin (promo only)		
(1) Blue Brave (AKA Why Should We Not)/	Prestige 45 - 314	6/**/64
Brother Jack (promo only)		
(1) Do Wah Diddy Diddy (edit)/What You Gonna Do?	Ascot AS 2157	8/03/64
(1) Sha La La/John Hardy	Ascot AS 2165	10/13/64
(1) Come Tomorrow/What Did I Do Wrong	Ascot AS 2170	1/07/65
(1) I Can't Believe What You Say/Poison Ivy (cancelled)	Ascot AS 2181	4/21/65
(1) My Little Red Book (All I Do Is Talk About You)/	Ascot AS 2184	5/26/65
What Am I Doing Wrong (edit)		
(1) If You Gotta Go, Go Now/The One In The Middle	Ascot AS 2194	8/26/65
(1) Do Wah Diddy Diddy (edit)/What You Gonna Do?	United Artists "Silver Spotlight Series" UA 1644	10/27/65
(1) Sha La La/John Hardy	United Artists "Silver Spotlight Series" UA 1656	10/27/65
(1) She Needs Company/Hi Lili, Hi Lo	Ascot AS 2210	2/28/66
(1) Pretty Flamingo/You're Standing By	United Artists UA 50040	5/18/66
(1) Just Like A Woman/I Wanna Be Rich	Mercury 72607	7/28/66
(1) When Will I Be Loved/Did You Have To Do That	United Artists UA 50066	8/17/66
(1) Semi-Detached Suburban Mr. James/	Mercury 72629	10/07/66
Each And Every Day		

[**NOTE:** Some copies of the above are shown as "Semi-Detached Surburban Mr. Jones" or "Semi-Detached Surburban Mr. James."]

(1) Ha! Ha! Said The Clown/Feeling So Good	Mercury 72675	3/30/67
(1) The Mighty Quinn (Quinn The Eskimo)/	Mercury 72770	2/08/68
By Request - Edwin Garvey		

[**NOTE:** Some copies of the above are shown as "Quinn The Eskimo" or "Mighty Quinn (Quinn The Eskimo)."]

(1) My Little Red Book (All I Do Is Talk About You)/	Ascot AS 2241	4/17/68
I Can't Believe What You Say		
(1) My Little Red Book (All I Do Is Talk About You)/	Ascot SAS 2241	4/17/68
I Can't Believe What You Say (stereo promo)		
(1) My Name Is Jack (Version 2)/There Is A Man	Mercury 72822	6/14/68
(1) Fox On The Run/Too Many People	Mercury 72879	11/20/68
(1) Ragamuffin Man/A 'B' Side	Mercury 72921	4/17/69
(4) Please Mrs. Henry (2:32 edited mono remix with	Polydor PD 14097	9/10/71
extra guitar overdub)/Prayer (mono)		

(6) Living Without You/Tribute	Polydor PD 14113	1/28/72

[**NOTE:** "Living Without You" was sped up on the US single only.]

(6) I'm Up And I'm Leaving/Part Time Man	Polydor PD 14130	6/14/72
(1) Do Wah Diddy Diddy (edit)/Sha La La	United Artists "Silver Spotlight Series" XW048	12/22/72
(1) Pretty Flamingo/Come Tomorrow	United Artists "Silver Spotlight Series" XW049	12/22/72
(6) It's All Over Now Baby Blue/ Ashes (AKA Ashes To The Wind)	Polydor PD 14164	1/24/73

[**NOTE:** Promo copies of the above record had mono and stereo 3:08 edits of the A-side, but regular copies featured the 4:26 LP version.]

(6) Mardi Gras Day/Sadjoy	Polydor PD 14173	4/16/73
(6) Get Your Rocks Off/Wind	Polydor PD 14191	7/25/73
(6) Joybringer (edit)/Cloudy Eyes (edit)	Polydor PD 14205	10/16/73
(6) Father Of Night (AKA Father Of Day, Father Of Night) (edited remix)/Solar Fire Two (AKA Solar Fire) (edit)	Polydor PD 14225	4/01/74
(1) Do Wah Diddy Diddy (edit)/(B-side by other artist)	Chess "Blue Chip Series" 9036	6/**/75
(6) Spirit In The Night (Version 1 - 2:56 edit)/ As Above So Below	Warner Bros. WBS 8152	10/27/75
(1) The Mighty Quinn (Quinn The Eskimo)/ 98.6 (by Keith)	Mercury "Celebrity Series" C-30167	12/29/75
(6) Spirit In The Night (Version 1 - 3:13 edit)/ As Above So Below	Warner Bros. WBS 8176	1/26/76

[**NOTE:** Promo copies of the above record had the 3:13 edit on one side, and the 6:26 LP version on the other.]

(6) Blinded By The Light (edit)/Starbird No. 2 (AKA Starbird)	Warner Bros. WBS 8252	8/31/76

[**NOTE:** Promo copies of the above record had a lyric sleeve.]

(6) Spirit In The Night (Version 2 - 3:20)/Questions	Warner Bros. WBS 8355	4/04/77

[**NOTE:** Early promo copies of the above were incorrectly titled "Spirit."]

(6) Blinded By The Light (edit)/Spirit In The Night (Version 2 - 3:20)	Warner Bros. "Back To Back Hits" GWB 0350	7/**/77
(6) California (3:55 edit)/Bouillabaisse (AKA Drowning On Dry Land/ Fish Soup - edit)	Warner Bros. WBS 8574	4/24/78
(6) Davy's On The Road Again (edited remix)/ Bouillabaisse (AKA Drowning On Dry Land/ Fish Soup - edit)	Warner Bros. WBS 8620	7/17/78
(6) You Angel You/"Belle" Of The Earth	Warner Bros.	

	WBS 8850	5/28/79
(6) For You (edited remix)/A Fool I Am	Warner Bros.	
	WBS 49678	3/02/81
(6) Lies (Through The 80's) (edit)/	Warner Bros.	
Adolescent Dream (edited remix)	WBS 49762	6/22/81
(6) Demolition Man (edited remix)/Demolition Man	Arista ADP-9110	10/31/83
(edited remix) (promo 12")		
(6) Runner (edit)/Where Do They Send Them	Arista AS1-9143	1/09/84
(AKA To Bantustan?)		
(6) Runner (LP version)/Runner (LP version) (promo 12")	Arista ADP-9147	1/09/84
(6) Rebel (remix)/Rebel (remix) (promo 12")	Arista ADP-9202	4/30/84
(6) Rebel (remix)/Figures On A Page	Arista AS1-9203	4/30/84
(AKA Tribal Statistics)		
(6) Runner (edit)/Rebel (remix)	Flashback/Arista	
	AFS-9240	8/13/84

EPs

ALBUMS

ARTIST CODE:
(1) Manfred Mann
(2) Manfred Mann Chapter Three
(3) Manfred Mann, prior to name change to Manfred Mann's Earth Band
(4) Manfred Mann's Earth Band
(5) Manfred Mann's Earth Band with Chris Thompson
(6) Manfred Mann's Plain Music

UK & FOREIGN:		RELEASE DATE
(1) The Five Faces Of Manfred Mann (stereo version cancelled)	HMV CLP 1731/ CSD 1539	9/11/64
(1) The Five Faces Of Manfred Mann (rechanneled stereo version available)	Canadian Capitol T/ST-6093	9/**/64
(1) The Manfred Mann Return	Canadian Capitol T-6102 (mono)	3/**/65
(1) What's New Pussycat? (Original Motion Picture Score; one track - "My Little Red Book [All I Do Is Talk About You]")	United Artists ULP/SULP 1096	9/03/65
(1) Mann Made	HMV CLP 1911/ CSD 1628	10/15/65
(1) Mann Made	Canadian Capitol T-6187 (mono)	4/**/66
(1) Mann Made Hits	HMV CLP 3559 (mono)	9/09/66
(1) As Is	Fontana TL/STL 5377	10/21/66
(1) Soul Of Mann	HMV CLP/CSD 3594	1/13/67
(1) Manfred Mann	Swedish HMV SGLP 533 (mono)	1/**/67
(1) Soul Of Mann	Canadian Capitol T-6199 (mono)	4/**/67
(1) Mann Made Hits!	Canadian Capitol T-6230 (mono)	9/**/67
(1) One Way	Dutch Fontana 858 037 FPY	11/**/67
(1) Up The Junction - Original Soundtrack Recording	Fontana TL/STL 5460	2/23/68
(1) What A Mann	Fontana SFL 13003	3/16/68

(1) The Charge Of The Light Brigade (Original Motion Picture Score; one track - "The Charge Of The Light Brigade")	United Artists ULP/SULP 1189	4/06/68
(1) Mighty Garvey!	Fontana TL/STL 5470	6/28/68
(2) Manfred Mann Chapter Three	Vertigo VO 3	11/07/69
(1) Mann Made (reissue)	Regal Starline SRS 5007	11/14/69
(2) Manfred Mann Chapter Three Volume Two	Vertigo 6360 012	10/23/70
(1) What's New Pussycat? (Original Motion Picture Score: reissue; one track - "My Little Red Book [All I Do Is Talk About You]")	Sunset SLS 50202	2/26/71
(3) Stepping Sideways (cancelled)	Philips 6308 062	8/06/71
(1) This Is . . . Manfred Mann	Philips 6382 020	11/12/71

[**NOTE:** The above album contains first time stereo on "My Name Is Jack" (Version 1) and "Semi-Detached Suburban Mr. James."]

(4) Manfred Mann's Earth Band	Philips 6308 086	2/18/72
(1) Up The Junction - Original Soundtrack Recording (reissue)	Fontana 6852 005	4/14/72
(1) The Greatest Hits Of Manfred Mann	Music For Pleasure MFP 5269	5/12/72

[**NOTE:** The above album contains first time stereo on "If You Gotta Go, Go Now" and "Do Wah Diddy Diddy" (edit).]

(1) Attention! Manfred Mann!	German Fontana 6438 063	6/**/72
(1) Attention! Manfred Mann! Vol. 2	German Fontana 6438 079	6/**/72
(4) Glorified Magnified	Philips 6308 125	9/29/72
(4) Suck It And See (2LP; one track: "Buddah" - its first appearance)	Vertigo 6641 116	5/18/73
(4) Messin'	Vertigo 6360 087	6/15/73
(4) Solar Fire	Bronze/Island ILPS 9265	11/30/73
(4) The Good Earth	Bronze/Island ILPS 9306	10/11/74
(4) Nightingales And Bombers	Bronze/Island ILPS 9337	8/22/75
(1) Mannerisms	Philips SON 016	7/30/76
(4) The Roaring Silence	Bronze/Island ILPS 9357	8/27/76
(4) EMI Introduce The New Bronze Age (promo; contains 4 MMEB tracks)	Bronze/Island PSLP 209	4/22/77
(4) Solar Fire (reissue)	Bronze/EMI	

	BRON 265	4/22/77
(4) The Good Earth (reissue)	Bronze/EMI	
	BRON 306	4/22/77
(4) Nightingales And Bombers (reissue)	Bronze/EMI	
	BRON 337	4/22/77
(4) The Roaring Silence (reissue)	Bronze/EMI	
	BRON 357	4/22/77
(4) Manfred Mann's Earth Band (reissue)	Bronze/EMI	
	BRON 252	5/27/77
(4) Glorified Magnified (reissue)	Bronze/EMI	
	BRON 257	5/27/77
(4) Messin' (reissue)	Bronze/EMI	
	BRON 261	5/27/77

[**NOTE:** The above reissues were released in Germany in January 1977.]

(4) Manfred Mann's Earth Band 1971-1973	Vertigo 9199 107	7/29/77
(1) The Best Of Manfred Mann	EMI NUT 7	8/12/77
(4) Watch	Bronze/EMI	
	BRON 507	2/24/78
(1) Superstars Of The 60s And 70s (10LP; Manfred Mann on one LP side)	Reader's Digest GSUP-10A	9/**/78
(2) Manfred Mann Chapter Three (reissue)	German Bronze/ Ariola	
	200 383-320	1/**/79
(2) Manfred Mann Chapter Three Volume Two (reissue)	German Bronze/ Ariola	
	200 384-320	1/**/79
(4) Angel Station	Bronze/EMI	
	BRON 516	3/09/79

[**NOTE:** The above album was released in Germany in February 1979.]

(1) Semi-Detached Suburban (20 Great Hits Of The Sixties)	EMI EMTV 19	8/24/79
(4) The Best Of Manfred Mann's Earth Band	New Zealand Bronze BRON 001	9/**/79
(4) Chance	Bronze/EMI	
	BRON 529	10/10/80
(4) Manfred Mann's Earth Band (reissue)	Bronze/Polydor	
	BRON 252	6/19/81
(4) Glorified Magnified (reissue)	Bronze/Polydor	
	BRON 257	6/19/81
(4) Messin' (reissue)	Bronze/Polydor	
	BRON 261	6/19/81
(4) Solar Fire (reissue)	Bronze/Polydor	
	BRON 265	6/19/81
(4) The Good Earth (reissue)	Bronze/Polydor	

	BRON 306	6/19/81
(4) Nightingales And Bombers (reissue)	Bronze/Polydor	
	BRON 337	6/19/81
(4) The Roaring Silence (reissue)	Bronze/Polydor	
	BRON 357	6/19/81
(4) Watch (reissue)	Bronze/Polydor	
	BRON 507	6/19/81
(4) Angel Station (reissue)	Bronze/Polydor	
	BRON 516	6/19/81
(4) Chance (reissue)	Bronze/Polydor	
	BRON 529	6/19/81
(1) The R & B Years	See For Miles	
	CM 105	2/26/82
(1) The History Of Rock Volume 7 (2LP; contains 10 Manfred Mann tracks, plus tracks by The Kinks, The Hollies and The Searchers)	Orbis HRL 007	6/**/82
(4) Somewhere In Afrika	South African Bronze ML 4645	11/15/82
(4) Somewhere In Afrika (different back cover)	Bronze/Polydor BRON 543	2/18/83

[NOTE: The above album was released in Germany in October 1982.]

(1) The Best Of Manfred Mann	Music For Pleasure/ Conifer	
	1A 222 58029	5/06/83
(1) The Five Faces Of Manfred Mann/ Mann Made (reissue; 2LP)	HMV EDP 1546363	8/05/83
(4) Budapest (LP/cassette) (The cassette contains the live bonus tracks "Brothers And Sisters Of Africa," "Where Do They Send Them" [[AKA "No Transkei" [long version]], and "Don't Kill It Carol")	Bronze/Polydor BRON 550 (LP)/ BRONC 550 (cassette)	2/17/84

[NOTE: The above album was released in Germany in January 1984.]

(1) The Very Best Of Manfred Mann 1963-1966	Music For Pleasure MFP 41 5651 1	6/01/84
(4) Budapest (CD; reissue)	German Bronze/ Ariola 610 163-222	9/**/84
(1) Soul Of Mann (reissue)	See For Miles SEE 52	7/**/85
(4) Watch (CD; reissue)	German Bronze/ Ariola 610 588-222	12/**/85
(4) Angel Station (CD; reissue)	German Bronze/ Ariola	

	610 589-222	12/**/85
(4) Solar Fire (CD; reissue)	German Bronze/	
	Ariola	
	610 590-222	12/**/85
(1) The Singles Album	EMI EMS 1121	1/**/86

[NOTE: The album contains first time stereo on "Now You're Needing Me" and "What Am I Doing Wrong."]

(1) The R & B Years (reissue; different cover)	See For Miles	
	CM 105	3/**/86
(1) Hit Records 1966-1969	Fontana PRICE 66	3/**/86
(2) Manfred Mann Chapter Three (CD; reissue)	German Bronze/BMG	
	250 383-217	3/**/86
(2) Manfred Mann Chapter Three Volume Two (CD; reissue)	German Bronze/BMG	
	250 384-217	3/**/86
(4) Chance (CD; reissue)	German Bronze/BMG	
	252 970-217	3/**/86
(4) Somewhere In Afrika (CD; reissue)	German Bronze/BMG	
	255 077-222	3/**/86
(5) Criminal Tango (LP/CD)	10/Virgin DIX 35 (LP)/	
	DIXCD 35 (CD)	6/13/86

[NOTE: The above album was released in Germany in April 1986.]

(1) The Singles Plus (CD)	EMI CDP 7 46603 2	7/**/87

[NOTE: The above CD is the same as "The Singles Album" plus 5 tracks. In addition, it contains first time stereo on "Cock-A-Hoop" and "What Did I Do Wrong."]

(4) Masque (LP/CD)	10/Virgin DIX 69 (LP)/	
	DIXCD 69 (CD)	10/16/87

[NOTE: The above album was released in Germany in September 1987.]

(4) The Roaring Silence (CD; reissue)	German Bronze/BMG	
	258 729-217	10/**/87
(4) Nightingales And Bombers (CD; reissue)	German Bronze/BMG	
	258 730-217	10/**/87
(4) Messin' (CD; reissue)	German Bronze/BMG	
	258 731-217	10/**/87
(4) Glorified Magnified (CD; reissue)	German Bronze/BMG	
	258 732-217	10/**/87
(4) Manfred Mann's Earth Band (CD; reissue)	German Bronze/BMG	
	258 733-217	10/**/87
(4) The Good Earth (CD; reissue)	German Bronze/BMG	
	258 734-217	10/**/87
(4) Chance (LP/CD; reissue)	Castle Communications	
	CLALP 133 (LP)/	
	CLACD 133 (CD)	11/06/87
(4) Solar Fire (LP/CD; reissue)	Legacy LLP 121 (LP)/	
	LLCD 121 (CD)	11/**/87

(4) The Roaring Silence (LP/CD; reissue)	Legacy LLP 122 (LP)/
	LLCD 122 (CD) 11/**/87
(4) Watch (LP/CD; reissue)	Legacy LLP 123 (LP)/
	LLCD 123 (CD) 11/**/87
(4) Angel Station (LP/CD; reissue)	Legacy LLP 124 (LP)/
	LLCD 124 (CD) 11/**/87
(4) Somewhere In Afrika (LP/CD; reissue)	Legacy LLP 125 (LP)/
	LLCD 125 (CD) 11/**/87
(4) Nightingales And Bombers (LP/CD; reissue)	Castle Communications
	CLALP 137 (LP)/
	CLACD 137 (CD) 1/29/88
(4) Messin' (LP/CD; reissue)	Castle Communications
	CLALP 150 (LP)/
	CLACD 150 (CD) 4/**/89
(4) Manfred Mann's Earth Band (LP/CD; reissue)	Castle Communications
	CLALP 151 (LP)/
	CLACD 151 (CD) 4/**/89
(1) The EP Collection (LP/CD)	See For Miles
	SEE 252 (LP)/ 7/**/89
	SEECD 252 (CD)

[**NOTE:** The above album contains first time stereo on "I Can't Believe What You Say."]

(1) The Collection (2LP; single CD)	Castle Communications
	CCSLP 245 (LP)/
	CCSCD 245 (CD) 6/**/90
(4) Solar Fire (LP/CD; reissue)	Cohesion/Pacific
	COMME 1 (LP)/
	COMMECD 1
	(CD) 8/20/90
(4) The Roaring Silence (LP/CD; reissue)	Cohesion/Pacific
	COMME 2 (LP)/
	COMMECD 2
	(CD) 8/20/90
(4) Watch (LP/CD; reissue)	Cohesion/Pacific
	COMME 3 (LP)/
	COMMECD 3
	(CD) 8/20/90
(4) Angel Station (LP/CD; reissue)	Cohesion/Pacific
	COMME 4 (LP)/
	COMMECD 4
	(CD) 8/20/90
(4) Somewhere In Afrika (LP/CD; reissue)	Cohesion/Pacific
	COMME 5 (LP)/
	COMMECD 5
	(CD) 8/20/90

(4) Manfred Mann's Earth Band (LP/CD; reissue)	Cohesion/Pacific COMME 6 (LP)/ COMMECD 6 (CD)	8/20/90
(4) Messin' (LP/CD; reissue)	Cohesion/Pacific COMME 7 (LP)/ COMMECD 7 (CD)	8/20/90
(4) Nightingales And Bombers (LP/CD; reissue)	Cohesion/Pacific COMME 8 (LP)/ COMMECD 8 (CD)	8/20/90
(4) Chance (LP/CD; reissue)	Cohesion/Pacific COMME 9 (LP)/ COMMECD 9 (CD)	8/20/90
(4) Budapest (LP/CD; reissue)	Cohesion/Pacific COMME 10 (LP)/ COMMECD 10 (CD)	8/20/90
(4) 20 Years Of Manfred Mann's Earth Band 1971-1991 (LP: 10 tracks; CD: 13 tracks)	Cohesion/Pacific BOMME 1 (LP)/ BOMME CD 1 (CD)	11/12/90
(6) Plains Music (LP/CD)	German Intuition INT 3062 1 (LP)/ INT 3062 2 (CD)	5/**/91
(6) Plains Music (LP/CD; different front and back covers than above)	South African PVB PVBC 13 (LP)/ PVBCD 13 (CD)	5/**/91
(4) Solar Fire (LP/CD; reissue)	Cohesion/Rio COMME 1 (LP)/ COMMECD 1 (CD)	12/23/91
(4) The Roaring Silence (LP/CD; reissue)	Cohesion/Rio COMME 2 (LP)/ COMMECD 2 (CD)	12/23/91
(4) Watch (LP/CD; reissue)	Cohesion/Rio COMME 3 (LP)/ COMMECD 3 (CD)	12/23/91
(4) Angel Station (LP/CD; reissue)	Cohesion/Rio COMME 4 (LP)/	

	COMMECD 4	
	(CD)	12/23/91
(4) Somewhere In Afrika (LP/CD; reissue)	Cohesion/Rio	
	COMME 5 (LP)/	
	COMMECD 5	
	(CD)	12/23/91
(4) Manfred Mann's Earth Band (LP/CD; reissue)	Cohesion/Rio	
	COMME 6 (LP)/	
	COMMECD 6	
	(CD)	12/23/91
(4) Messin' (LP/CD; reissue)	Cohesion/Rio	
	COMME 7 (LP)/	
	COMMECD 7	
	(CD)	12/23/91
(4) Nightingales And Bombers (LP/CD; reissue)	Cohesion/Rio	
	COMME 8 (LP)/	
	COMMECD 8	
	(CD)	12/23/91
(4) Chance (LP/CD; reissue)	Cohesion/Rio	
	COMME 9 (LP)/	
	COMMECD 9	
	(CD)	12/23/91
(4) Budapest (LP/CD; reissue)	Cohesion/Rio	
	COMME 10 (LP)/	
	COMMECD 10	
	(CD)	12/23/91
(4) 20 Years Of Manfred Mann's Earth Band 1971-1991 (LP/CD; reissue - LP: 10 tracks; CD: 13 tracks)	Cohesion/Rio BOMME 1 (LP)/ BOMME CD 1	
	(CD)	12/23/91
(1) The Most Of Manfred Mann (CD)	Australian EMI	
	4380082	8/**/92
(6) Plains Music (CD)	Kaz KAZ CD 902	8/17/92
(1) The Collection (CD; reissue - different cover)	Castle Communications	
	CCSCD 245	8/17/92
(1) 1 And Only - 25 Years Of Radio 1 (2CD; contains BBC version of "Pretty Flamingo")	Band Of Joy BOJ CD 25	9/07/92
(4) Spotlight (CD)	Cohesion/Rio	
	COMME CD 13	9/14/92
(4) Manfred Mann's Earth Band (13CD box set; contains CDs COMME 1 through COMME 10 **plus the following 3 CDs:**	Cohesion/Rio MM BOX 1	10/12/92
(4) Glorified Magnified (CD; reissue)	Cohesion/Rio	
	COMME CD 11	10/12/92

(4) The Good Earth (CD; reissue)	Cohesion/Rio	
	COMME CD 12	10/12/92
(4) Plain Talking (Manfred Mann Interview with	Cohesion/Rio	
Andy Taylor) (CD)	MM INT 1	10/12/92
(4) Blinded By The Light - The Very Best Of	German Arcade	
Manfred Mann's Earth Band (CD; 2 different covers)	8800068	12/**/92
(1) Ages Of Mann (LP/CD)	PolyGram TV	
	514 326-1 (LP)/	
	514 326-2 (CD)	1/11/93
(1) The Five Faces Of Manfred Mann (CD; reissue)	Japanese EMI	
	TOCP-7547	1/27/93
(1) The Best Of The EMI Years (CD)	EMI 7 89490 2	6/07/93

[**NOTE:** This CD is the first to contain the previously unreleased track "Sticks And Stones."]

(4) The Very Best Of Manfred Mann's Earth Band	Dutch Arcade	
(CD; different track listing than above)	01 8040.61	6/**/93
(1) Soul Of Mann (CD; reissue)	Japanese EMI	
	TOCP-7943	9/08/93
(4) The Very Best Of Manfred Mann's Earth Band	German Arcade	
Vol. 2 (CD)	8800182	12/**/93
(4) The Very Best Of Manfred Mann's Earth Band	German Arcade	
Volumes 1 & 2 (2CD - limited edition)	8800184	12/**/93
(4) Solar Fire (CD; reissue)	Cohesion/Grapevine	
	MFMCD 1	12/13/93
(4) The Roaring Silence (CD; reissue)	Cohesion/Grapevine	
	MFMCD 2	12/13/93
(4) The Roaring Silence (special package with	Cohesion/Grapevine	
CD and cassette - unreleased)	MFMBX 2	12/13/93
(4) Watch (CD; reissue)	Cohesion/Grapevine	
	MFMCD 3	12/13/93
(4) Watch (special package with CD and cassette -	Cohesion/Grapevine	
unreleased)	MFMBX 3	12/13/93
(4) Angel Station (CD; reissue)	Cohesion/Grapevine	
	MFMCD 4	12/13/93
(4) Angel Station (special package with CD and	Cohesion/Grapevine	
cassette - unreleased)	MFMBX 4	12/13/93
(4) Somewhere In Afrika (CD; reissue)	Cohesion/Grapevine	
	MFMCD 5	12/13/93
(4) Manfred Mann's Earth Band (CD; reissue)	Cohesion/Grapevine	
	MFMCD 6	12/13/93
(4) Messin' (CD; reissue)	Cohesion/Grapevine	
	MFMCD 7	12/13/93
(4) Nightingales And Bombers (CD; reissue)	Cohesion/Grapevine	
	MFMCD 8	12/13/93
(4) Chance (CD; reissue)	Cohesion/Grapevine	

(4) Budapest (CD; reissue)	MFMCD 9 Cohesion/Grapevine	12/13/93
(4) Glorified Magnified (CD; reissue)	MFMCD 10 Cohesion/Grapevine	12/13/93
(4) The Good Earth (CD; reissue)	MFMCD 11 Cohesion/Grapevine	12/13/93
(4) Spotlight (CD; reissue)	MFMCD 12 Cohesion/Grapevine	12/13/93
(4) 20 Years Of Manfred Mann's Earth Band 1971-1991 (CD; reissue - 13 tracks)	MFMCD 13 Cohesion/Grapevine BOMCD 1	12/13/93 12/13/93
(1) The Best Of Manfred Mann 1964-1966 (CD)	Music For Pleasure CDMFP 5994	12/20/93
(2) Manfred Mann Chapter Three Volume One (CD; retitled reissue of "Manfred Mann Chapter Three")	Cohesion/Grapevine MFMCD 14	2/14/94
(2) Manfred Mann Chapter Three Volume Two (CD; reissue)	Cohesion/Grapevine MFMCD 15	2/14/94
(4) The Very Best Of Manfred Mann's Earth Band (CD)	Arcade ARC 3100162	8/29/94
(1) Mann Made Hits And Other Delicacies 1966-1969 (CD)	Australian Fontana 522 644-2	9/12/94

		RELEASE
		DATE

US:

(1) The Manfred Mann Album — Ascot ALM 13015/ ALS 16015 — 9/17/64

(1) Manfred Mann Radio Interview (promo - shown as Side 1 and Side 2) — United Artists UAL 94 (mono) — 9/18/64

(1) The Five Faces Of Manfred Mann — Ascot ALM 13018/ ALS 16018 — 2/08/65

(1) What's New Pussycat? (Original Motion Picture Score; one track - "My Little Red Book [All I Do Is Talk About You]") — United Artists UAL 4128/ UAS 5128 — 5/25/65

(1) My Little Red Book Of Winners! — Ascot ALM 13021/ ALS 16021 — 9/13/65

(1) Mann Made — Ascot ALM 13024/ ALS 16024 — 11/05/65

(1) Pretty Flamingo — United Artists UAL 3549/ UAS 6549 — 7/19/66

(1) Manfred Mann's Greatest Hits — United Artists UAL 3551/ UAS 6551 — 10/13/66

(1) Up The Junction - Original Soundtrack Recording — Mercury SR 61159 — 3/11/68

(1) The Mighty Quinn — Mercury SR 61168 — 5/06/68

(1) The Charge Of The Light Brigade (Original Motion Picture Score; one track - "The Charge Of The Light Brigade") — United Artists UAL 4177/ UAS 5177 — 9/26/68

(2) Manfred Mann Chapter Three — Polydor 24-4013 — 2/16/70

(4) Manfred Mann's Earth Band — Polydor PD 5015 — 1/24/72

(4) Glorified Magnified — Polydor PD 5031 — 10/23/72

(4) Get Your Rocks Off — Polydor PD 5050 — 5/14/73

(4) Solar Fire — Polydor PD 6019 — 1/21/74

(1) The Best Of Manfred Mann — Janus JLS 3064 — 7/15/74

(1) What's New Pussycat? (Original Motion Picture Score: reissue; one track - "My Little Red Book [All I Do Is Talk About You]") — United Artists UA-LA278-G — 7/15/74

(4) The Good Earth — Warner Bros. BS 2826 — 10/28/74

(4) Nightingales And Bombers — Warner Bros. BS 2877 — 8/25/75

(4) The Roaring Silence — Warner Bros. BS 2965 — 8/30/76

(4) The Roaring Silence (reissue with extra track - — Warner Bros.

"Spirits In The Night" [Version 2])	BSK 3055	5/09/77
(1) The Best Of Manfred Mann	Capitol M-11688	7/25/77
(4) Watch	Warner Bros.	
	BSK 3157	2/20/78
(4) Angel Station	Warner Bros.	
	BSK 3302	4/30/79
(1) The Best Of Manfred Mann (reissue)	Capitol N-16073	10/13/80
(4) Chance	Warner Bros.	
	BSK 3498	1/12/81
(4) Somewhere In Afrika	Arista AL8-8194	11/14/83
(1) The Best Of Manfred Mann (reissue; cassette only)	EMI America	
	L4N-10338	2/23/87
(4) Highs Of The Seventies (CD) (only US CD to contain the long version of "Blinded By The Light")	Warner Special Products 9-27614-2	6/15/87
(4) The Roaring Silence (CD; reissue - cancelled)	Warner Bros. (no #)	6/07/88
(1) The Best Of Manfred Mann (CD; reissue)	EMI CDP 7 48397 2	8/14/89
(4) The Best Of King Biscuit Live - Volume 3 (CD) (contains one live MMEB track - "Spirits In The Night," recorded 11/23/78 in New York)	Sandstone D233007-2	9/24/91
(6) Plains Music (CD)	Rhythm Safari CDL 57123	10/15/91
(1) The Best Of Manfred Mann - A Definitive Collection (CD)	EMI CDP 7 96096 2	6/02/92

[**NOTE:** The above CD is the first to contain the radio-only "Group Interview," the unreleased track "Come Home Baby," an unreleased stereo mix of "When Will I Be Loved," a different stereo mix of "Tired Of Trying, Bored With Lying, Scared Of Dying," the unedited version of "Do Wah Diddy Diddy," and the TV version of "5-4-3-2-1." "She" and "Machines" also have studio talk.]

(1) Legends Of Christmas Past - A Rock n' R&B Holiday Collection (CD; contains the stereo mix of "God Rest Ye Merry Gentlemenn")	EMI CDP 7 99987 2	9/22/92
(1) Chapter Two: The Best Of The Fontana Years	Fontana 314 522 665-2	10/11/94

RADIO SHOWS

except where noted, all programs are credited to Manfred Mann, but program contents are almost exclusively by MMEB

SINGLES

		RELEASE DATE
UK & FOREIGN:		
none		none

		RELEASE DATE
US:		
Get Your Rocks Off (with interview)/	What's It All About?	
(b-side by Smokey Robinson - Sweet Harmony with interview)	Program #189/ #190	8/**/73
Manfred Mann (Medley with interview)/	What's It All About?	
(b-side by Gary S. Paxton - medley with interview)	Program #382/ #381	8/**/77

ALBUMS

		RELEASE DATE
UK & FOREIGN:		
John Peel In Concert with Manfred Mann's Earth Band (25 min. live concert from 1972)	BBC Transcription Service 128812-S	11/10/72
Pop Spectacular featuring Manfred Mann's Earth Band (51 min. live concert from 1973)	BBC Transcription Service 134457-S	1/**/74

US:

		RELEASE DATE
The Mann In Question (interview with studio tracks)	Rock Around The World Program #137	3/20/77 to 3/26/77
A Tale Of Mann And Gold (1977 live concert and interview; side two features 5 live tracks by Andrew Gold)	Rock Around The World Program #138	3/27/77 to 4/02/77
Manfred Mann (interview; plus interviews with other artists)	Billboard Report 3/2/81-3/8/1981	3/02/81 to 3/08/81
Manfred Mann (live concert from 1973)	The Best Of The BBC Rock Hour Program #211	week of 3/15/81
Manfred Mann (2LP; live Paris concert from 1980 on 3 LP sides, 1 LP side by Ry Cooder)	King Biscuit Flower Hour Program KB 362	4/12/81
Manfred Mann (live concert from 1977)	Retro Rock #RR 81-14	11/23/81
Manfred Mann (2 interview segments; plus interviews with other artists)	Earth News wk. of 2/27/84	2/27/84
Manfred Mann (2LP; live concert from "Budapest" LP on 3 LP sides. Contains an otherwise unavailable live/studio version of "Runner")	King Biscuit Flower Hour Program KB 516	3/25/84
Manfred Mann (2LP; interviews and music)	Off The Record OTRSP#84-15	week of 4/02/84
Manfred Mann (3LP; Manfred plays and speaks about his favorite records on 3 LP sides. The other 3 LP sides are by Rick Wright of Pink Floyd.)	Guest D.J. Show #107	4/09/84
Manfred Mann (2LP; edited from Program KB 516 over 3 LP sides - one 1 LP side by Clarence Clemons. Also includes live/studio version of "Runner")	Best Of The Biscuit Program BOB 536	8/12/84
Manfred Mann (4LP; Manfred speaks about "Do Wah Diddy Diddy" and "Blinded By The Light")	Dick Clark's Rock Roll & Remember RRR-12-12-87	12/12/87

NOTE: In addition to the above BBC material, the following tracks have been recorded by Manfred Mann for the BBC:

Paul Jones era: Oh No Not My Baby; L.S.D.; That's The Way I Feel; You Better Be Sure; I'm A Longhaired, Unsweared Dude Called Jack; It Took A Little While; Pretty Flamingo; Watermelon Man; Sticks And Stones (TV appearance introduced by Jimmy Saville)

Mike d'Abo era: Just Like A Woman; Abraham, Martin & John; Orange Peel; Ragamuffin Man; Pretty Flamingo (1966 "Top Of The Pops" Christmas show - Jones singing with Fontana lineup); Handbags And Gladrags; I'm Your Hoochie Coochie Man; Nitty Gritty; She's A Woman; Fox On The Run; Clair; So Long; Each And Every Day; The Letter; My Name Is Jack; So Long, Dad; Hound Dog; Mighty Quinn; Cubist Town; Sleepy Hollow; The Vicar's Daughter; Fever; Sweet Pea; You Got It Made; Summertime; Oh What A Day; Bare Hugg; Little Miss Understood ("Clair" and "So Long" were recorded for the "Top Gear" program that aired 12/22/68.)

Manfred Mann Chapter Three: Time; One Way Glass; Jump Before You Think; Breakdown

Manfred Mann's Earth Band: Bubblegum And Kipling (AKA "Earth The Circle, Part 2"); Dealer; Glorified Magnified; Messin'; Meat; Mighty Quinn; Get Your Rocks Off; Joybringer; Cloudy Eyes; Father Of Day, Father Of Night; Solar Fire

Interviews with the band were also recorded by the BBC, and at least 2 other d'Abo era BBC tracks have yet to be identified.

MANFRED MANN PRODUCTIONS/ WRITER CREDITS/ SESSIONS

SINGLES

UK & FOREIGN:		RELEASE DATE
THE MARK LEEMAN FIVE - Portland Town/ Gotta Get Myself Together (Manfred produced both sides)	Columbia DB 7452	1/08/65
JOHN MANTELL - Remember Child/ I'll See You Around (Manfred produced both sides)	CBS 201783	6/18/65
THE LUVVERS - House On The Hill/Most Unlovely (Manfred and Mike Hugg wrote the A-side, which was not released by Manfred Mann)	Parlophone R 5459	6/03/66
ROB HOEKE'S R & B GROUP - Jolita/ Jolita (instrumental) (Manfred and Mike Hugg wrote both sides, which were not released by Manfred Mann)	Dutch Jolita 113 129 F	2/09/68
UNIT 4 PLUS 2 - You Ain't Goin' Nowhere/ So You Want To Be A Blues-Player (Manfred produced both sides)	Fontana TF 931	5/03/68
PERFECT PEOPLE - House In The Country/Polyanna (Manfred and Mike Hugg wrote the A-side, which was not released by Manfred Mann)	MCA MU 1079	5/09/69
COULSON, DEAN, McGUINNESS, FLINT - Lay Down Your Weary Tune/Tiny Montgomery - I Wanna Be Your Lover (In addition to producing all of the above tracks [both B-side tracks are non-album], Manfred plays on "Tiny Montgomery")	DJM DJS.267	5/26/72
FULL ALERT - Sheer Enjoyment/Jinx On Me (Manfred and Mike Hugg originally wrote the A-side under the titles "A 'B' Side" and	Polydor 2058 848	3/25/77

"Travelling Lady." Mike Hugg, who was the
only member of this "group," wrote new lyrics
for the song)

		RELEASE DATE
COULSON, DEAN, McGUINNESS, FLINT - Lay Down Your Weary Tune/Let Me Die In My Footsteps	Sire SAA-711	10/08/73

ALBUMS

UK & FOREIGN:		RELEASE DATE
URIAH HEEP - Look At Yourself (Manfred plays on the tracks "July Morning" and "Tears In My Eyes")	Bronze/Island ILPS 9169	9/03/71
COULSON, DEAN, McGUINNESS, FLINT - Lo And Behold (Manfred produced the entire album)	DJM DJLPS 424	7/14/72
MIKE HUGG - Somewhere (Manfred plays on the tracks "Love Is Waiting" and "Bessie Don't You Cry")	Polydor 2383 140	9/01/72

"PETER AND THE WOLF" (Children's album with music and English narration. Manfred plays on the track "Peter's Theme")	RSO 2479 167	11/28/75
"PETER AND THE WOLF (DEUTSCH GESPROCHENE VERSION)" (German-language narration. Manfred plays on the track "Peter's Theme")	German RSO 2394 164	11/28/75
"PETER AND THE WOLF" (Italian-language narration. Manfred plays on the track "Peter's Theme")	Italian RSO 2394 162 A	1/**/76
"PETER AND THE WOLF" (French-language narration. Manfred plays on the track "Peter's Theme")	French RSO 2394 162	1/**/76
"PETER AND THE WOLF" (Spanish-language narration. Manfred plays on the track "Peter's Theme")	Spanish RSO 2394 162	1/**/76
URIAH HEEP - Look At Yourself (reissue) (Manfred plays on the tracks "July Morning" and "Tears In My Eyes")	Bronze/EMI BRON 169	4/22/77
THE YARDBIRDS - Shapes Of Things (2LP) (Manfred produced one track, "Sweet Music")	Charly CDX 1	12/09/77
JIMMY HIBBERT - Jimmy Hibbert's Heavy Duty (Manfred plays with many Earth Band members on the tracks "Telephone," "Out Of Control," "Heavy Duty" and "Pop Your Cherry")	Logo 1021	4/25/80
TREVOR RABIN - Wolf (Manfred plays on the tracks "Lost In Love" and "Looking For A Lady [Wolfman]")	Chrysalis CHR 1293	1/16/81
URIAH HEEP - Look At Yourself (reissue) (Manfred plays on the tracks "July Morning" and "Tears In My Eyes")	Bronze/Polydor BRON 169	6/19/81
THE YARDBIRDS - Shapes Of Things (7LP) (Contains a demo version of "Sweet Music," which Manfred produced)	Charly CHARLY BOX 104	11/**/84

URIAH HEEP - Look At Yourself (CD; reissue)   Castle Communications
(Manfred plays on the tracks "July Morning" and   CLACD 107   4/**/89
"Tears In My Eyes")

THE YARDBIRDS - The Studio Sessions 1964-1967   Decal CHARLY 187   6/**/90
(CD; contains a demo version of "Sweet Music,"
which Manfred produced)

THE YARDBIRDS - Shapes Of Things (4CD reissue;   Charly LIK BOX 1   5/13/91
contains a demo version of "Sweet Music," which
Manfred produced)

THE MARK LEEMAN FIVE - The Mark Leeman   See For Miles
   Five Memorial Album   SEE 317 (LP)/
(LP has 20 tracks, CD has 25 tracks. Both LP and CD   SEECD 317 (CD)   5/20/91
contain both sides of the Manfred Mann-produced
single "Portland Town." The CD also has a longer,
unreleased stereo mix of "Portland Town" and an
unreleased stereo mix of "Gotta Get Myself
Together," which is incorrectly listed as a different
version)

THE YARDBIRDS - Shapes Of Things (4CD;   Japanese Alfa
contains a demo version of "Sweet Music,"   ALCB-527/528/
which Manfred produced)   529/530   6/01/92

UNIT 4+2 - Concrete And Clay (CD; contains   German Repertoire
"You Ain't Goin' Nowhere," which Manfred produced)   REP 4191-WY   2/08/93

THE YARDBIRDS - Train Kept A-Rollin' - The   Charly CD LIK
   Complete Giorgio Gomelsky Productions (4CD;   BOX 3   5/11/93
Manfred produced both versions of the track "Sweet
Music." **NOTE: This album presents both versions
in stereo and in the best quality and longest length
anywhere.)**

"PETER AND THE WOLF" (CD; reissue with   German Viceroy
different cover - children's album with music and   Music VIC 6006-2   5/24/93
English narration. Manfred plays on the track
"Peter's Theme")

US:

THE YARDBIRDS - For Your Love   Epic LN 24167/
(Manfred produced one track, "Sweet Music")   BN 26167   6/13/65

URIAH HEEP - Look At Yourself   Mercury
(Manfred plays on the tracks "July Morning" and   SRM-1-614   9/13/71
"Tears In My Eyes")

"SWEDISH FLY GIRLS" -
Original Soundtrack Recording   Juno S-1003   12/18/72
(Manfred produced the entire album, and wrote
the track "One Way Glass," which was retitled
"Broken-Glass Lives" on this album)

COULSON, DEAN, McGUINNESS, FLINT -   Sire SAS 7405   8/06/73
  Lo And Behold
(Manfred produced the entire album)

"PETER AND THE WOLF"   RSO RS-1-3001   1/26/76
(Children's album with music and English narration.
Manfred plays on the track "Peter's Theme")

THE YARDBIRDS - Heart Full Of Soul   Accord SN 7237   1/**/83
(Contains a demo version of "Sweet Music,"
which Manfred produced)

URIAH HEEP - Look At Yourself (reissue)   Mercury
(Manfred plays on the tracks "July Morning" and   814 180-1   9/05/83
"Tears In My Eyes")

URIAH HEEP - Look At Yourself (CD; reissue)   Mercury
(Manfred plays on the tracks "July Morning" and   814 180-2   3/20/89
"Tears In My Eyes")

THE YARDBIRDS - The Yardbirds, Volume 1/   Sony Music
  Smokestack Lightning (2CD;   Special Products
contains a demo version of "Sweet Music,"   A2K 48655   9/24/91
which Manfred produced)

"PETER AND THE WOLF" (CD; reissue -   Viceroy Music
children's album with music and English narration.   VIC 6006-2   5/25/93
Manfred plays on the track "Peter's Theme")

PUBLICATIONS

Platform End - The Official Manfred Mann Fan Club Magazine

Issue 1 - released 12/92
Issue 2 - released 7/93
Issue 3 - released 11/93
Issue 4 - released 4/94
Issue 5 - released 10/94
Issue 6 - released 4/95

For information on subscribing to Platform End, the official publication of the Manfred Mann fan club, please write to:

THE MANFRED MANN FAN CLUB, 29 LYNDHURST ROAD, WALLASEY, WIRRAL, MERSEYSIDE L45 6XB, ENGLAND

OFFICIAL VIDEOS

(only authorized tapes featuring complete songs included)

		RELEASE DATE
UK & FOREIGN:		
none		none

		RELEASE DATE
US:		
"Casey Kasem Rock 'N' Roll Goldmine - The British Invasion" (one track: "Mighty Quinn")	Vestron Music Video 1118	**/**/88
"What's New Pussycat?" (one track: "My Little Red Book [All I Do Is Talk About You]" - film version)	MGM/UA Home Video M 202079	**/**/90
"Rock Archives" (one track: lip-synch version of "Blinded By The Light" on "The Captain And Tennille Show")	Entertainment Weekly/ Billboard Entertainment Mktg., Inc. (no #)	7/**/92
"Shindig! Presents British Invasion Vol. 1" (includes a live version of "Do Wah Diddy Diddy")	Rhino Home Video RNVD 1454	9/**/92
"Shindig! Presents British Invasion Vol. 2" (includes a live version of "Sha La La")	Rhino Home Video RNVD 1460	10/16/92
"Rock In The U.K." (one track: "Mighty Quinn")	Rhino Home Video R3 2073	2/23/94

US "SHINDIG!" TV PERFORMANCES

Show #: N/A (9/64)   - Do Wah Diddy Diddy (lip-synch)
Show #: 11 (11/18/64) - Sha La La (lip-synch)
Show #: 14 (12/09/64) - Do Wah Diddy Diddy (live); Sha La La (live)
Show #: 17 (1965)   - Got My Mojo Working (live); Come Tomorrow (lip-synch)
Show #: 49 (1965)   - The One In The Middle (live)
Show #: 61 (1965)   - If You Gotta Go, Go Now (live from the Richmond Jazz Festival)
Show #: 67 (1965)   - Watermelon Man (live); 5-4-3-2-1 (live)

BOOTLEGS

ARTIST CODE:
(1) Manfred Mann
(2) Manfred Mann's Earth Band

SINGLES

UK & FOREIGN:		RELEASE DATE
(2) Somewhere In The Land Of Wet Lips And Big Tits (contains 6 live tracks, including the unreleased titles "Eastbound Train" and "Step By Step")	French Exterieur Musidisques E.T. 8308	1/**/84

US:		RELEASE DATE
none		none

ALBUMS

UK & FOREIGN:		RELEASE DATE
(1) Manfred Mann (CD) (contains HMV and Fontana hits and LP tracks)	German Laserlight 15 114	6/**/88
(1) The Early Days Of Rock - Volume 2 (CD) (contains the following live tracks: "Nitty Gritty," "You Don't Know Me," "Semi-Detached Suburban Mr. James" and "Hound Dog," plus live tracks by other artists)	Italian Living Legend LLR-CD022	6/**/89

182

(2) Quinn The Escimo (sic) (CD) Luxembourg Oh Boy
    (contains the entire BBC Rock Hour program 1-9044 9/24/90
    without pre-song introductions)

(2) Live In Stockholm 1974 (CD) Italian SGRS 015 6/**/91

(2) Road To Babylon (CD) Italian Great Live
    (contains the entire "Retro Rock" program) Records GLR 9244 7/**/92

		RELEASE
		DATE
US:		
none		none

The Supporting Cast -
Life Before, During and After Manfred Mann

Mike Hugg

Tom McGuinness' description of Mike Hugg as a chameleon couldn't have been a better one for this vastly underrated co-founder of Manfred Mann. Hugg's tremendous contributions to all aspects of the Manfred Mann repertoire have proven to be the most durable of all the Manfred Mann members. After finally parting professionally from Manfred in 1972, Mike went through many different performing guises before settling into his behind-the-scenes audio/visual projects.

Hugg has had many career highlights, but none as important as the revered minor classic, "Blue Suede Shoes Again." Mike's studio group The Highly Likely scored a lone UK Top 40 hit with "The Likely Lads'" theme "Whatever Happened To You?". Another notable Hugg composition is the original theme of the long-running British show "Minder" in 1979. This theme was later performed by the UK artist Kenny until the show's conclusion in March 1994. Hugg's last album appearance on drums was on the 1973 Apple Records album "Brother" by Lon & Derrek Van Eaton. Hugg has since been making his noise from behind the keyboards, and Mike's talents are also heavily featured in the touring Manfreds.

ARTIST CODE:
(1) Mike Hugg
(2) The Highly Likely
(3) Hug
(4) Mike Hugg's Freeway
(5) Full Alert

SINGLES

UK & FOREIGN:		RELEASE DATE
(1) Blue Suede Shoes Again/Fool No More	Polydor 2058 265	8/04/72
(1) Bonnie Charlie + 1 Slade track/(one-sided flexi issued free with "Music Scene" magazine)	Music Scene SF1 122	11/**/72
(1) Stress And Strain/Tonight	Polydor 2058 359	5/04/73
(2) Whatever Happened To You?/God Bless Everyone	BBC RESL 10	1/18/74
(3) Keep Pushing On/City	Polydor 2058 553	3/07/75
(4) Same Old Fantasy/Those Days	Polydor 2058 691	2/20/76
(1) Bet You're Gonna Like Them/(one-sided flexi; advert theme for "Rock 'N Rollers")	Lyntone LYN 3393	**/**/76
(4) Wichita/No Love In The City	Polydor 2058 805	11/05/76
(5) Sheer Enjoyment/Jinx On Me	Polydor 2058 848	3/25/77

US:		RELEASE DATE
(1) Blue Suede Shoes Again/Fool No More	Verve VK 10691	8/14/72
(1) Stress And Strain/Tonight	MGM K 14544	5/14/73

ALBUMS

UK & FOREIGN:		RELEASE DATE
(1) Somewhere	Polydor 2383 140	9/01/72
(1) Stress And Strain	Polydor 2383 213	7/06/73
(3) Neon Dream	Polydor 2383 330	5/09/75
(4) True Grip (cancelled)	Polydor 2383 386	5/14/76
(2) BBC Comedy Themes (one track: "Whatever Happened To You?")	BBC REH 387	12/12/80

US:		RELEASE DATE
none		none

Mike Vickers

Mike Vickers' contributions to the British music industry have been overlooked for many years. This is mainly because his name has usually appeared in small print on numerous albums and singles over the years. Groups such as The Scaffold, The Zombies and Gentle Giant have received Mike Vickers arrangement and production treatments. These recordings have turned out to be the most enduring of their careers.

After leaving Manfred Mann in 1965, Vickers had aspirations to conduct and arrange, and his Columbia output clearly reflected this goal. Vickers even assisted with the production of Manfred Mann's "Up The Junction" soundtrack. A little known fact about Vickers is that he was a British synthesizer pioneer two years before Manfred bought his Moog! Vickers' rented synthesizer enabled him to prepare for the British progressive movement in the early 1970s.

Vickers even had a taste of British Top 40 success with "Captain Kremmen (Retribution)" by teaming up with radio personality Kenny Everett. Currently, Mike has been enjoying himself in The Manfreds.

ARTIST CODE:
(1) Mike Vickers & Orchestra
(2) Mike Vickers
(3) Mike Vickers Orchestra
(4) Kenny Everett & Mike Vickers

SINGLES

ALBUMS

Paul Jones

Calling a Paul Jones a multiple threat would be an understatement. His output of records and compositions is impressive. However, his appearances on TV, radio, video and the stage is nothing short of monumental! After his '60s pop career wound down, Jones went into acting while occasionally dabbling in recording. Jones' acting success was extremely surprising, as his only pre-Manfreds acting experience was playing "Duncan" in his school's production of "Macbeth."

After giving the Manfreds his notice in 1965, Paul Jones' last session with the group took place on March 18, 1966. Following this, Jones brought his harmonica into the studio that same month with Eric Clapton, Steve Winwood (vocals), Jack Bruce (bass), Ben Palmer (piano) and Pete York (drums). This group was dubbed Eric Clapton & The Powerhouse. This star-studded session ("I Want To Know," "Crossroads" and "Steppin' Out") appeared on the Elektra album "What's Shakin'."

Jones' solo career began with a bang with the hits "High Time" and "I've Been A Bad Bad Boy." However, no large successes followed. (Jones re-recorded "High Time" and "I've Been A Bad Bad Boy" later for the K-Tel owned Key Seven company.) The film "Privilege," in which Jones starred,

was not universally accepted but its accompanying EP did well. The follow-up single "Thinkin' Ain't For Me" succeeded to a lesser extent. Still, Jones found it difficult to compete in the rapidly changing British music scene. In October 1967, Jones was forced to switch over to EMI's Columbia label because EMI was reserving HMV for classical releases, but this label change did not change his fortunes. The only exception was the #7 Australian success of his biggest single there - "Sons & Lovers." A highlight among Jones' non-hits was the Gibb brothers' song "And The Sun Will Shine," and this single featured help from such notables as Paul McCartney, Jeff Beck and others. Paul Jones' solo material after 1969 became extremely erratic, reflecting rapid changes in musical styles. At this point, Jones switched over to mainly non-musical activities. On February 25, 1969, Jones made his London stage debut in two Open Space Theatre plays: "Fun War" and "Muzeeka."

Of his acting pursuits, Paul's stage appearances have been his most plentiful and consistently successful. The Andrew Lloyd Webber musical "Evita" was an exception, combining Jones and d'Abo's voices for the first time on record. This project commemorated the short but eventful life of Argentine leader Evita Peron, and was a tremendous success.

In December 1978, Paul Jones' surprise appearance at a Peter Gabriel/Tom Robinson benefit at London's Hammersmith Odeon won over the crowds. As Tom McGuinness has noted, "He (Jones) got an amazing response from the audience . . . finding that he was valid and welcome gave him a tremendous boost!" McGuinness and Jones then spoke on the telephone about forming a blues-based band, and that became The Blues Band. Their most commercially successful records were their first two albums and only EP. The biggest impact they had was on the audiences that were treated to the finest, most energetic blues available anywhere. After the late 1982 breakup of The Blues Band, Paul Jones resumed acting full-time. In 1989, The Blues Band's members all got the itch to play again. They have been going ever since. Like Tom McGuinness, Jones also moonlights with The Manfreds and enjoys it immensely.

The following is a list (and I dare say it must be incomplete) of Paul Jones' activities outside Manfred Mann:

Theatre:
o   Noel Park in "The Banana Box" (West End)
o   MacHeath in "The Beggar's Opera" (National Theatre)
o   Rum Tum Tugger in "Cats"
o   Lieut. Arthur Drake in "Conduct Unbecoming" (late 1968, lasted 2 years - first West End appearance)
o   Lieut. Arthur Drake in New York's Broadway production of "Conduct Unbecoming"
o   Francis Drake in "Drake's Dream" (West End - Shaftesbury Theatre)
o   "Fun War" (Jones' London stage debut at the Open Space Theatre)
o   Sky Masterson in "Guys And Dolls" (National Theatre)
o   Title role in "Hamlet" (at the Ludlow Festival)
o   "Hooray For Hollywood" (1992)
o   Joseph in "Joseph And The Amazing Technicolour Dreamcoat"
o   Edmund in "King Lear"
o   Fred Graham & Petruchio in "Kiss Me Kate" (Royal Shakespeare Company at Stratford and The Old Vic in 1987)
o   Claudio in Peter Gill's production of "Measure For Measure" at the Riverside Theatre
o   Frank in "Mrs. Warren's Profession"
o   "Muzeeka" (Jones' London stage debut at the Open Space Theatre)
o   Cassio in "Othello"
o   Sid Sorokin in "The Pajama Game" (at the Leicester Haymarket and national tour)
o   Christian in "Pilgrim" (at the Edinburgh Festival)
o   Title role in "Pippin" (West End)

o   Jim in "Pump Boys And Dinettes" (Piccadilly, London)
o   The Twins in "Ring Around The Moon"
o   Romeo in "Romeo And Juliet" (in The Young Vic)
o   Trench in "Widower's Houses"
o   Orestes in Anouilh's "You Were So Sweet When You Were Little"

plus: seasons at Coventry, Bristol, Nottingham, Ludlow, Edinburgh, Watford & Chichester
Television: includes "A Bit Of Indiscretion," "Square One," "The Beggar's Opera," "John Lennon -

A Day In The Life," "Top Of The Pops," "Z-Cars," Ready Steady Go," "The Sweeney," "Hammer,"
"The Protectors," "Space 1999," "A Matter Of Taste" (directed by Peter Gill), "The Songwriters"
(1978), host of Granada TV's "Weekend," Channel 4's "A Plus 4," BBC's "Beat The Teacher," "Juke
Box Jury," "Looking For An Answer" (a religious program by ABC-TV on Sunday, 7/16/67, where
Jones argued religion with Cliff Richard), live from The Palladium, "Let's Face The Music," "The
South Bank Show," "Starburst," "Showcase," "Celebrity Squares," the green activist of BBC1's
children comedy thriller "Uncle Jack . . . And Operation Green," and an advert with Manfred for Ty-
Phoo Tea.

Film: "Privilege," "The Committee," "Demons Of The Mind."

Radio: presenter of "Counterpoint" (BBC World Service), presenter of "Sing Gospel" (BBC World
Service), host of "Rhythm And Blues" program presented on BBC Radio Two (Network) at 9:00PM,
"Jazz Me Blues" (Jazz FM), "Take It As Gospel" (Jazz FM).

Composing: including theme and/or incidental music for "The Wednesday Plays," "Fighting Back" (BBC TV/drama series), "Privilege," "The Committee" (film), and "Intimate Reflections" (film), "The Last Vacation," and other TV programs and commercials. Other compositions have been recorded by John Mantell (on his lone CBS single), and major artists from Helen Shapiro to Eric Clapton.

Jones' stage debut in "Fun War"

Sessions: "Evita" with Mike d'Abo, playing harmonica on albums by Tina Turner, Carla Bley, Eric Clapton, Radio Stars, Dave Kelly, Alexis Korner, Memphis Slim (video/CD), Gerry Rafferty, Su Pollard, etc., and work on "Dempsey And Makepeace" and jeans commercials.

194

ARTIST CODE:
all records by Paul Jones, except:
(1) Paul Jones Urbana
also see The Blues Band listing under Tom McGuinness

SINGLES

EPs

UK & FOREIGN:

		RELEASE DATE
Songs From The Film "Privilege"	HMV 7EG 8974	6/16/67

[tracks: Free Me; I've Been A Bad Bad Boy;/ Privilege; (My Poor Heart Is Surely) Breaking]

US:

		RELEASE DATE
none		none

ALBUMS

UK & FOREIGN:

		RELEASE DATE
"What's Shakin'" (3 tracks by Eric Clapton & The Powerhouse)	Elektra EUK 260/ EUKS 7260	8/12/66
My Way	HMV CLP/CSD 3586	12/09/66
Love Me, Love My Friends	HMV CLP/CSD 3602	7/14/67
"Privilege" (soundtrack; with George Bean Group and Mike Leander)	HMV CLP 3623	9/08/67
Come Into My Music Box	Columbia SCX 6347	9/05/69
Crucifix In A Horseshoe	Vertigo 6360 059	10/29/71
"Evita" (2LP)	MCA MCX 503	11/19/76
"Joseph And The Amazing Technicolor Dreamcoat" (cast recording; Paul Jones as Joseph on all tracks, also features Tim Rice, Gordon Waller, The Mike Sammes Singers, and Geoff Love And His Orchestra)	Music For Pleasure MFP 50455	11/16/79
Hits & Blues	One Up OU 2231	5/23/80
"Music Of Quality And Distinction (Volume 1)" (one track: "There's A Ghost In My House")	Virgin V 2219	4/09/82
"Drake's Dream" (cast recording)	President PTLS 1068	**/**/85
"Kiss Me Kate" (CD; cast recording)	First Night CAST CD 10	10/**/87
"What's Shakin'" (LP/CD; reissue - 3 tracks by The Powerhouse)	Edsel ED 249 (LP)/ EDCD 249 (CD)	1/**/88
"Joseph And The Amazing Technicolor Dreamcoat" (CD; reissue - cast recording)	Music For Pleasure CC 242/ CDB 7 92038 2	2/**/90
Paul Jones Rhythm & Blues Show - American Guests Vol. 3 (CD)	JSP JSPCD 235	4/**/90
"Evita" (2CD; reissue)	MCA DMCX 503	11/**/90

Crucifix In A Horseshoe (CD; reissue)   German Repertoire
                                                          REP 4196-WP   8/**/91
"B.E.F. - Music Of Quality And Distinction   Ten/Virgin CDBEF 1   8/**/92
    (Volume 1)" (CD; reissue - one track:
    "There's A Ghost In My House")
(1) I Need A Storm (CD)   Flying Fish
                                                          FF 606CD   2/**/93
"Sons And Lovers - Four British Rock Masters"   Australian Raven
    (CD; 7 Paul Jones tracks, plus 7 tracks each by   RVCD 27   4/**/93
    Chris Farlowe, Wayne Fontana and Chris Andrews)

		RELEASE DATE
US:		
"What's Shakin'" (3 tracks by The Powerhouse)	Elektra EKL-4002/ EKS-74002	7/11/66
"Privilege" - Original Soundtrack Album	Uni 3005/ 73005	7/24/67
Paul Jones Sings Songs From "Privilege" And Others...	Capitol T/ST-2795	7/31/67
Crucifix In A Horseshoe	London XPS 605	2/07/72
"Evita" (2LP)	MCA MCA2-11003	1/17/77
"Evita" (2CD; reissue)	MCA MCAD2-11003	1/**/85
"What's Shakin'" (CD; reissue)	Elektra 9 61343-2	5/11/93

[Paul Jones tracks on "Evita": "She Is A Diamond" (with Officers); "Dice Are Rolling/ Eva's Sonnet" (with Julie Covington); A New Argentina (with Covington, Mike Smith and Mike d'Abo); On The Balcony Of The Casa Rosada/ Don't Cry For Me Argentina (with C.T. Wilkinson and Covington); Rainbow Tour (with Wilkinson and Covington)]

[Paul Jones tracks on "Drake's Dream": I've Always Had A Dream; Take A Little Time (with Janet Shaw); When The Winds Command Us Away (and the Company); Sedition (with David Burt and the Company); Nova Albion; Sailing Around (with the Company); plus some other tracks with the Company]

McGuinness (right) with Eric Clapton (left) in The Roosters
(photo credit: Roy Bainton)

Tom McGuinness

What would Manfred Mann be without Tom McGuinness' levity to loosen things up? Any time Tom was called upon to provide liner notes for a record, Tom's cutting comments caused all targets to run for cover. Whether on stage, on TV or in the studio, this sense of humor was always prevalent. In essence, McGuinness was the glue that held the Manfreds together.

McGuinness' path to the Manfreds was a very frustrating one. Tom and writing partner Mark Newell had some success on UK TV's "That Was The Week That Was" and the lesser known "Private Eye," but Tom really wanted to attack the music business. His first group never got beyond the rehearsal stage but lasted from the summer to the fall of 1962. McGuinness quickly moved through many underachieving R&B bands, namely The Talismen, The Ravens and The London Thunderbirds. During the life of his original rehearsal group, McGuinness had run into Paul Jones and both kept contact. Tom's girlfriend at the time was attending the Kingston College Of Art, and she introduced him to fellow student Eric Clapton. From this meeting in March 1963, Tom started the band The Roosters with Clapton on guitar and pianist Ben Palmer. The Roosters lasted until October 1963, when McGuinness and Clapton made the incorrect decision of joining Merseybeat group Casey Jones And The Engineers for a disastrous tour that month. Clapton was quickly off to The Yardbirds, and McGuinness was moving furniture in Bentalls.

This is where McGuinness pulled off his first big joke. McGuinness knew of bassist Dave Richmond's problems with Manfred Mann, and spoke with Paul Jones about it. McGuinness conned Paul Jones into thinking that he switched over to bass and that he was the man for the job. McGuinness also convinced Manfred Mann and Mike Hugg of his skills, and amazingly, he was never asked to play during his "audition." In fact, the first time he played bass was on stage with Manfred Mann, since there was no time for rehearsals. By the time his bandmembers discovered that he deceived them all, they all had a good laugh since he worked in so well!

Tom played bass until Mike Vickers left in 1965, then turned over his bass to Jack Bruce and later Klaus Voorman. At this point, Tom was able to switch back to guitar, his natural instrument. After Manfred Mann ran out in 1969, Tom joined friend Hughie Flint to form McGuinness Flint. Their band scored two major hits in England, "When I'm Dead And Gone" and "Malt And Barley Blues."

Changing their musical styles after leaving Capitol Records signaled the end of their success. This was compounded by a BBC ban of the single "Let The People Go" due to its lyrical jabs at Britain's internment policy in Ireland. Songwriters and McGuinness Flint members Benny Gallagher and Graham Lyle were mainly responsible for the band's success, and their frustration caused them to quit the group. They soon became a successful duo. McGuinness and Flint then joined up with Dennis Coulson and Dixie Dean to record the 1972 album "Lo And Behold." "Lo And Behold" was a collection of then-unreleased Bob Dylan songs. The album was produced by Manfred Mann, and also included session work by Mike Hugg. McGuinness also did a Christmas single with Rob Townsend and Lou Stonebridge that came out using three different spellings of the artist's name (obviously another joke!).

Spurred on by Paul Jones' surprise performance in 1978, Tom got a call from Jones to form The Blues Band with Dave Kelly, Hughie Flint and Gary Fletcher. The first Blues Band concert was at The Bridge House in Canning Town in April 1979. Their first EP and first two albums were extremely successful, and all noticed their honest and spirited treatment of the blues. This ride lasted until December 18, 1982, when the band wanted some time to do other projects. McGuinness went into TV production/direction, such as The South Bank Show's Hendrix biography. He also wrote the serious (for once) liner notes for MMEB's LP "Somewhere In Afrika." Tom also humorously documented his career in his book "So You Want To Be A Rock & Roll Star."

While still with The Blues Band, Tom teamed up with Lou Stonebridge to do a single on Chrysalis and an album for RCA. After the dissolution of The Blues Band, McGuinness joined The Dave Kelly Band in time for their re-recording of the McGuinness Flint hit "When I'm Dead And Gone." Tom was replaced in this band by none other than Mick Rogers. Other McGuinness projects include the Lyle McGuinness Band and a single with Terry Oldfield. The Blues Band reunited in 1989 for more action, and Tom has doubled his pleasure by touring with The Manfreds.

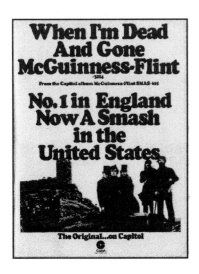

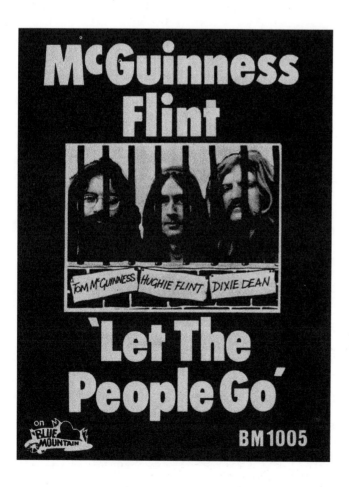

ARTIST CODE:
(1) McGuinness Flint
(2) Coulson, Dean, McGuinness, Flint
(3) Ruddie & The Rialtos featuring Wolfman Jack
(4) Rudy & The Rialtos
(5) Rudi And The Rialtos
(6) Stonebridge McGuinness
(7) The Blues Band
(8) The Dave Kelly Band
(9) Lyle McGuinness Band
(a) Terry Oldfield & Tom McGuinness

SINGLES

(7) Hey, Hey Little Girl (live)/Sus Blues (live)	Arista BLUES 2	6/18/82
(the above single only came in a limited edition double 7" pack)		
(8) When I'm Dead And Gone/Time After Time	Cool King CK 009	10/15/82
(7) Seemed Like A Good Idea (At The Time)/ Rolling Log	Arista BOOT 7	11/05/82
(9) Elise/What Does It Take	Cool King CK 011	5/20/83
(1) When I'm Dead And Gone/Malt And Barley Blues	EMI G45 29	7/20/84
(a) Main Theme From "John Silver's Return To Treasure Island"/Isabella - Island Of Dreams	Towerbell TVP 8	8/01/86
(7) Blue Collar/ (one-sided promo)	Ariola 112836	10/16/89
(7) Blue Collar/Duisberg Blues (promo only)	Ariola 112838	10/16/89

		RELEASE DATE
US:		
(1) When I'm Dead And Gone/Lazy Afternoon	Capitol 3014	12/14/70
(1) Malt And Barley Blues/Rock On	Capitol 3139	6/28/71
(1) Friends Of Mine/Happy Birthday, Ruthy Baby	Capitol 3186	9/06/71
(2) Lay Down Your Weary Tune/Let Me Die In My Footsteps	Sire SAA-711	10/08/73

ALBUMS

		RELEASE DATE
UK & FOREIGN:		
(1) McGuinness Flint	Capitol EA-ST 22625	12/04/70
(1) Happy Birthday, Ruthy Baby	Capitol ST 22794	7/09/71
(2) Lo And Behold	DJM DJLPS 424	7/14/72
(1) Greatest Hits	Dutch Sounds Superb SPR 80537	**/**/73
(1) Rainbow	Bronze/Island ILPS 9244	10/26/73
(1) C'est La Vie	Bronze/Island ILPS 9302	11/22/74
(2) Lo And Behold (cassette with different cover and tracks)	DJM DJM 44320	12/10/76
(7) Official Blues Band Bootleg Album (autographed)	Blues Band BBBP 101	1/18/80
(7) "The London R&B Sessions" (one track: "Death Letter" [live])	Albion DAI 2	2/22/80
(7) Official Blues Band Bootleg Album (reissue)	Arista BBBP 101	2/29/80
(6) Corporate Madness	RCA PL 25275	3/14/80
(7) Ready (with free single)	Arista BB 2	10/03/80

(7) Itchy Feet	Arista BB 3	9/25/81
(7) Brand Loyalty	Arista 204 922	9/03/82
(7) Official Blues Band Bootleg Album (reissue)	Fame FA 3059	2/18/83
(7) Bye Bye Blues	Arista 205 256	5/20/83
(9) Acting On Impulse	Cool King CKLP 03	6/**/83
(7) "The London R&B Sessions" (CD; reissue - one track: "Death Letter" [live])	German Line	**/**/85
(1) Rainbow (CD; reissue)	German Bronze/ Ariola	**/**/87
(7) These Kind Of Blues (LP/CD)	German Date/Line DALP 4001160 J (LP)/DACD 9.00180 O (CD)	10/**/88
(7) Back For More (LP/CD)	Ariola 210 095 (LP)/ 260 095 (CD)	10/16/89
(7) Official Blues Band Bootleg Album (LP/CD; reissue - first 500 copies autographed)	Ariola 210 497 (LP)/ 260 497 (CD)	2/05/90
(7) Ready (LP/CD; reissue - with bonus tracks)	Ariola 210 498 (LP)/ 260 498 (CD)	2/05/90
(7) Itchy Feet (LP/CD; reissue - with bonus tracks)	Ariola 210 697 (LP)/ 260 697 (CD)	5/21/90
(1) Heart On My Sleeve - The Very Best Of Gallagher & Lyle (CD; 2 tracks by McGuinness Flint: "When I'm Dead And Gone" and "Malt And Barley Blues")	A&M 3971232	4/01/91
(7) Brand Loyalty (LP/CD; reissue - with bonus tracks)	Ariola 211 319 (LP)/ 261 319 (CD)	4/22/91
(7) Fat City (LP/CD)	RCA PL/PD 75100	9/16/91
(1) Heart On My Sleeve - The Very Best Of Gallagher & Lyle (CD; reissue - 2 tracks by McGuinness Flint: "When I'm Dead And Gone" and "Malt And Barley Blues")	A&M CDMID 172	10/19/92
(7) Live (CD; repackage of "Bye Bye Blues" with bonus tracks)	Mau Mau MAUCD 629	11/**/92
(7) Homage (CD)	Essential ESSCD 202	9/20/93
(8) Acting On Impulse (CD; reissue)	RPM RPM 123	1/17/94
(7) Wire-Less (LP/CD)	Cobalt COBLP 1 (LP)/ COBCD 1 (CD)	3/06/95
(7) Fat City (CD; reissue)	Cobalt COBCM 1	3/06/95
(7) Official Blues Band Bootleg Album (CD; reissue)	Cobalt COBCM 2	3/06/95
(7) Ready (CD; reissue)	Cobalt COBCM 3	3/06/95

		RELEASE DATE
US:		
(1) McGuinness Flint	Capitol SMAS-625	12/28/70

(1) Happy Birthday, Ruthy Baby   Capitol ST-794   7/19/71
(2) Lo And Behold   Sire SAS 7405   8/06/73

Klaus Voorman

Bassist Klaus Voorman's friendship with the pre-fame Beatles prepared him for later success with Manfred Mann and his other Beatles-related activities. Klaus was first in the group The Blue Sounds before he formed Paddy, Klaus & Gibson. This Liverpool-based trio followed The Beatles into Hamburg, Germany to gain the necessary experience to succeed in England. Besides Klaus, this group consisted of Paddy Chambers (formerly in The Big 3; vocals and guitar) and Gibson Kemp, former drummer for Rory Storm and Kingsize Taylor. After three unsuccessful Pye singles, Klaus accepted an offer to join Manfred Mann, which had just signed with Fontana.

After his tenure with Manfred Mann, Voorman renewed his ties with John Lennon by joining The Plastic Ono Band. His appearances included the Lennon albums "Live Peace In Toronto," "Plastic Ono Band," "Imagine," "Some Time In New York City," "Walls And Bridges" and "Rock 'N' Roll," in addition to many other sessions. In 1982, Klaus produced the German/UK hit "Da Da" by German group Trio. Voorman now runs a hotel in northern Germany.

all records by Paddy, Klaus & Gibson:
SINGLES

UK & FOREIGN:		RELEASE DATE
I Wanna Know/I Tried	Pye 7N 15906	7/09/65
No Good Without You Baby/Rejected	Pye 7N 17060	2/18/66
Teresa/Quick Before They Catch Us	Pye 7N 17112	5/19/66

US:		RELEASE DATE
none		none

ALBUMS

UK & FOREIGN:

"Some Other Guys - Merseybeat Nuggets '63 - '66" (LP/CD; one track: "I Wanna Know")	Sequel NEX 102 (LP)/NEXCD 102 (CD)	2/**/90
"Quick Before They Catch Us - The Pop Era Vol. 1" (LP/CD; one track: "Quick Before They Catch Us")	Sequel NEX 108 (LP)/NEXCD 108 (CD)	2/**/90
"Footsteps To Fame Vol. 2" (CD; 2 tracks by Paddy, Klaus & Gibson: "I Wanna Know" and "I Tried")	German Repertoire REP 4185-WZ	**/**/91
"Hippy Hippy Shake - The Beat Era Vol. 2" (CD; one track: "I Tried")	Sequel NEXCD 218	4/19/93

RELEASE
DATE

US:

"Some Other Guys - Merseybeat Nuggets '63-'66" (CD; one track: "I Wanna Know")	Collectables COL-0564	5/**/94
"Quick Before They Catch Us - The Pop Era Vol. 1" (CD; one track: "Quick Before They Catch Us")	Collectables COL-0566	5/**/94

Mike d'Abo

d'Abo (right) with A Band Of Angels

Replacing Paul Jones as vocalist of the Manfreds was obviously a tall order to fill. While not quite matching the stage persona of Jones, d'Abo kept the Fontana version of Manfred Mann fresh until the end of the decade. Fulfilling his musical dreams at Harrow School, keyboardist/vocalist Mike d'Abo formed A Band Of Angels. This group also featured Christian (John) Gaydon (guitar/vocals), guitarist John Baker, Dave Wilkinson (bass) and drummer James Rugge-Price. Besides an appearance on the various artist album "Just For You," A Band Of Angels released two singles each on Piccadilly and United Artists. The Manfreds spotted d'Abo in 1966 and he quickly became the band's new vocalist.

Before Manfred Mann officially announced their disbanding, d'Abo released a quickly recalled single on Immediate. Since Fontana sued by claiming that d'Abo had exclusive recording rights with their label, the record had no chance. Despite this, d'Abo went on to perform in the studio production of "Jesus Christ Superstar." This production was an immediate smash in the US in 1970, but it inexplicably took two years to catch on in the UK.

Mike d'Abo's hit songwriting credits have been plentiful. These include "Build Me Up Buttercup" (The Foundations' hit), "Handbags And Gladrags" (Rod Stewart and Chris Farlowe) and "Storm In A Teacup" (The Fortunes' success). Two of Mike's projects were a collaboration with former Dave Clark Five vocalist Mike Smith in the mid-'70s, and the "Evita" studio album with Paul Jones. Also along the way, d'Abo has scored for film ("There's A Girl In My Soup"), the stage, and for commercials ("Finger Of Fudge" for Cadbury Fingers, Ty-Phoo Tea and Rowntree's Jelly Tots). He also appears on Radio Gloucester (a regular show) and Radio Two (occasionally), and hosts the 2-hour "Late Night West" show.

Mike has performed with His Mighty Quintet and The Manfreds in later years, and his productive interactions with Paul Jones in the latter group reinforce just how strong Mike d'Abo remains to this day.

ARTIST CODE:
(1) A Band Of Angels
(2) Mike d'Abo
(3) Smith/d'Abo
(4) Smith & d'Abo
(5) Mike d'Abo & His Mighty Quintet

SINGLES

UK & FOREIGN:		RELEASE DATE
(1) Me/Not True As Yet	United Artists UP 1049	4/17/64
(1) Gonna Make A Woman Of You/She'll Never Be You	United Artists UP 1066	9/25/64
(1) Leave It To Me/Too Late My Love	Piccadilly 7N 35279	11/19/65
(1) Invitation/Cheat And Lie	Piccadilly 7N 35292	2/04/66
(2) (See The Little People) Gulliver's Travels/ Anthology Of Gulliver's Travels	Immediate IM 075	2/14/69
(2) Let It Roar/California Line	Uni UNS 525	7/17/70
(2) Miss Me In The Morning/Arabella, Cinderella	Bell BLL 1134	12/11/70
(2) Belinda/Little Miss Understood	A&M AMS 7016	7/21/72
(2) Fuel To Burn/Hold On Darlin'	A&M AMS 7121	7/05/74
(3) Running Away From Love/Rockin' Chair	CBS 4417	6/25/76
(4) Free As A Bird/Only Love	CBS 4587	9/03/76
(4) Ray Of Sunshine/Loving You (Came So Easy)	CBS 4754	11/05/76
(1) Invitation/ Michael (by Geno Washington) - Our Love Is Getting Stronger (by Jason Knight)	Soul Supply/PRT 7SS 101	10/28/83
(1) Invitation/ Michael (by Geno Washington) - Our Love Is Getting Stronger (by Jason Knight) (12")	Soul Supply/PRT 12SS 101	10/28/83
(2) Loving On A Shoestring/Thank You	President PT 559	4/**/87

US:		RELEASE DATE
(2) King Herod's Song/Superstar (by Murray Head)	Decca 34803	10/27/70

[**NOTE:** This single was only available in a box set of singles from "Jesus Christ Superstar" - d'Abo played King Herod.]

(2) Miss Me In The Morning/Arabella, Cinderella	Bell 956	12/28/70
(2) Belinda/Little Miss Understood	A&M 1374	8/14/72

EPs

UK & FOREIGN:

RELEASE
DATE

(1) A Band Of Angels   French United

           Artists 36050   10/**/64

(tracks: She'll Never Be You; Gonna Make A Woman Of You;/ Me; Not True As Yet)

(1) A Band Of Angels   French Vogue

           PNV.24162   2/**/66

(tracks: Invitation; Too Late My Love;/ Cheat And Lie; Leave It To Me)

US:
           RELEASE DATE

none   none

ALBUMS

UK & FOREIGN:

		RELEASE DATE
(1) "Just For You" (one track: "Hide 'n' Seek")	Decca LK 4620	8/28/64
(2) d'Abo	Uni UNLS 114	7/31/70
(2) "Jesus Christ Superstar" (2LP)	MCA MKPS 2011/2	10/16/70
(2) Down At Rachel's Place	A&M AMLH 68097	5/05/72
(2) Broken Rainbows	A&M AMLH 63634	8/02/74
(4) Smith & d'Abo	CBS 81583	10/01/76
(2) "Jesus Christ Superstar" (2LP; reissue)	MCA MCX 501	11/19/76
(2) "Evita" (2LP)	MCA MCX 503	11/19/76
(2) Gulliver's Travels	Instant INLP 003	**/**/82
(2) Indestructible	President PTLS 1084	**/**/87
(5) Tomorrow's Troubadour	President PTLS 1090	**/**/88
(2) "Jesus Christ Superstar" (2CD; reissue)	MCA DMCX 501	11/**/90
(2) "Evita" (2CD; reissue)	MCA DMCX 503	11/**/90
(1) "Footsteps To Fame Vol. 2" (CD; 2 tracks by A Band Of Angels: "Invitation" and "Cheat And Lie")	German Repertoire REP 4185-WZ	**/**/91
(2) Mike d'Abo Relives Manfred Mania! (cassette; 500 copies only)	MD 0001	**/**/93

US:

		RELEASE DATE
(2) "Jesus Christ Superstar" (2LP)	Decca DXSA-7206	10/27/70
(2) Down At Rachel's Place	A&M SP-4346	7/24/72
(2) Broken Rainbows	A&M SP-3634	8/12/74
(2) "Evita" (2LP)	MCA MCA2-11003	1/17/77
(2) "Jesus Christ Superstar" (2LP; reissue)	MCA MCA2-79179	**/**/79

(2) "Jesus Christ Superstar" (2CD; reissue)	MCA MCAD2-10000	**/**/84
(2) "Evita" (2CD; reissue)	MCA MCAD2-11003	1/**/85
(2) "Jesus Christ Superstar" (2CD; reissue - Ultimate Master Disc, 24 karat gold CDs)	MCA MCAD2-10950	12/07/93

Chris Slade

Chris Slade (left) with Tom Jones (top) and The Playboys

Welchman Chris Slade's rock steady beats and occasional blasts of power during his time with MMEB are two of the reasons why most fans hold the original lineup in such high esteem. Chris started playing drums on a semi-professional basis with The Bright Boys. This group included his father Danny Slade, a dancer, and Thomas Woodward, a new singer who used the name Tommy Scott. Scott later became known as Tom Jones. Slade's association with Tom Jones lasted for eight years, as Slade was incorporated in Tom's backing groups. These groups were The Senators, The Playboys and finally The Squires, Jones' backing band during his breakthrough 1965 tour. Chris is also on the artificial live EP "Tom Jones On Stage" and hit single "It's Not Unusual." On the latter record, Slade played with session guitarist Jimmy Page. Tom Jones also performed this song on "Top Of The Pops" with Slade. Tom Jones' success was universal, and Slade made three 6-month US tours with Jones. On the same tours, Slade even backed the Ted Heath and Count Basie bands!

Chris worked as a shoe salesman, played on other sessions and stayed six months with The Squires after Tom Jones got another backing band. The most notable session was with Toomorrow, the disastrous studio group that included Olivia Newton-John. Thankfully, Slade was only with the band a few months. He was not heavily involved with the album or the film this group made. Soon after, Manfred Mann got Chris Slade to help him on the aborted third Manfred Mann Chapter Three album. Four months after Manfred Mann Chapter Three broke up, Manfred called up Slade to form another band with Mick Rogers. Slade then brought in bassist Colin Pattenden, and the lineup of MMEB was complete.

Slade stayed with the Earth Band until late 1978, when he formed the short-lived Terra Nova ("new earth") with Colin Pattenden. This group did not have any records, but recorded at least one track, "Black Rose."

Uriah Heep called Chris Slade in November 1979, and he stayed with them until September 1980. Unfortunately, this was the weakest lineup of the band, since Slade replaced longtime drummer Lee Kerslake and Ken Hensley had just left. Lead singer John Sloman did not work out, and the band's recordings and live shows bore this out. Uriah Heep was then out of business until 1982.

 After a session with Pink Floyd guitarist Dave Gilmour, Gilmour got Slade into the swing of things again. Through Gilmour, Slade was brought back into contact with his friend on the nearly 20 year-old "It's Not Unusual" session - Jimmy Page. Their resulting group was The Firm, and it also included former Free and Bad Company vocalist Paul Rodgers and bass player Tony Franklin. After an initial splash with their first album, The Firm did not meet the expectations of music fans and of themselves. They broke up soon after their second album.

Slade was out of action until AC/DC gave him a call to play on their 1990 album, "The Razors Edge" (please note the intentional misspelling). This album and the resulting tour were massive, and Slade has been involved with AC/DC ever since. This album spun off many strong songs, including "Thunderstruck" and "Moneytalks." AC/DC's one-dimensional rock approach continues to work, and Slade got his wish to be a part of a well-functioning group. On this album's tour, this success continued with the album "Live," available in single and double CD formats. The last recording that AC/DC produced was "Big Gun," recorded for the Arnold Schwarzenegger movie "Last Action Hero."

ARTIST CODE:
(1) Tom Jones
(2) Toomorrow
(3) Uriah Heep
(4) The Firm
(5) AC/DC

SINGLES

UK & FOREIGN:		RELEASE DATE
(1) It's Not Unusual/To Wait For Love (Is To Waste Your Life Away)	Decca F 12062	1/22/65
(2) I Could Never Live Without Your Love/ Roll Like A River	Decca F 13070	8/28/70
(3) Carry On/Been Hurt	Bronze BRO 88	1/25/80
(3) Love Stealer/No Return	Bronze BRO 96	6/20/80
(3) Think It Over/My Joanna Needs Tuning	Bronze BRO 112	1/16/81
(4) Radioactive/Together (7")	Atlantic A9586	3/01/85
(4) Radioactive/Together (7" shaped picture disc)	Atlantic A9586P	3/01/85
(4) Radioactive (remix)/City Sirens (live) - Live In Peace (live) (12")	Atlantic A9586T	3/01/85
(4) Radioactive - Together/City Sirens (live) - Live In Peace (live) (12")	Atlantic A9586TE	3/01/85
(4) All The King's Horses/Fortune Hunter	Atlantic A9458	4/18/86

(5) Thunderstruck/Fire Your Guns (7")	Atco B 8907	9/14/90
(5) Thunderstruck - Fire Your Guns - Chase The Ace (CD5)	Atco B 8907 CD	9/14/90
(5) Moneytalks/Mistress For Christmas (7")	Atco B 8886	11/16/90
(5) Moneytalks - Mistress For Christmas - Borrowed Time (CD5)	Atco B 8886 CD	11/16/90
(5) Are You Ready/Got You By The Balls (7")	Atco B 8830	4/13/91
(5) Are You Ready - Got You By The Balls (CD5)	Atco B 8830 CD	4/13/91
(5) Are You Ready/Got You By The Balls (specially packaged 7")	Atco 1B 8830W	5/07/91
(5) Highway To Hell (live)/Hell's Bells (live) (7")	Atco B 8479	10/05/92
(5) Highway To Hell (live)/Hell's Bells (live) - Bonnie Intro (live) - High Voltage (live) (12")	Atco B 8479T	10/05/92
(5) Highway To Hell (live) - Hell's Bells (live) - Bonnie Intro (live) - High Voltage (live) (first CD5)	Atco B 8479CDX	10/05/92
(5) Highway To Hell (live) - Hell Ain't A Bad Place To Be (live) - If You Want Blood You've Got It (live) - The Jack (live) (second CD5)	Atco B 8479CD	10/05/92
(5) Dirty Deeds Done Dirt Cheap (live)/ Shoot To Thrill (live) (12")	Atco B 6073T	2/22/93
(5) Dirty Deeds Done Dirt Cheap (live) - Shoot To Thrill (live) (CD5)	Atco B 6073CD	2/22/93
(5) Big Gun/For Those About To Rock (live in Moscow) - Back In Black (live in Moscow) (7")	Atco B 8396	6/28/93
(5) Big Gun/For Those About To Rock (live in Moscow) - Back In Black (live in Moscow) (12")	Atco B 8396T	6/28/93
(5) Big Gun/For Those About To Rock (live in Moscow) - Back In Black (live in Moscow) (CD5)	Atco B 8396CD	6/28/93
(5) Big Gun/For Those About To Rock (live in Moscow) - Back In Black (live in Moscow) (MC)	Atco B 8396C	6/28/93

		RELEASE DATE
US:		
(1) It's Not Unusual/To Wait For Love (Is To Waste Your Life Away)	Parrot 45 PAR 9737	3/08/65
(4) Radioactive/Together	Atlantic 7-89586	1/28/85
(4) Radioactive (remix)/City Sirens (live) - Live In Peace (live) (12")	Atlantic 0-86896	1/28/85
(4) Satisfaction Guaranteed/Closer	Atlantic 7-89561	4/22/85
(4) All The King's Horses/Fortune Hunter	Atlantic 7-89458	2/03/86
(4) Live In Peace/Spirit Of Love	Atlantic 7-89421	4/07/86
(5) Moneytalks/Borrowed Time	Atco 98881	11/19/90
(5) Big Gun/For Those About To Rock (live in Moscow) (cassette single)	Atco 98406	5/25/93

EPs

UK & FOREIGN:

		RELEASE DATE
(1) Tom Jones On Stage	Decca DFE 8617	4/09/65

(tracks: Bama Lama Bama Loo; I Can't Stop Loving You;/ Lucille; Little By Little.
NOTE: All tracks are studio recordings with overdubbed applause.)

US:

		RELEASE DATE
none		none

ALBUMS

UK & FOREIGN:

		RELEASE DATE
(1) Along Came Jones	Decca LK 4693	5/28/65
(3) Conquest	Bronze BRNA 524	3/14/80
(4) The Firm (LP/CD)	Atlantic 7 81239 1/2	2/22/85
(4) Mean Business (LP/CD)	Atlantic WX 35/ 7 81628 2	2/14/86
(1) The Golden Hits: Tom Jones (CD)	London 810 192-2	3/**/87

[**NOTE:** Although "It's Not Unusual" has appeared on numerous CDs, this is its first CD appearance.]

(1) What's New Pussycat? (CD; reissue - contains "Bama Lama Bama Loo" and "Little By Little" without overdubbed applause)	London 820 523-2	6/**/88
(5) The Razors Edge (sic) (LP/CD)	Atco 91413-1/2	9/24/90
(1) Tom Jones (CD; contains "I Can't Stop Loving You" and "Lucille" without overdubbed applause)	Deram 820 772-2	11/**/90
(3) Conquest (CD; reissue)	Castle Communications CLACD 208	12/**/90
(1) Along Came Jones (CD; reissue)	Decca 8440252	7/15/91
(5) The Razors Edge (picture disc LP)	Atco XW 364P	8/26/91
(3) Rarities From The Bronze Age	Sequel NEX CD 184	11/**/91
(5) Live (CD)	Atco 7567922152	10/26/92
(5) Live (Special Collector's Edition) (2LP/2CD)	Atco 7567922121/ 7567922122	10/26/92
(5) "Last Action Hero" - Music From The Original Motion Picture (CD)	Columbia 4739902	7/05/93

US:

		RELEASE DATE
(1) It's Not Unusual	Parrot PA 61004/ PAS 71004	6/07/65
(1) What's New Pussycat? (contains "Bama Lama Bama Loo" and "Little By Little" without overdubbed applause)	Parrot PA 61006/ PAS 71006	7/26/65
(3) Wonderful (same as "Conquest"; cancelled)	Chrysalis CHR 1227	3/**/80
(4) The Firm (LP/CD)	Atlantic 81239-1/2	2/18/85
(4) Mean Business (LP/CD)	Atlantic 81628-1/2	2/10/86
(5) The Razors Edge (sic) (LP/CD)	Atco 91413-1/2	9/25/90
(5) Live (CD)	Atco 92215-2	10/27/92
(5) Live (Special Collector's Edition) (2CD)	Atco 92212-2	10/27/92
(5) "Last Action Hero" - Music From The Original Motion Picture (CD)	Columbia CK 57127	6/08/93
(1) The Complete Tom Jones (CD; only US Tom Jones CD to contain "It's Not Unusual")	Deram 844 286-2	8/17/93

VIDEOS

UK & FOREIGN:

		RELEASE DATE
(4) The Firm	Atlantic	**/**/85
(5) Clipped	Atco Video	**/**/90
(5) Live At Donnington	A*Vision Entertainment	**/**/92
(5) "For Those About To Rock" (5 AC/DC tracks performed live in Moscow; with other artists)	Warner Home Video	**/**/92

US:

		RELEASE DATE
(4) The Firm	Atlantic	**/**/85
(5) Clipped	Atco Video 50234-3	**/**/90
(5) Live At Donnington	A* Vision Entertainment	10/27/92
(5) "For Those About To Rock" (5 AC/DC tracks performed live in Moscow; with other artists)	Warner Home Video 35514	**/**/92

Mick Rogers

For nearly every MMEB fan, Mick Rogers was responsible for blazing incredible musical fires over the band's '70s audiences. Mick's departure in 1975 marked the end of an era for the Earth Band, but Mick was never far away from the Earth Band's actions. Upon his return to the Earth Band in 1983, a new fire was set.

Mick's interest in music was inspired by his father Ted (a drummer) and uncle Ernie Norman (string bass and guitar). With his family's talent, Mick's excitement with '50s rock and roll formed his musical dreams. Mick's first jobs after leaving school included a 3-month stint as an apprentice engineer and a period as a shoe salesman. Mick started playing double bass and switched to guitar between 1964 and 1965. The local holiday spot Warner's Holiday Camp required a band, so Mick put one together for the summer. With this firmly behind him, Mick went to Expo '67 in Montreal and then to Australia on one of the dreaded package tours, playing with Adam Faith for a one-year period and then Gene Pitney. Also on this tour was the enormously successful Australian singer Normie Rowe and his band The Playboys. Mick's group backed all the artists except Rowe, and this group also played a 20-minute set of its own. Normie Rowe's guitar player was leaving, so Rowe asked Mick to join The Playboys. When Mick and fellow Playboys guitarist Brian Peacock started their work with Rowe in September 1966, the band played in Montreal and throughout Australia for a few months. Normie Rowe & The Playboys made some recordings before the effects of the Vietnam War broke up the band in December 1966. Peacock had been the author of Normie Rowe's hit "Penelope" before Mick Rogers' joining, and this song was later recorded by Procession.

Before this, Brian Peacock and drummer Craig Collinge were founding members of The Librettos, a successful New Zealand group that did not survive in Australia. In late 1966, Collinge headed a Cream-influenced power trio in Brisbane called The Knack. Meanwhile, The Playboys without Normie Rowe issued their own single on the Australian Sunshine label, "Sad." Soon, Collinge and Trevor Griffin (keyboards and vocals) were part of this new Playboys group, now called Procession. Griffin was previously with the London group The Question Marks. All of Procession's members wanted to tap into progressive territory, which included snatches of jazz within a pop format.

Procession set out to dominate the Australian music scene. They appeared every week on the new four-hour, Saturday morning Australian TV show "Uptight." This program was conveniently produced by their manager David Joseph, who also managed to work the band into a special segment of the show on a weekly basis.

Procession's goal was to present the band in some premiere setting each time out. For example, their first single "Anthem" (which was shown as by The Procession) was recorded without any instrumental accompaniment. Also, another unique occurrence was their first TV appearance, backed by a 40-member choir. Procession then received three-week assignments at Sebastian's and Bertie's commencing on December 17, 1967. These gigs built upon their "Uptight" fan base into early 1968.

The third premiere by the band was the recording of their first album. "Live At Sebastian's" (with "Penelope") was recorded on April 3, 1968, becoming the first live debut album by an Australian act. Procession was also the first Australian group to use an 8-track Scully recorder. This equipment was used to lay down their second single, "Listen."

 The unfortunate part of all this effort by the band is that their records did not sell. The Australian public was very confused and overwhelmed by the sheer diversity and musical structure of Procession's records. As a result, a complete lack of response occurred. The band decided that Australia wasn't advanced enough to appreciate their work, so they ventured to a place where they thought people had more open minds - London. This decision was helped by their manager, who obtained a large advance for the group from UK Mercury Records to record an album. The band had the good fortune to work with Mike Hugg in London for most of their first (and only) studio album. Hugg had just finished recording "Fox On The Run" with Manfred Mann, and was ready for this project. This was when Manfred heard Mick sing for the first time.

Australian "Procession" LP   UK "Procession" LP   US "Procession" LP

Procession's self-titled album (with different tracks on the Australian and UK editions) was by far the most progressive album by an Australian band. It reflected their jazz tendencies with a firm pop basis. Despite heavy promotion, the British radio and public now ignored their records. Fed up with this ignorance, Peacock formed the group The Party Machine in early 1969. Ross Wilson became Peacock's replacement on guitar, but this lineup folded before any other recordings were made.

Mick Rogers went back to Australia and formed a blues-based trio, Bulldog, with Peter Miles and Bob Daly. Bulldog released the single "A Man Of Constant Sorrow," and then Mick departed the group, which then evolved into Drummond. Drummond was a one-hit band in Australia, producing the #1 record "Daddy Cool." After this, Mick immersed himself in sessions.

Mick's opinion of the "Procession" album is not favorable: "The album was a pretty strange mixture of Jack Bruce, and free music bordering on jazz. After signing a UK contract, Mercury tried to turn us into a pop band."

Meanwhile, Collinge joined Manfred Mann Chapter Three for two albums before leaving to join an imitation Fleetwood Mac group, and the bands Shoot and Third World War. Collinge was replaced by Chris Slade, who started work on the abortive third Manfred Mann Chapter Three album.

(In the summer of 1978, a very frustrating thing occurred to the former members of Procession. The Australian vocal group The New Seekers hit #21 in the UK with "Anthem [One Day In Every Week]." This was the same song that Procession released without success as "Anthem" on a single, their Australian studio LP and live album, and as "One Day In Every Week" on their UK album. If anything, it proved the lasting impression the song truly had.)

Manager David Joseph helped Mick Rogers again in late 1970. While attending a record reception, Joseph discovered that Manfred Mann was forming a new band. Joseph called Mick and asked him to come from Australia to London to see if the project would work. Mick accepted the offer immediately.

After his long stint with the Earth Band, Mick returned to Australia and formed Eclipse. This band recorded a remake of "Get Your Rocks Off." Lillian Bron from Bronze Records called Mick up and asked if he would join Uriah Heep. Heep's singer (David Byron) and bass player (John Wetton) were leaving, so it would have been a great opportunity for Mick. After writing some songs with Uriah Heep member Ken Hensley for a couple of weeks, Mick decided that Heep wasn't for him. Mick did some MMEB sessions and then formed Aviator with Clive Bunker, Jack Lancaster and John G. Perry. Aviator then went on tour supporting guitarist Steve Hillage. Mick's take on Aviator was more positive: "I loved that band. It just ran out of money. Originally, Jack Lancaster was on horns - Jack was in a different area than we were. We wanted more of a rock band. I loved that band (Aviator) live - you talk about not capturing it on record . . . on a couple of things, that band sounded enormous. However, 'Turbulence,' our second album, came close. To cut a long story short, I met up with Manfred - we never lost contact."

During the '70s, Mick played on Mike Hugg's LPs "Somewhere" and "Stress And Strain." Mick also played with Dave Greenslade, Simon Phillips and bassist Tony Reeves. A short stint with Colosseum II also appeared on Mick's resume. Between his Earth Band stints, Mick played guitar on Jack Lancaster's 1981 LP "Skinningrove Bay" and he replaced Tom McGuinness in The Dave Kelly Band in 1982. He has also played off and on with Joan Armatrading. On weekends, Mick plays at a small Brentford pub with Willy Finlayson and Matt Irving on keyboards and vocals.

Mick's opinion of the albums on which he was not a member is equally favorable: "'The Roaring Silence' and 'Watch' were probably the closest that Manfred recorded to live albums. They bridged the gap more than any other album I think, and 'Solar Fire' (a Mick Rogers era MMEB album) still sells. I have done something on most MMEB albums, and the Earth Band (in 1986) were going through another change."

A lot of things for the Earth Band changed between 1975 and 1983. Mick likes the way it works now: "What changed was that I was no longer the singer. I was working alongside Chris Thompson, which was great. Manfred has employed the two singer system, so although Noel McCalla is now the main singer, I do my things . . . two totally different voices, but when we sing together, it all comes together.

"I think because Manfred and I are very close in interests, and because I know him from the early days as well, when he says he needs something, I can lock into it. Even now, we help one another, so that association carries on."

ARTIST CODE:
(1) Normie Rowe; actually by Normie Rowe & The Playboys
(2) The Playboys
(3) The Procession
(4) Procession
(5) Bulldog
(6) Mick Rogers & Eclipse
(7) Aviator
(8) The Dave Kelly Band
(9) Mick Rogers

SINGLES

UK & FOREIGN:		RELEASE DATE
(1) Ooh La La/Ain't Nobody Home	Australian Sunshine QK 1565	11/**/66
(1) It's Not Easy/Mary Mary	Polydor BM 56132	11/25/66
(1) It's Not Easy/Mary Mary	Australian Sunshine QIK 1605	12/**/66
(1) Ooh La La/Ain't Nobody Home	Polydor BM 56144	1/27/67
(2) Sad/Black Sheep R.I.P.	Australian Sunshine QIK	**/**/67
(3) Anthem/Take Time	Australian Festival FK 2126	1/**/68
(4) Listen/Minuets For Moderns	Australian Festival FK 2247	4/**/68

(4) Every American Citizen/Essentially Susan	Australian Festival	
	FK 2575	9/**/68
(4) Every American Citizen/Essentially Susan	Mercury MF 1053	9/20/68
(4) One Day In Every Week/Wigwam City	Australian Festival	
	FK	12/**/68
(4) One Day In Every Week/Wigwam City	Mercury MF 1070	12/12/68
(5) Man Of Constant Sorrow/Inner Spring	Australian Fable	
	FB 038	12/**/70
(6) Get Your Rocks Off/TCS	Australian OZ OZ 3	8/02/76
(7) Lay Down Your Weary Tune/Greed	Harvest HAR 5171	10/27/78
(7) Time Traveller/Rocking Chair	Harvest HAR 5180	2/16/79
(7) Way Of The World/Wood Wharf Gumbo	Harvest HAR 5202	2/22/80
(7) All Your Love Is Gone/Wood Wharf Gumbo	Harvest HAR 5208	7/11/80
(9) Bring Back The Night/Too Late	Trojan MR 1	3/07/86
(9) Rivers/Gold In My Pocket	Mooncrest	
	MOON 1001	**/**/86

		RELEASE DATE
US:		
(4) Adelaide, Adelaide/One Day In Every Week	Smash 2225	6/04/69
(4) Every American Citizen/You - Me	Smash 2239	8/08/69

ALBUMS

		RELEASE DATE
UK & FOREIGN:		
(4) Live At Sebastian's	Australian Festival	
	FL-32903/	
	SFL-932903	6/**/68
(4) Procession	Australian Festival	
	FL-33091/	
	SFL-933091	9/**/68
(4) Procession (different tracks and cover than above)	Mercury 20132	3/12/69
	SMCL	
(4) "So You Wanna Be A Rock 'N' Roll Star Volume 2" (2LP; one track - "Listen")	Australian Festival	
	L45705/6	**/**/77
(7) Aviator	Harvest SHSP 4096	4/13/79
(7) Turbulence	Harvest SHSP 4107	4/11/80
(8) Dave Kelly Band - Live!	Appaloosa AP 033	**/**/83
(4) Minuets For Moderns	Australian Raven	
	RVLP-32	**/**/89
(4) "Down Under Dreamtime - Australian 60's Psychedelia" (one track - "Listen")	Australian Raven	
	RVLP-35	**/**/89
(8) Dave Kelly Band - Live! (CD; reissue)	Appaloosa APCD	

		RELEASE DATE

US:

(4) Procession (same tracks as Australian LP, but with different cover)	Smash SRS-67122	5/30/69
(7) Aviator	EMI America ST-17012	5/21/79

[**NOTE:** Normie Rowe & The Playboys also recorded a "Things Go Better With Coke" commercial. It is not known if Mick Rogers is on this recording.]

Chris Thompson

Were it not the case that Chris Thompson's vocal talents received exposure via Manfred Mann's Earth Band, would he be the most in-demand vocalist on the British scene? Probably not. Thompson has appeared just about everywhere in projects that reflect his numerous talents and interests.

Born in England, vocalist/guitarist Chris Thompson grew up in New Zealand and started singing in high school folk bands. Another interest of Chris' was teaching, and he was qualified to deal with learning-disabled primary school children. He soon became a member of Hillberry Walker, a New Zealand based backup band for touring professionals such as Chuck Berry and Little Richard.

Thompson returned to England in 1974 to do TV commercials and sessions, including work with Ike and Tina Turner. Thompson soon joined up with Brian Keith (from the group Plastic Penny) and became the duo Central Park Reunion, issuing two singles. With the experience that he gained from these works, Thompson had learned from his past mistakes. Six years before he replaced Mick Rogers in the Earth Band in 1975, Chris auditioned for Argent. Thompson did not get the job despite being the best vocalist because at the time he was considered "overweight and bald" by the band. Chris found out about Manfred's audition and sang "Joybringer" and "Spirits In The Night." This time, he succeeded at the audition![93]

While still with MMEB, Thompson formed Filthy McNasty with the vastly underrated Stevie Lange on vocals and percussion, Billy Kristian (bass/vocals), Mike Walker (keyboards) and drummer Clive Edwards. Their residency at The Bridge House in London brought fans to their knees with their overwhelming and roughly sensual sound. The only fruit from this band was documented on their three live tracks on the 1978 double album "A Week At The Bridge E16."

At this point, Chris' lead vocal session work started to flourish. (These sessions, as well as Chris' compositions, have been listed in the following discography.) Thompson sang "Thunderchild" on Jeff Wayne's tremendously successful "The War Of The Worlds" 2LP concept album, released in the summer of 1978. This UK platinum album also did well in the States, reaching the Top 100. "Thunderchild" appeared as a single in the 12" format only, a rarity at the time.

Due to the success of Filthy McNasty and "The War Of The Worlds," Chris Thompson had given Manfred his notice. Chris Thompson was starting to write songs that he felt would be more suitable outside the Earth Band. After the Earth Band's 1979 European tour for "Angel Station," Chris formed the band Night. Night was formed from the Thompson/Lange/Kristian nucleus of Filthy McNasty plus Nicky Hopkins on piano, guitar man Robbie McIntosh and Rick Marrotta on drums.

Night's eponymous debut LP featured four Thompson written or co-written songs, and the entire album was a sensual pleasure due to Stevie Lange and her steamy interactions with Chris. The US public noticed this, and rewarded Night with the Top 20 hits "Hot Summer Nights" and "If You Remember Me."[94] The former was written by Walter Egan, who had released his modestly-selling version the year before.

A 3-week tour of the US with The Doobie Brothers from September 21 to October 14, 1979 gave the band greater exposure. For the tour, Peter Baron replaced Rick Marrotta on drums, and Chris struck up a productive friendship with Doobie Brothers member Patrick Simmons.

The band's next (and final) album was "Long Distance" in 1980. Keyboardist Bobby Wright replaced Nicky Hopkins, while Bobby Giudotti became the new drummer. More of Thompson's songs were used on this album, but the album and the singles from it (including the excellent "Love On The Airwaves") did not catch on. A tour followed, and a half-hour promo was done for Britain's Radio One. On this promo, the band ripped through their songs and a version of "Blinded By The Light."

The campy 1981 film "The Monster Club" offered Night an opportunity to expose themselves in the video medium, and Stevie Lange very nearly did that![95] The footage of the song they performed, "The Stripper," proved to be the most classic sequence of the film. The band then became The Island before finally grinding to a halt in 1983 when Robbie McIntosh accepted an offer to join The Pretenders.

In 1983, Chris released his first solo album, the German release "Out Of The Night." The album's title was a play on his past group, and was recorded at Manfred's Workhouse studio. In addition to Chris, Robbie McIntosh (guitar), Malcolm Foster (bass), Mic Clews (drums) and Paul Wickens (aka Wix; keyboards) formed the group. This band became The Islands. Chris and McIntosh wrote nearly the entire album, which did not sell.

Chris went on Radio One and on the road in 1984 to promote his single "Bye Bye Love" on Simple Records. Some of the tour material ended up on his 1985 European LP release "Radio Voices." This album featured a re-recording of Night's "Dr. Rock" and "A Shift In The Wind," a collaboration of Thompson and Queen guitarist Brian May.

"The High Cost Of Living" became Chris Thompson's next album in 1986. This time he was on Atlantic, and it became his only US and UK album release. Again, Chris joined Stevie Lange, Robbie McIntosh and others to create a uniformly strong album. The Motors' hit "Love And Loneliness" and "It's Not Over" did not make any singles impact.[96]

In 1987 John Farnham issued "You're The Voice," a song co-written by Chris, Andy Qunta, Keith Reid and Maggie Ryder. "You're The Voice" was a hit every place except North America.[97] Chris and Procol Harum lyricist Keith Reid contributed in 1988 to "Tabaluga And The Magic Jadestone," a child's tale of a dragon narrated by Hayley Mills with Chris Thompson on vocals. "One Step At A Time" and "To Hell With Love" were also issued as singles, and the album was also available in a German-narrated version.

With little notice, Thompson received a call from Harold Faltermeyer (known for his "Beverly Hills Cop" hit "Axel F") to write lyrics for a tennis-oriented song. Chris delivered, and the heavily synthesized single "The Challenge (Face It)" went into release just in time for Wimbledon. "The Challenge (Face It)" hit the top of the German singles charts, and the Wimbledon success of German tennis stars Steffi Graf and Boris Becker figured in the single's healthy sales.[98]

During the closing ceremony of the 1990 Commonwealth Games, Chris led a band including Billy Kristian on bass. The song recorded for the games, "This Is The Moment," received a New Zealand release. Thompson's next album "Beat Of Love" was released in Germany. Another synthesizer-based collaboration with Harold Faltermeyer, "Beat Of Love," enabled Thompson to tour Germany with former MMEB drummer John Lingwood, keyboard player Don Airey, Brett Sawyer on guitar and Kevin Reynolds (sax). On this tour, the band played the MMEB favorites "For You" and "Blinded By The Light," as well as The Blue Nile's "Stay."

Chris' most recent recorded appearance was on Alan Parsons' neglected "Try Anything Once" album in 1993. After years of studio work, Alan Parsons finally explored the live arena in 1994 with Thompson by his side.

At the time of this writing, Thompson has his sights set on securing a London pub residency with the incomparable Stevie Lange. In addition, Chris is also trying to get a US album deal with a new band and repertoire that he is putting the final touches on.

Still, Thompson sings on. He also has done TV ads for Corn Flakes and Rank Xerox (singing The Eagles' hit "Take It To The Limit").[99] At this moment, he is in a studio somewhere singing his heart out.

ARTIST CODE:
(1) Central Park Reunion
(2) Filthy McNasty
(3) Chris Thompson
(4) Night
(5) Chris Thompson, actually with Night
(6) Night featuring Chris Thompson
(7) Patrick Simmons
(8) Jennifer Warnes/Chris Thompson
(9) Hazel O'Connor & Chris Thompson
(a) Don Airey/K2
(b) SOS United featuring Chris Thompson
(c) Mike Oldfield
(d) Artists United For Nature
(e) Farfarello featuring Chris Thompson
(f) Jeff Wayne
(g) Brian May
(h) Jan Hammer
(i) Alan Parsons

SINGLES

UK & FOREIGN:		RELEASE DATE
(1) Deep Into The Night/Babe, I'm Your Man	MCA MCA178	3/07/75
(1) Don't Go/Kicking Up Stones	MCA MCA209	9/19/75
(3) Thunderchild (with narration by Richard Burton)/ Dead London - Thunderchild (edit) (12")	CBS 12-6477	1/19/79
(4) Hot Summer Nights/Party Shuffle	Dutch Planet K12366	6/29/79
(4) Hot Summer Nights/Love Message	Planet K12367	6/29/79
(4) Party Shuffle/Come Around (If You Want Me)	Planet K12382	9/21/79
(5) If You Remember Me/Theme From "The Champ" (by Dave Grusin)	Planet K12389	10/05/79
(6) If You Remember Me/You Ain't Pretty Enough	Dutch Planet PL 12405	11/16/79
(4) Cold Wind Across My Heart (Version #2)/ You Ain't Pretty Enough	Planet K12420	2/15/80
(4) Love On The Airwaves/Day After Day	Planet K12492	12/12/80
(4) Good To Be Back In Your Arms (edit)/Look At You	Planet K12507	2/13/81
(7) So Wrong/If You Want A Little Love	WEA E9839	5/27/83
(7) So Wrong/If You Want A Little Love (12")	WEA E9839T	5/27/83
(3) Do What You Wanna Do/Movin' On	German Ultra Phone 6.13805	**/**/83

(3) Bye Bye Love/Blue Water (7")	Simple SIM3	4/**/84
(3) Bye Bye Love/Blue Water - Lies (12")	Simple 12 SIM3	4/**/84
(3) Bye Bye Love/Eight Letters Three Words One	German Teldec	
Meaning	6.14489 TS	**/**/85
(9) Push And Shove/Safe (non-Thompson track) (7")	Towerbell FND 1	6/21/85
(9) Push And Shove (extended mix)/Push And Shove -	Towerbell FND 12	6/21/85
Moments On A Lever (non-Thompson track) (12")		
(3) Love And Loneliness/Empty House (7")	Atlantic A9384	9/05/86
(3) Love And Loneliness/Empty House (12")	Atlantic A9384T	9/05/86
(3) Love And Loneliness/Empty House - Missing (12")	German Atlantic	
	7 86785-0	9/05/86
(3) It's Not Over/Make It A Holiday (7")	Parlophone R6152	4/**/87
(3) It's Not Over (extended mix)/It's Not Over	Parlophone 12 R6152	4/**/87
(extended dub mix) - Make It A Holiday (12")		
(3) To Hell With Love/Man Of Steel	German Teldec	
	6.15136	**/**/88
(3) One Step At A Time/Bridge Across The River	German Teldec	
	6.15189	**/**/88
(3) The Challenge (Face It)/The Challenge (Face It)	German Ariola	
(instrumental) (7")	112485	7/**/89
(3) The Challenge (Face It) (Centre Court Mix)/	German Ariola	
The Challenge (Face It) (single mix) - The Challenge	612485	7/**/89
(Face It) (Strawberries & Cream Mix) (12")		
(3) The Challenge (Face It) - The Challenge (Face It)	German Ariola	7/**/89
(instrumental) (CD3)	162485	
(3) The Challenge (Face It) (Centre Court Mix) -	German Ariola	7/**/89
The Challenge (Face It) (Strawberries & Cream	662485	
Mix) - The Challenge (Face It) (instrumental) (CD5)		
(3) Take Me To Heaven/Take Me To Heaven	German Ariola	
(instrumental)	112755	9/**/89
(3) Take Me To Heaven (Uptown Mix) - Take Me To	German Ariola	
Heaven (Heavenly Mix) (CD5)	162755	9/**/89
(d) Yes We Can/Yes We Can (Native Sounds)	German Virgin	
	112764	9/**/89
(b) Lullaby For Grown Ups (Good Night)/	German EMI	
Blessed Are (7")	203489 7	**/**/89
(b) Lullaby For Grown Ups (Good Night)/Blessed	German EMI	
Are - two non-Chris Thompson tracks (12")	203489 6	**/**/89
(b) Lullaby For Grown Ups (Good Night) - Blessed	German EMI	
Are - two non-Chris Thompson tracks (CD3)	203489 3	**/**/89
(3) This Is The Moment/	New Zealand	**/**/90
(e) Sea Of Emotion/Mephisto	German Ariola	
	113419	8/**/90
(e) Sea Of Emotion - Mephisto - Evening In Cassis -	German Ariola	

Savanah (CD5)	663419	8/**/90
(e) Sea Of Emotion/Mephisto (with gatefold sleeve)	German Ariola 113711	10/**/90
(3) Beat Of Love/When The Wind Blows (7")	German Ariola 114129	3/**/91
(3) Beat Of Love (Extended Version) - When The Wind Blows (12")	German Ariola 614129-213	3/**/91
(3) Beat Of Love (Extended Version)/When The Wind Blows - Beat Of Love (single version) (CD5)	German Ariola 664129	3/**/91
(3) Tower Of Love/The Revolution Man (7")	German Ariola 114644	11/**/91
(3) Tower Of Love - The Revolution Man + 1 (CD5)	German Ariola 664644	11/**/91
(d) Yes We Can/Yes We Can (Instrumental Mix) (7")	ELF/Polygram TV AUN 1	6/22/92
(d) Yes We Can - Yes We Can (Extended Version featuring Brian May) - Yes We Can (Instrumental Mix) (CD5)	ELF/Polygram TV AUND 1	6/22/92
(i) Turn It Up (Radio Edit) - Turn It Up (CD5)	Arista 74321167262	10/18/93

US:

		RELEASE DATE
(4) Hot Summer Nights/Party Shuffle	Planet P-45903	5/21/79
(5) If You Remember Me/Theme From "The Champ" (by Dave Grusin)	Planet P-45904	5/28/79
(4) Cold Wind Across My Heart (Version #2)/ Come Around (If You Want Me)	Planet P-45907	10/15/79
(6) If You Remember Me/You Ain't Pretty Enough	Planet P-45909	12/03/79
(4) Love On The Airwaves/Day After Day	Planet P-47921	11/24/80
(4) Love On The Airwaves/Love On The Airwaves (promo 12")	Planet AS 11474-A	11/24/80
(7) So Wrong/If You Want A Little Love	Elektra 7-69839	3/07/83
(8) All The Right Moves (edit)/Love Theme From "All The Right Moves" (by David Campbell)	Casablanca 814 603-7	10/24/83
(3) Love And Loneliness/Empty House	Atlantic 7-89384	7/14/86
(3) What A Woman Wants/She's Dangerous	Atlantic 7-89368	8/04/86
(3) It Don't Bother Me/This Is Not A World Of Our Making	Atlantic 7-89287	2/02/87
(i) Turn It Up (Radio Edit) - Turn It Up (promo CD5)	Arista 2623	11/02/93

ALBUMS

UK & FOREIGN:

(3) "The War Of The Worlds" (2LP)	CBS 96000	6/09/78
(3) "The War Of The Worlds" (2LP; Spanish narration)	Spanish CBS	6/09/78
(3) "The War Of The Worlds" (2LP; Italian narration)	Italian CBS	6/09/78
(3) "The War Of The Worlds" (2LP; French narration)	French CBS	6/09/78
(2) "A Week At The Bridge E16" (2LP; 3 tracks: "Move Over," "The Fire Down Below" and "Can't Get Next To You")	Bridge House BHLP 001/ BHEP1	**/**/78
(3) "The War Of The Worlds" (2LP box set)	CBS WOW 100	1/**/79
(4) Night (with revised track listing)	Planet K52200	12/07/79
(4) Long Distance	Planet K52251	12/05/80
(4) "Monster Club" - The Original Soundtrack (one track: "The Stripper")	Chips CHILP 2	5/08/81
(3) "Highlights Of 'The War Of The Worlds'" (LP)	CBS 85337	10/09/81
(3) "Arrested" by the Royal Philharmonic Orchestra (Thompson lead vocals on "De Do Do Do, De Da Da Da" and "Don't Stand So Close To Me")	RCA RCALP 8001	4/**/83
(3) Out Of The Night	German Ultra Phone 6.25484	**/**/83
(7) Arcade (dual lead vocals with Patrick Simmons)	WEA 60225-1	6/10/83
(3) "The War Of The Worlds" (2CD; reissue)	CBS CD-96000	5/**/85
(3) "Highlights Of 'The War Of The Worlds'" (LP; reissue)	CBS 32356	5/**/85
(9) "Greenpeace - The Album"	Towerbell/EMI FUND 1	6/**/85
(3) Radio Voices	German Ultra Phone 6.25922	6/**/85
(3) "Wind In The Willows" (two tracks: "The Badger" and "Piper At The Gates Of Dawn")	President PTLS 1078	7/**/85
(3) The High Cost Of Living	Atlantic 81665-1	9/**/86
(a) Triumphs And Tragedies (CD; Thompson provides lead vocals on "Can't Make Up Your Mind" and "Song For Al")	German MCA Int'l. MCD 15457	1/**/88
(9) "Greenpeace - The Album" (CD; reissue)	PolyGram 827 351-2	**/**/88
(3) Tabaluga And The Magic Jadestone (English Version) (LP/CD)	German Teldec 6.26847AS (LP)/ 8.26847 ZP (CD) (243 880-2)	11/**/88
(3) Tabaluga And The Magic Jadestone (German Version) (LP/CD)	German Teldec	11/**/88
(3) Tabaluga And The Magic Jadestone (promo LP;	German Teldec	

no narration, substitutes the otherwise unavailable "Red Light" for the track "World's Conductor")	6.26849AS	11/**/88
(c) Earth Moving (LP; two tracks: "Runaway Son" and "See The Light")	Virgin V 2610	7/10/89
(3) "Highlights Of 'The War Of The Worlds'" (CD; reissue)	CBS 85337	2/04/91
(3) Beat Of Love (CD)	German Ariola 261 417	5/**/91
(c) Earth Moving (CD; reissue - two tracks: "Runaway Son" and "See The Light")	Virgin CDV 2610	4/**/92
(d) "Earthrise" (LP/CD; one track: "Yes We Can")	ELF/PolyGram TV 515 419-1 (LP)/ 515 419-2 (CD)	6/15/92
(f) "Spartacus" (2CD) (Thompson portrays Oenomaus)	Columbia 4720302	9/21/92
(g) Back To The Light (LP/CD; one Thompson lead vocal)	Parlophone PCSD 123 (LP)/ CDPCSD 123 (CD)	9/28/92
(h) Beyond The Mind's Eye (CD; one track: "Seeds Of Life")	MCA MCD 10752	3/01/93
(3) "Classic Police" by the Royal Philharmonic Orchestra (CD; retitled reissue of UK LP "Arrested")	Icon ICOCD 001	3/08/93
(g) Back To The Light (limited edition gold CD - one Thompson lead vocal)	Parlophone CDPCSDX 123	6/07/93
(i) Try Anything Once (CD; two tracks: "Turn It Up" and "Back Against The Wall")	Arista 74321167302	10/25/93
(i) Alan Parsons Live (CD; four lead vocals: "Limelight," "Psychobabble," "You're Gonna Get Your Fingers Burned" and "Standing On Higher Ground," plus two shared lead vocals with Gary Howard on "The Raven" and "Don't Answer Me")	German Arcade 9902230	12/**/94
(3) "Original Soundtrack Part II - Florida Lady" (one track: "Florida Lady")	German Jupiter/BMG 74321-21387.2	**/**/95

US:		RELEASE DATE
(3) "The War Of The Worlds" (2LP)	Columbia PC2 35290	6/19/78
(4) Night	Planet P-2	6/04/79
(4) Night (with revised track listing)	Planet P-3	11/12/79
(4) Long Distance	Planet P-10	1/05/81
(7) Arcade (dual lead vocals with Patrick Simmons)	Elektra 60225-1	4/18/83
(8) "All The Right Moves" - Original Soundtrack From The Motion Picture	Casablanca 814 449-1 M-1	11/07/83
(3) "The War Of The Worlds" (2CD; reissue)	Columbia C2K	

	35290	5/**/85
(9) "Greenpeace - The Album"	A&M SP-5091	8/**/85
(3) The High Cost Of Living	Atlantic 81665-1	7/14/86
(3) Royal Philharmonic Orchestra Plays THE POLICE (CD; retitled version of UK LP "Arrested")	Dunhill DZS 001	**/**/87
(c) Earth Moving (CD; two tracks: "Runaway Son" and "See The Light")	Virgin 91270-2	2/20/90
(g) Back To The Light (CD; one Thompson lead vocal)	Hollywood HR-61404-2	2/02/93
(i) Try Anything Once (CD; two tracks: "Turn It Up" and "Back Against The Wall")	Arista 09026-18741-2	10/26/93
(i) Try Anything Once (CD; 20-bit mastered version - two tracks: "Turn It Up" and "Back Against The Wall")	Arista 09026-18744-2	10/26/93
(i) The Very Best Live (CD; in addition to the Thompson tracks on the Arcade release, this disc contains three additional studio tracks not on that album: "Take The Money And Run," "When" and "You're The Voice." The latter two tracks feature Thompson lead vocals.)	RCA Victor/ BMG 09026-68229-2	6/27/95

CHRIS THOMPSON - COMPOSITIONS AND OTHER SESSIONS

ARTIST - Song (involvement by Chris Thompson)	Album	Year
NOEL McCALLA (Chris Thompson on backing vocals on most of album)	Night Time Emotion	1979
THE DOOBIE BROTHERS - No Stoppin' Us Now (Chris Thompson, Patrick Simmons and Michael McDonald wrote the song, and Thompson is on backing vocals)	One Step Closer	1980
TIM GOODMAN - Little Too Late (Chris Thompson on backing vocals)	Footsteps	1980
TREVOR RABIN (Chris Thompson on backing vocals on most of album)	Wolf	1981
ROGER DALTREY - Move Better In The Night (Chris Thompson, Stevie Lange, Robbie McIntosh and Roger Daltrey wrote the song)	Under A Raging Moon	1985
JOHN FARNHAM - You're The Voice (Chris Thompson, Andy Qunta, Keith Reid and Maggie Ryder wrote the song; Thompson later recorded it with Alan Parsons)	Whispering Jack	1987

JOHN FARNHAM - The Fire (Chris Thompson wrote the song; he later recorded it himself)	Age Of Reason	1988
JOHN FARNHAM - Don't Tell Me It Can't Be Done (Chris Thompson wrote the song)	Age Of Reason	1988
THE DOOBIE BROTHERS - I Can Read Your Mind (Chris Thompson, Patrick Simmons and Dale Okerman wrote the song)	Cycles	1989
STARSHIP - Blaze Of Love (Chris Thompson wrote the song)	Love Among The Cannibals	1989
JOHN FARNHAM - The First Step (Chris Thompson wrote the song; he later recorded it himself)	Chain Reaction	1990
PROCOL HARUM - The Hand That Rocks The Cradle (Chris Thompson wrote the song with Keith Reid)	The Prodigal Stranger	1991
HALE & PACE & THE STONKERS - The Stonk (Chris Thompson on backing vocals)	UK single	1991
FREDDIE MERCURY TRIBUTE CONCERT (Chris Thompson assisted Brian May with this concert)	none	1992
ANDY QUNTA	singles	

RADIO SHOWS

UK:		RELEASE DATE
none		none

Although Chris and Stevie Lange have appeared on British radio, none of these recordings were made available on record.

US:		RELEASE DATE
Star Trak (3 interview segments with Chris and Stevie Lange)	Westwood One ST 10-8-79	wk. of 10/08/79

Chris and Stevie Lange also appeared on the radio program "The Great American Radio Show" in 1979.

Steve Waller

Steve Waller could be described as the "big bear" of the Earth Band. Waller dutifully played his guitar and sang his growly vocals during the band's post-1978 rebuilding. Though not as proficient as his fiery predecessor Dave Flett, Waller made the best of his abilities based on his strong grounding in jazz and blues. Waller was a self-taught musician with B.B. King as his idol. His debut at 12 on the pub circuit was with The Little Stevie Smith Band. Steve left school to work solo in folk clubs, then moved back to pubs with the bands Asland, The Sunshine Jazz Trio, and Gerry McAvoy Jam. The latter was captured live on the album "Live At The Bridge E16" by album producer/MMEB lead vocalist Chris Thompson. The year before, Steve played with the venerable British band Gonzalez. This band scored a UK and US hit with a 1978 remix of "Haven't Stopped Dancing Yet." Waller has also played on many sessions, including early dates for the Trojan label. Steve has also played with The Bonzo Dog Doo Dah Band and Kevin Coyne. While playing with the Earth Band, Steve also made a single with No Man's Band. Recently, Waller has been playing the London pub circuit.

ARTIST CODE:
(1) Gerry McAvoy Jam
(2) Gonzalez
(3) No Man's Band

SINGLES

UK & FOREIGN:		RELEASE DATE
(2) I Haven't Stopped Dancing Yet/Carnival	EMI EMI 2706	9/30/77
(2) Just Let It Lay/Just Let It Lay (instrumental)	EMI EMI 2868	10/27/78
(2) Haven't Stopped Dancing Yet (remix)/You're All I Need (To See Me Through The Day) (7")	Sidewalk SID 102	2/23/79
(2) Haven't Stopped Dancing Yet (remix)/You're All I Need (To See Me Through The Day) (12")	Sidewalk 12SID 102	2/23/79
(3) Hey Joe/Tears Have To Fall	Energy NRG006	7/09/82
(2) Haven't Stopped Dancing Yet (remix)/Ain't No	Dance On Wax	

Way To Treat A Lady (12")	DANCE 112	6/**/87

		RELEASE DATE
US:		
(2) Haven't Stopped Dancing Yet (3:45 remix)/ Baby, Baby, Baby	Capitol 4647	10/23/78
(2) Haven't Stopped Dancing Yet (4:23 remix)/ Just Let It Lay (6:19 remix) (12" promo)	Capitol SPRO-8942/8941	10/23/78
(2) Haven't Stopped Dancing Yet (3:45 remix)/ Just Let It Lay (3:40 remix - edit)	Capitol 4674	12/11/78
(2) Haven't Stopped Dancing Yet (remix)/ Haven't Stopped Dancing Yet (remix) (12" promo)	Capitol SPRO-8984	12/11/78
(2) Haven't Stopped Dancing Yet (4:23 remix)/ Just Let It Lay (6:19 remix) (12")	Capitol 8508	1/02/79

ALBUMS

		RELEASE DATE
UK & FOREIGN:		
(1) "A Week At The Bridge E16" (2LP; 2 tracks)	Bridge House BHLP 001/ BHEP1	**/**/78
(2) Haven't Stopped Dancin'	Sidewalk UK 2001	3/23/79

		RELEASE DATE
US:		
(2) Shipwrecked	Capitol SW-11855	9/18/78
(2) Haven't Stopped Dancin'	Capitol SW-11855	1/22/79

[**NOTE:** "Shipwrecked" and "Haven't Stopped Dancin'" are the same album except that the former has a 4:23 version of "Haven't Stopped Dancing Yet," while the latter has a 8:02 version. The albums have entirely different covers, and "Haven't Stopped Dancing Yet" and "Just Let It Lay" are different mixes than the ones that appeared on the original British EMI singles.]

Noel McCalla

For those who have seen MMEB's recent live shows, Noel McCalla's powerful vocals have breathed new life into the songs that have been solely associated with Chris Thompson. Among these are "Blinded By The Light," "Martha's Madman" and "Davy's On The Road Again." Despite this exposure, McCalla is practically unknown.

Noel started singing on a professional basis in the Midlands in 1974. He formed the band Moon after moving to London. Two of the members of Moon were Loz Netto and Luigi (Lou) Salvoni, both later of the band Sniff 'N' The Tears. Two Moon albums for Epic Records did not sell very well, and Noel went solo with an Epic album produced by Trevor Rabin. Trevor, as usual, was involved in nearly all aspects of its production, including playing most of the instruments. Chris Thompson and Stevie Lange also contributed their usual strong backing vocals, but this album was ignored. McCalla did a single for Direction Records, then immersed himself in sessions. He immediately got a backing vocalist slot with his friends in Sniff 'N The Tears on their debut LP "Fickle Heart." This album included the US Top 20 hit "Driver's Seat." The success of "Fickle Heart" took Noel on a tour of the US and Europe with the band.

Another successful project for Noel was the lead vocalist slot on Genesis guitarist Mike Rutherford's solo album "Smallcreep's Day." Noel has also contributed to projects with Mezzoforte, Morrissey Mullen, Paul Weller, Bomb The Bass, Curiosity, Betty Boo, and jingles (such as Boneo). In 1986, Noel also recorded a single with Viola Wills. In between these jobs, Noel finally formed his own band in early 1987 and had it going for about two years. Noel tells what happened next: "Manfred heard of me through a friend and came to see me at the jazz venue The Bass Clef, Hoxton Square. He said that he had some tracks to try out, but it was not immediately in Manfred's mind for me to join MMEB. I was just a working musician working at my craft for a long time without pretensions or aspirations. I molded in very well and so 'Plains Music' was the first introduction. Manfred then told me that he had some gigs to do and asked me if I could sing 'Blinded By The Light' and 'Mighty Quinn.' I wasn't sure but I tried, even though they weren't my type of songs. 'Plains Music,' however, made me think that this experience wasn't going to be just rock - it was more organic, and since then, it has become a lot more than that."

Noel's band was originally called Noel McCalla's Contact and is now simply called McCalla. The band is still going strong and works around Manfred's schedule. Noel McCalla's Contact released a self-produced cassette, with backing tracks recorded at Manfred's Workhouse and overdubs at the band's 16-track studio. Noel re-recorded many of the cassette's tracks for the release of the CD "Push & Pull." Noel describes what both the album and the band are all about: "The album 'Push & Pull' is hard to describe - blues, soul, jazz with good lyrics, nice rhythms. The guitarist is bluesy, the sax player is jazzy, the drummer is rocky and steady, the bass player is like Bill Wyman. The band does as much live work as it can."

As a humorous sideline, Noel McCalla released the 1993 single "Let's Go Deeper" under the name Nuf-El-Tee. Most recently, McCalla's powerful "Hot From The Smoke" album has won over many new fans. With his band and MMEB work, one thing is certain: McCalla will continue to be a very busy singer.

ARTIST CODE:
(1) Moon
(2) Noel McCalla
(3) Mike Rutherford
(4) Viola Wills & Noel McCalla
(5) Noel McCalla's Contact
(6) Nuf-El-Tee
(7) McCalla

SINGLES

UK & FOREIGN:		RELEASE DATE
(1) Lone Ranger/Back To Your Old Ways	Epic EPC 4418	7/02/76
(1) Daydreaming/Desolation Alley	Epic EPC 4667	10/08/76
(1) Name Of The Game/White Paper Time	Epic EPC 5327	6/03/77
(1) All Night/Back Rooms	Epic EPC 5508	7/29/77
(1) All Night/Back Rooms (with picture sleeve)	Epic SHOTS 1	7/29/77
(2) Where Is Our Love/Midnight Girl	Epic EPC 6725	9/29/78
(2) Where Is Our Love/Midnight Girl	Epic EPC 7041	2/16/79
(2) Ain't Nothin' But A House Party/Midnight Girl	Epic EPC 7486	7/20/79
(2) Night Life On Venus/Loving Arms	Epic EPC 7855	9/21/79
(3) Working In Line/Compression	Charisma CB 353	2/08/80
(2) Beggin' - Ain't That Peculiar/ One More Heartache - Shake Me, Wake Me	Direction 58 8731	7/04/80
(3) Time And Time Again/At The End Of The Day	Charisma CB 364	7/25/80
(4) Take One Step Forward/Take One Step Forward (Nightmare Dub Mix) (7")	Nightmare MARES 7	12/19/86
(4) Take One Step Forward/Take One Step Forward (Nightmare Dub Mix) (12")	Nightmare MARE 7	12/19/86
(6) Let's Go Deeper/Let's Go Deeper (instrumental) (7")	Huge HUG 5	3/15/93

		RELEASE DATE
(6) Let's Go Deeper/Let's Go Deeper (instrumental) (12")	Huge HUG 5T	3/15/93
(6) Let's Go Deeper/Let's Go Deeper (instrumental) (CD5)	Huge HUG 5CD	3/15/93
(7) Pull Together - Trouble - Full Circle (promo only CD5)	German EWM 4041	9/27/93

US & FOREIGN:		RELEASE DATE
(3) Working In Line/Compression	Passport PS 7919	5/12/80

ALBUMS

UK & FOREIGN:		RELEASE DATE
(1) Too Close For Comfort	Epic EPC 81456	8/27/76
(1) Turning The Tide (original title: "Second To None")	Epic EPC 82084	6/24/77
(2) Night Time Emotion	Epic EPC 83838	10/05/79
(3) Smallcreep's Day	Charisma CAS 1149	2/15/80
(3) Smallcreep's Day (CD; reissue)	Charisma CASCD 1149	6/**/89
(5) Noel McCalla's Contact (cassette)	no label or #	**/**/91
(7) Push & Pull (CD)	German EWM 4038	9/27/93
(7) Push & Pull (CD)	Uplands 00012	3/07/94
(7) Hot From The Smoke (CD)	Uplands EDM 41622	4/**/95

US:		RELEASE DATE
(3) Smallcreep's Day	Passport PB 9843	3/10/80

Clive Bunker

Clive Bunker (top center) with Mick Abrahams
(top left) in The Toggery Five
(photo credit: Martin Webb)

Even though Clive Bunker is a relatively new member of Manfred Mann's Earth Band, his career is one that every musician would envy. Many fans hold Clive in high esteem, thanks to his participation in the formation and breakthrough of Jethro Tull.

Clive describes his early start: "I started with music at school, originally having a bash on guitar and quickly being transferred behind the drum kit (or what passed as one then). The band quickly became one of the popular bands in the area. After a couple of years, I got the chance to turn professional (in The Toggery Five) and moved to Manchester. I stayed for just over a year, in which time we did the German clubs and a lot of Northern halls - quite a good grounding, really looking back on it. With my future firmly behind me, I returned to my roots fixing commercial vehicles and the usual round of rushing around doing pubs and clubs in the evenings."

During 1965 and 1966, Clive Bunker and guitarist Michael (Mick) Abrahams were in the Manchester-based The Toggery Five after the band released two Parlophone singles between 1964-1965. The full lineup of The Toggery Five was Abrahams, Bunker, Graham Waller (piano), Paul Young (vocals), Arthur Hasford (trumpet), Dave Cakebread (bass), and Bernie Hetherington (saxes). After this group broke up, Bunker and Abrahams appeared with Andy Pyle (bass) and Pete Fensome (vocals) in McGregor's Engine in 1967.

In November 1967, McGregor's Engine was playing on the same bill as The John Evan Smash. The John Evan Smash played a combination of jazz, blues and soul, and consisted of Ian Anderson (vocals/flute), drummer Barrie Barlow, John Evans (keyboards; later known as John Evan), bassist Glenn Cornick, Neil Smith (aka Chick Murray; guitar), Tony Wilkinson (baritone sax) and Neil Valentine (tenor sax). Both bands were on the verge of breaking up. Upon seeing McGregor's Engine, Ian Anderson asked Mick Abrahams and Clive Bunker if they would join his band to replace Barlow and Smith. Clive and Mick were located in Luton, so they relocated to London at the end of 1967 to get gigs. Ian Anderson then handled the booking arrangements, which first involved satisfying the remaining John Evan Smash dates in soul clubs. To be able to play more than once at the same clubs, this new band played using several names to build up their reputation. The name that was the most successful with club owners was Jethro Tull, the real name of an 18th Century agriculturist and inventor of the seed drill. Jethro Tull's personnel now included Ian Anderson (vocals, flute), Mick Abrahams (guitar), Glenn Cornick (bass) and Clive Bunker (drums).

The John Evan Smash had already recorded two sessions with producer Derek Lawrence in 1967: the first was a demo session for EMI under the name Candy Coloured Rain, and the second featured the songs "Aeroplane," "Blues For The 18th" and a couple of others. By the time "Aeroplane" was completed, the sax players were dismissed and were not included on the track. Nothing happened with these songs until Bunker and Abrahams were brought into the fold.

The second Derek Lawrence session had Jethro Tull recording the Mick Abrahams pop composition "Sunshine Day." This song, combined with the previous John Evan Smash track "Aeroplane," formed the respective A-side and B-side of their debut single released by MGM on February 16, 1968. The MGM single was bound to fail, since Derek Lawrence changed the band's name to Jethro Toe on the record label. MGM and Derek Lawrence were soon out of the picture. After this disastrous experience, bookers Chris Wright and Terry Ellis got Jethro Tull signed to Island Records and their newly formed Chrysalis production company, which soon evolved into Chrysalis Records.

Jethro Tull played pubs and small clubs through the summer of 1968, but their residency at London's Marquee Club was the ideal location for them to expand their fan base. Thanks to the Marquee's manager John Gee, Tull took off like a rocket. The band was booked at the August 1968 Sunbury Jazz and Blues Festival, and they became the festival's smash hit. Everyone took notice of the band's amazing stage presence, especially that of front man Ian Anderson.

The combination of Ian Anderson's writing and playing talents and the entire band's live excitement formed the blueprint for success with their first LP "This Was." The album, a Top 10 seller in England (#62 in the US), had a lot of powerful material to offer. Bunker's showcase on the album was the drum heavy "Dharma For One." The next offering by the band was the Top 30 UK single "Love Story."

For the most part, Anderson and Abrahams did their writing apart. This situation, combined with management squabbles, put Abrahams in the middle between Anderson and management. Abrahams finally had enough of an unpleasant situation and left the band in December 1968 - just after they made plans to tour the US![100] Mick Abrahams formed the group Blodwyn Pig and did some solo albums during the '70s.

After making its first BBC radio session recordings with new guitarist Martin Barre, Jethro Tull arranged a 1969 US tour, opening up for Led Zeppelin and Fleetwood Mac. Again, in a short time, Jethro Tull had won over the US as they had done in England. Now they were ready for their big breakthrough.

Jethro Tull certainly made the most out of their first trip to the US. In February 1969, in the middle of their US stay, Jethro Tull recorded the song "Living In The Past" in a small New Jersey studio. Released as a single in May of that year, "Living In The Past" provided the major hit (#3) that the band was looking for in England. Capitalizing on this hit, Jethro Tull appeared on BBC TV's "Top Of The Pops" and achieved full acclaim across the board. Suddenly, Tull had graduated from the underground rock scene. In the US, this single was not a big seller but it helped to cultivate the band's growing American audience. When the band headed west in March 1969, it stopped in a Los Angeles studio to lay down the single's B-side, "Driving Song."

With the appearance of the "Stand Up" LP in 1969, Jethro Tull was finally able to present a full album's worth of material coinciding with Ian Anderson's musical visions. Jethro Tull was rewarded with a #1 British album and their first gold album in the US (a Top 20 item). Now since Jethro Tull had success on both the album and singles fronts, it was now time to build on that success. The follow-up single "Sweet Dream" provided Tull with another Top 10 UK single in late 1969, but US singles success was still in the wings.

The start of the seventies brought with it a new Tull single: "The Witch's Promise" b/w "Teacher." A #4 double-sided British hit, the single included an appearance by old friend (and current college student) John Evans (aka John Evan) on keyboards. "Benefit" was a May 1970 release, and furthered the band's success throughout the world. British and American sales were strong, and the band advanced to concert headlining status in the US. Before setting out for this tour, John Evans made a guest appearance on "Benefit" and was convinced to give up his studies to join the band full-time. Glenn Cornick left at the end of 1970 to form the group Wild Turkey, and he was replaced by Jeffrey Hammond-Hammond (a joke!).

The issuance of the "Aqualung" LP in March 1971 (US: May 1971) was the realization of all that the band strove for, and remains Jethro Tull's landmark LP. Presented in two parts, "Aqualung" presented Anderson's views on life and organized religion, and included the rock anthems "Aqualung," "Cross-Eyed Mary," "Hymn 43" and "Locomotive Breath." "Aqualung" hit #4 and #7 respectively on the UK and US album charts.[101]

Clive Bunker left the band in May 1971 to get married. In 1974, Clive joined Mick Abrahams in a reformation of Blodwyn Pig, but this didn't last long. He later played on numerous sessions, with albums by Steve Hillage ("Live Herald") and Steve Howe ("The Steve Howe Album") being the most notable. Clive relates his situation: "In 1971, I left to practice all the bits they had shown me . . . no seriously, I actually left to get married and take some time off to get it all together, and practice, of course!" After about six months, Clive Bunker was asked by Chrysalis if he would join up with Robin Trower. This didn't work out due to musical differences. He started doing varied sessions like Generation X to Demis Roussos. Loads of singles sessions were also on Clive's schedule, but his enjoyment of touring was also satisfied by this work.

After missing that "band feeling," Bunker joined Mick Rogers (ex-MMEB) and Jack Lancaster (ex-Blodwyn Pig) to form Aviator in 1979. Aviator released two albums: "Aviator" (1979) and "Turbulence" (1980), the latter being a UK-only release. This turned out to be musically self-indulgent for him, and Clive was back to doing sessions. Again, this included another reformation of Blodwyn Pig! Clive recalls that with Aviator, "We just could not pull that band out of the bag, and its shelf life ran out."

In 1991, Manfred Mann called Clive and asked him if he wanted to join the Earth Band. Clive had never seen the band live despite knowing Mick Rogers, but he was told that MMEB was really good live. Bunker joined up, and he also plays with Mick's Abrahams' Blodwyn Pig on occasion. He also played with Jethro Tull in London for some shows during their 25th anniversary tour in 1993.

ARTIST CODE:
all records by Jethro Tull, except:
(1) Mick Abrahams' Blodwyn Pig
(2) Clive Bunker

also see the Aviator listing under Mick Rogers

SINGLES

UK & FOREIGN:		RELEASE DATE
Sunshine Day/Aeroplane (shown as JETHRO TOE)	MGM 1384	2/16/68
A Song For Jeffrey/One For John Gee	Island WIP 6043	9/27/68
Love Story/A Christmas Song	Island WIP 6048	11/29/68
Living In The Past/Driving Song	Island WIP 6056	5/02/69
Sweet Dream/17	Chrysalis WIP 6070	10/10/69
The Witch's Promise/Teacher	Chrysalis WIP 6077	1/16/70
Inside/Alive And Well And Living In	Chrysalis WIP 6081	5/29/70
Lick Your Fingers Clean/Up To Me (cancelled)	Chrysalis WIP 6098	1/29/71
Living In The Past/Requiem	Chrysalis CHS 2081	1/16/76
Coronach (from the Channel 4 TV Series "The Blood Of The British") - Jack Frost And The Hooded Crow/ Living In The Past - Elegy (12")	Chrysalis TULLX 2	6/27/86
Another Christmas Song/A Christmas Song	Chrysalis TULL 5	11/27/89
Living In The Past/Hard Liner (7")	Chrysalis CHS 3970	5/10/93
Living In The Past (12" Club Mix) - Living In The Past (7" Mix)/Living In The Past (Ravey Master Mix) - Living In The Past (N.Y. Tip Mix) (12")	Chrysalis 12CHS 3970	5/10/93

Living In The Past - Truck Stop Runner -   Chrysalis 3 23971 2   5/10/93
   Piece Of Cake - Man Of Principle (CD5)

US:
   Love Story/A Song For Jeffrey   Reprise 0815   2/12/69
   Living In The Past/Driving Song   Reprise 0845   7/28/69
   Living In The Past (stereo)/Driving Song (stereo)   Reprise 0845   7/28/69
      (promo only)
   Sweet Dream/Reasons For Waiting   Reprise 0886   11/26/69
      (mislabelled B-side; record plays "Back To The Family")
   The Witch's Promise/Teacher   Reprise 0899   3/11/70
   Inside/A Time For Everything   Reprise 0927   6/10/70
   Hymn 43/Mother Goose   Reprise 1024   6/16/71
   Locomotive Breath/Wind-Up   Reprise 1054   11/17/71
   Living In The Past/A Christmas Song   Chrysalis CHS 2006   10/30/72
   Living In The Past/Cross-Eyed Mary   Chrysalis "Back To
                                                     Back Hits"
                                                  GCH 0026   1/**/74
   Locomotive Breath/Fat Man   Chrysalis CRS 2110   1/12/76
   Ring Out Solstice Bells - March, The Mad   Chrysalis
      Scientist/Christmas Song - Pan Dance (promo 12")   CHS-3-PDJ   11/29/76
   Christmas Song/Skating Away On The Thin Ice   Chrysalis/CEMA
      Of The New Day (green vinyl jukebox issue)   Special Markets
                                                  S7-18211-A/B   11/10/94

EPs

UK & FOREIGN:
   Ring Out Solstice Bells - March, The Mad
      Scientist/Christmas Song - Pan Dance   Chrysalis CXP 2   12/03/76

US:
   Stand Up - Radio Spots (promo only)   Reprise PRO 353   9/29/69
   Aqualung (jukebox EP)   Chrysalis 1044   5/03/71

ALBUMS

UK & FOREIGN:

This Was	Island ILP/ILPS 9085	10/25/68
Stand Up	Island ILPS 9103	8/01/69
Benefit	Island ILPS 9123	5/01/70
Aqualung	Island ILPS 9145	3/19/71
Living In The Past (2LP)	Chrysalis CJT 1	6/23/72
This Was (reissue)	Chrysalis CHR 1041	8/01/73
Stand Up (reissue)	Chrysalis CHR 1042	8/01/73
Benefit (reissue)	Chrysalis CHR 1043	8/01/73
Aqualung (reissue)	Chrysalis CHR 1044	8/01/73
M.U. - The Best Of Jethro Tull	Chrysalis CHR 1078	1/09/76
"Rare Tracks" (one track: "Sunshine Day")	Polydor 2482 274	5/07/76
Repeat - The Best Of Jethro Tull - Vol. II	Chrysalis CHR 1135	9/09/77
Stand Up (reissue; recalled)	Fame/MFP FA 413086-1	2/17/84
Original Masters (LP)	Chrysalis JTTV 1	10/25/85
M.U. - The Best Of Jethro Tull (CD; reissue)	Chrysalis CCD 1078	12/**/85
This Was (CD; reissue)	Chrysalis CCD 1041	4/**/86
Stand Up (CD; reissue)	Chrysalis ACCD 1042	4/**/86
Aqualung (CD; reissue)	Chrysalis CCD 1044	4/**/86
Repeat - The Best Of Jethro Tull - Vol. II (CD; reissue)	Chrysalis CCD 1135	4/**/86
Original Masters (CD; reissue)	Chrysalis CCD 1515	4/**/86
Benefit (CD; reissue)	Chrysalis CCD 1043	6/**/87
Living In The Past (CD; reissue - incorrect track listing, 2 tracks missing)	Chrysalis CCD 1035	10/**/87
20 Years Of Jethro Tull (5LP/3CD)	Chrysalis TBOX 1 (LP)/TBOXCD 1 (CD)	7/01/88 7/01/88
20 Years Of Jethro Tull (single CD)	Chrysalis CCD 1655	1/16/89
Stand Up (CD; reissue)	Chrysalis/EMI CCD 1042	1/16/89
This Was (CD; reissue)	Chrysalis/EMI CCD 1041	3/23/92
Benefit (CD; reissue)	Chrysalis/EMI CCD 1043	3/23/92
Aqualung (CD; reissue)	Chrysalis/EMI CCD 1044	3/23/92
Living In The Past (CD; reissue - incorrect track	Chrysalis/EMI	

Title	Label / Catalog	Release Date
listing, 2 tracks missing)	CCD 1035	3/23/92
M.U. - The Best Of Jethro Tull (CD; reissue)	Chrysalis/EMI CCD 1078	3/23/92
Repeat - The Best Of Jethro Tull - Vol. II (CD; reissue)	Chrysalis/EMI CCD 1135	3/23/92
Original Masters (CD; reissue)	Chrysalis/EMI CCD 1515	3/23/92
20 Years Of Jethro Tull (single CD; reissue)	Chrysalis/EMI CCD 1655	3/23/92
"The Derek Lawrence Sessions - Take 4" (CD; one track: "Sunshine Day")	German Line LICD	10/**/92
25th Anniversary Box Set (4CD)	Chrysalis/EMI 3 26008 2	4/26/93
The Best Of Jethro Tull (2CD)	Chrysalis/EMI 3 21954 2	5/24/93
(1) Live/All Tore Down (CD)	Indigo IGOCD 2011	10/24/94

US:

Title	Label / Catalog	RELEASE DATE
This Was	Reprise RS 6336	2/10/69
Stand Up	Reprise RS 6360	9/29/69
Benefit	Reprise RS 6400	4/20/70
Aqualung	Reprise MS 2035	5/03/71
Living In The Past (2LP)	Chrysalis 2TS 2106	10/31/72
This Was (reissue)	Chrysalis CHR 1041	7/23/73
Stand Up (reissue)	Chrysalis CHR 1042	7/23/73
Benefit (reissue)	Chrysalis CHR 1043	7/23/73
Aqualung (reissue)	Chrysalis CHR 1044	7/23/73
Living In The Past (2LP; reissue)	Chrysalis CHR 1035	7/23/73
Aqualung (quad)	Chrysalis CH4 1044	4/02/75
M.U. - The Best Of Jethro Tull	Chrysalis CHR 1078	1/12/76
Repeat - The Best Of Jethro Tull - Vol. II	Chrysalis CHR 1135	11/07/77
Aqualung (half-speed master)	Mobile Fidelity Sound Labs MFSL 1-061	**/**/80
1982 Promotion Manual (promo only)	Chrysalis CHS-47-PDJ	8/**/82
This Was (reissue)	Chrysalis FV 41041	11/18/83
Stand Up (reissue)	Chrysalis FV 41042	11/18/83
Benefit (reissue)	Chrysalis FV 41043	11/18/83
Aqualung (reissue)	Chrysalis FV 41044	11/18/83
Living In The Past (2LP; reissue)	Chrysalis V2X 41035	11/18/83
M.U. - The Best Of Jethro Tull (reissue)	Chrysalis FV 41078	11/18/83
Repeat - The Best Of Jethro Tull - Vol. II (reissue)	Chrysalis PV 41135	11/18/83
Aqualung (CD; reissue)	Chrysalis VK 41044	3/**/84

M.U. - The Best Of Jethro Tull (CD; reissue)	Chrysalis VK 41078	7/**/85
This Was (CD; reissue)	Chrysalis VK 41041	8/**/85
Stand Up (CD; reissue)	Chrysalis VK 41042	8/**/85
Benefit (CD; reissue)	Chrysalis VK 41043	8/**/85
Original Masters (LP)	Chrysalis FV 41515	11/25/85
Repeat - The Best Of Jethro Tull - Vol. II (CD; reissue)	Chrysalis VK 41135	4/**/87
Living In The Past (CD; reissue - incorrect track listing, 2 tracks missing)	Chrysalis VK 41035	1/**/88
Original Masters (LP/CD; reissue)	Chrysalis PV 41515 (LP)/ VK 41515 (CD)	4/25/88
20 Years Of Jethro Tull (5LP/3CD)	Chrysalis V5K 41653 (LP)/ V3K 41653 (CD)	7/18/88
20 Years Of Jethro Tull (single CD)	Chrysalis VK 41655	1/16/89
Stand Up (CD; reissue - 24 karat gold CD)	Mobile Fidelity Sound Labs UDCD01-00524	9/**/89
This Was (CD; reissue)	Chrysalis/EMI F2 21041	3/24/92
Stand Up (CD; reissue)	Chrysalis/EMI F2 21042	3/24/92
Benefit (CD; reissue)	Chrysalis/EMI F2 21043	3/24/92
Aqualung (CD; reissue)	Chrysalis/EMI F2 21044	3/24/92
Living In The Past (CD; reissue - incorrect track listing, 2 tracks missing)	Chrysalis/EMI F2 21035	3/24/92
M.U. - The Best Of Jethro Tull (CD; reissue)	Chrysalis/EMI F2 21078	3/24/92
Repeat - The Best Of Jethro Tull - Vol. II (CD; reissue)	Chrysalis/EMI F2 21135	3/24/92
Original Masters (CD; reissue)	Chrysalis/EMI F2 21515	3/24/92
20 Years Of Jethro Tull (single CD; reissue)	Chrysalis/EMI F2 21655	3/24/92
25th Anniversary Box Set (4CD)	Chrysalis/EMI 3 26008 2	4/20/93
The Best Of Jethro Tull (2CD)	Chrysalis/EMI 3 26015 2	6/29/93

VIDEOS

UK & FOREIGN:

This Is . . . The First 20 Years   Virgin Vision
                                              VVD 398   8/**/88
25th Anniversary Video   PMI 7243 4911263 6   7/04/94
(2) Drum Tuition for Beginners   Masterfield Productions
                                              Ltd. MFD 0024   4/**/95
(2) Drum Tuition for Intermediates   Masterfield Productions
                                              Ltd. MFD 0025   4/**/95
(2) Drum Tuition for Advanced   Masterfield Productions
                                              Ltd. MFD 0026   4/**/95

US:

20 Years Of Jethro Tull (retitled version of   Virgin Music Video
    "This Is . . . The First 20 Years")   3-50136   8/**/88
"Rock In The U.K." (one track: "With You   Rhino Home Video
    There To Help Me")   R3 2073   2/23/94
25th Anniversary Video   EMI Records/
                                                    Chrysalis Video
                                                    F3-77790   10/21/94

Other Members

DAVE RICHMOND - After leaving Manfred Mann in 1963, Richmond became a session player. His most notable appearances were on Manfred Mann's "Instrumental Assassination" EP (1966), Elton John's self-titled album (1970), Bread, Love & Dreams' "Amaryllis" LP (1971) and Hank Marvin's "Second Opinion" album (1971). After these, Richmond quietly retired from the music scene.

JACK BRUCE - In 1965, Bruce moved from The Graham Bond Organisation to John Mayall's Bluesbreakers to Manfred Mann, while releasing a solo single that year ("I'm Gettin' Tired [Of Drinkin' And Gamblin']"). He left in 1966 to form Cream with Eric Clapton and Ginger Baker. After this band ran out its 2-year term, Bruce appeared with his bass in numerous solo and group settings.

COLIN PATTENDEN - Colin learned how to play bass from instructional guides, especially from American session player Carol Kaye. Pattenden started playing his bass with a group called Les Tekneeks (later known as Tekneek). This group was formed with his cousin Graham White. Pattenden and White did sessions and backed up numerous pop luminaries: Leapy Lee, Solomon King and Gerry Dorsey. The latter became famous afterward when he changed his name to Engelbert Humperdinck! When Tekneek broke up, Colin labored as a lathe turner and prototype wireman in an electronics company for six months until Chris Slade invited him to try out for MMEB.

After leaving the Earth Band in 1977, he and Chris Slade formed Terra Nova with Chris Slade in 1978. Despite recording the track "Black Rose," this band dissolved. Pattenden became a successful businessman, but his musical interests were still active. He joined a reformed Beggar's Opera and released the German-only LP "Life Line." Colin has also played with a touring version of The Nashville Teens.

DAVE FLETT - Scotsman Dave Flett was certainly an amazingly talented guitarist, but his sudden disappearance after MMEB's breakup even baffled the band. After this breakup, Flett joined Thin Lizzy on a tour of Japan in 1979. Fleet then formed a short-lived band with Matt Irving called Special Branch. Following this, Flett was nowhere to be found.

PAT KING - King, also born in Scotland, worked his way through the session grind, with Lulu and Cat Stevens dates to his credit. After leaving art school, Pat moved to London and played in many bands. One of these bands was Cliff Bennett's band Shanghai, which went on a British and European tour with Status Quo. King quit Shanghai in 1976 and joined MMEB the next year. Pat now works for Manfred Mann concert promoter Alec Leslie.

JOHN LINGWOOD - Lingwood sat behind the MMEB drum kit when Geoff Britton became ill in 1979. Another seasoned session man, Lingwood had played with Leo Sayer, Arthur Brown, Catherine Howe, Maddy Prior, Steamhammer and Stomu Yamashta's East Wind. He also played in the bands of the London stage productions of "Jesus Christ Superstar" and "Hair" during the mid-1970s. He co-wrote the theme to the "Gangsters" TV series with Greenslade in 1978. In between his Earth Band duties, Lingwood also appeared in Dave Greenslade's TV rock opera "Curricle, Curricla" in 1981. The next year, Lingwood recorded albums and tours with Roger Chapman and Elkie Brooks. Brooks' 1982 album "Pearls II" was a platinum seller, as was the video "Pearls - The Video Show." He has also played on two Roger Waters LPs with Matt Irving: "When The Wind Blows" and "Radio Kaos." Most recently, Lingwood worked on Chris Thompson's 1991 German tour, and has continued his projects with Thompson.

MATT IRVING - Another Scottish bassist, Irving has been in many groups as well: The Dream Police, a 1967 band featuring Hamish Stewart (who later formed Average White Band), The Crocodiles, Longdancer and The Babys. After forming Special Branch with Dave Flett, Irving played on sessions with Zaine Griff, Anthony Moore, The Lords Of The New Church, Roger Waters and Paul Young. Matt joined the Earth Band in 1981. Matt, who also plays keyboards and accordion, played the former with Squeeze, and he most recently has played with Chris Rea.

STEVE KINCH - The current MMEB bass player started playing guitar at the age of twelve, when his parents bought it for a Christmas present. Two years later, he was playing for the "Girl Guides." At sixteen, Steve left school to become a glassblower, and after four or five years, he started to play bass in some bands. Playing with Hazel O'Connor in 1980 gave Steve his first successful experience on tour in England, Europe and in the States. This group lasted for about two years.

In 1984, Kinch joined Jim Capaldi's band. He spent three months rehearsing for a US tour, but the tour was canceled at the last minute. Steve joined MMEB in 1985, and the story on how he passed the audition is humorous: "After about a year of trying to start up my own projects, a friend called me up to tell me that MMEB was looking for a bass player. Fortunately, my friend was also helping out with the auditions. After I took care of my friend (!), I found out what songs they were auditioning with, giving me an advantage over most of the other hopefuls and impressing the band by my ability to play on "previously unheard songs!" After succeeding at the audition, Kinch played in the 1986 touring band and appeared on the album "Criminal Tango."

Between 1987 and 1991 he toured the world with The Rubettes, but in 1991 he got Manfred's call to rejoin MMEB for some tours and to work on a new album.

MANFRED MANN
1960s SESSIONOGRAPHY
(+ = master tape has not been located)

EMI RECORDINGS

Date	First appearance
May 23, 1963 (DEMOS - MONO RECORDINGS)	
Why Should We Not (Take 1)	UNRELEASED
Why Should We Not (Take 2)	UNRELEASED
Why Should We Not (Take 3)	UNRELEASED
Why Should We Not (Take 4)	UNRELEASED
Why Should We Not (Take 5)	"Soul Of Mann" stereo LP
Why Should We Not (Take 6)	UK single
I Don't Want To Know	UNRELEASED
Let's Go	UNRELEASED
Tell Me What Did I Say (aka "Don't Ask Me What I Say")	UNRELEASED
Brother Jack (Frere Jacques)	UK single
Without You	UNRELEASED
June 13, 1963	
Words	+UNRELEASED
June 26, 1963	
Broken Wings	+UNRELEASED
Have You Ever Been To London Town	+UNRELEASED
September 30, 1963	
Now You're Needing Me	UK single
Chatterin'	UNRELEASED
Cock-A-Hoop	UK single
December 17, 1963	
5-4-3-2-1 (Version 1)	UK single
5-4-3-2-1 (Version 2)	Canadian "The Manfred Mann Return LP"
Without You	UK single

February 5, 1964
Mr. Anello (mono LP version)   "The Five Faces Of Manfred Mann" LP
Mr. Anello (stereo LP version)   "Soul Of Mann" stereo LP
Sack O'Woe   "The Five Faces Of Manfred Mann" LP
You've Got To Take It   "The Five Faces Of Manfred Mann" LP
Down The Road Apiece   see 3/13/64
Dimples   +UNRELEASED
I'm Your Hoochie Coochie Man   "The Five Faces Of Manfred Mann" LP

March 2, 1964
Hubble Bubble (Toil And Trouble)   UK single

March 6, 1964
Got My Mojo Working   "The Five Faces Of Manfred Mann" LP
Smokestack Lightning   "The Five Faces Of Manfred Mann" LP
I'm Your Kingpin   UK single

March 13, 1964
Down The Road Apiece (overdubbed)   "The Five Faces Of Manfred Mann" LP
Ain't That Love?   +UNRELEASED

April 10, 1964
Bring It To Jerome   "The Five Faces Of Manfred Mann" LP
I Just Want To Make Love To You   +UNRELEASED
Sticks And Stones   "The Best Of The EMI Years" CD
Untie Me (mono LP version)   "The Five Faces Of Manfred Mann" LP

May 5, 1964
Untie Me (stereo LP version)   US "The Manfred Mann Album" LP
Don't Ask Me What I Say   "The Five Faces Of Manfred Mann" LP

June 5, 1964
It's Gonna Work Out Fine   "The Five Faces Of Manfred Mann" LP
What You Gonna Do?   UK single
All Your Love   UNRELEASED

June 11, 1964
Do Wah Diddy Diddy (long version)   Canadian "Mann Made Hits!" LP
Do Wah Diddy Diddy (edited version)   UK single

June 23, 1964
Dashing Away With The Smoothing Iron   see 11/16/64
Groovin'   "Groovin'" EP
Five Long Years   +UNRELEASED
Can't Believe It   "Groovin'" EP

July 28, 1964
The One In The Middle   "The One In The Middle" EP
Did You Have To Do That   "Groovin'" EP
The Manfreds Doodlin'   +UNRELEASED

August 18, 1964
A Love Like Yours (Don't Come Knocking   US "My Little Red Book Of
    Every Day)   Winners!" LP

September 2, 1964
John Hardy   UK single
She   US "The Five Faces Of Manfred
                                                   Mann" LP

September 1964
Group Radio Interview Side I   US "Manfred Mann Radio
                                                   Interview" promo LP
Group Radio Interview Side II   US "Manfred Mann Radio
                                                   Interview" promo LP

September 22, 1964
Sha La La   see 9/23/64

September 23, 1964
Sha La La (overdubbed)   UK single

November 9, 1964
Come Tomorrow   see 11/16/64

November 16, 1964
Come Tomorrow (overdubbed)   UK single
Speak Love   +UNRELEASED
Dashing Away With The Smoothing Iron   US "The Five Faces Of Manfred
  (overdubbed)   Mann" LP
Watermelon Man   US "The Five Faces Of Manfred
                                                   Mann" LP

November 26, 1964
What Did I Do Wrong   UK single

January 11, 1965
I'll Make It Up To You   "Mann Made" LP
With God On Our Side   "The One In The Middle" EP

January 12, 1965
Sie (German speech only for "She" backing track)   German single
Wiene Nicht (German speech only for "Come Tomorrow"
   backing track)   German single

January 15, 1965
Look Away   "Mann Made" LP

March 4, 1965
Bare Hugg (originally titled "D.D.")   "Mann Made" LP

March 12, 1965
What Am I To Do   "The One In The Middle" EP
Oh No Not My Baby   UK single

March 16, 1965
L.S.D.   "Mann Made" LP
What Am I Doing Wrong   UK single
I Can't Believe What You Say   see 4/5/65

March 17, 1965
Poison Ivy   US "My Little Red Book Of
                                                          Winners!" LP

On The Horizon   +UNRELEASED
Play It   +UNRELEASED

April 5, 1965
I Can't Believe What You Say (overdubbed)   "My Little Red Book Of
                                                          Winners!" LP

April 8, 1965
I Really Do Believe   "Mann Made" LP
You Don't Know Me   "Mann Made" LP
The Way You Do The Things You Do   "Mann Made" LP
The Abominable Snowmann   "Mann Made" LP
Watch Your Step   "Mann Made" LP
Stormy Monday Blues   "Mann Made" LP

April 27, 1965
My Little Red Book (All I Do Is Talk About You)   US "What's New Pussycat?
                                                     (Original Motion Picture Score)" LP

My Little Red Book (All I Do Is Talk About You)
   (film version)   UNRELEASED

May 18, 1965
Since I Don't Have You   "Mann Made" LP

May 24, 1965
You Gave Me Somebody To Love (mono version) UK single
You Gave Me Somebody To Love (stereo version)   US "My Little Red Book Of
                                                  Winners!" LP
You're For Me   US "My Little Red Book Of
                                                  Winners!" LP

June 10, 1965
Hi Lili, Hi Lo   "Mann Made" LP

July 19, 1965
If You Gotta Go, Go Now   US single

August 2, 1965
Stay Around   UK single
There's No Living Without Your Loving   "No Living Without Loving" EP

August 25, 1965
Tired Of Trying, Bored With Lying, Scared Of Dying   "No Living Without Loving" EP
I Put A Spell On You   "No Living Without Loving" EP

September 8, 1965
God Rest Ye Merry Gentlemenn   "Soul Of Mann" LP
Something You've Got   +UNRELEASED

September 13, 1965
Let's Go Get Stoned   "No Living Without Loving" EP
Time   +UNRELEASED

December 15, 1965
That's All I Ever Want From You Baby   "As Was" EP
Spirit Feel   "Mann Made Hits" LP
Tennessee Waltz   "Machines" EP

December 20, 1965
You Can't Love 'Em All   +UNRELEASED

December 21, 1965
Tengo Tango   "Soul Of Mann" LP
She Needs Company (Version 1)   US single
When Will I Be Loved   "Machines" EP

January 12, 1966
Still I'm Sad   "Instrumental Asylum" EP
I Got You Babe   "Instrumental Asylum" EP
My Generation   "Instrumental Asylum" EP
(I Can't Get No) Satisfaction   "Instrumental Asylum" EP

January 24, 1966
You're Standing By   UK single

February 4, 1966
She Needs Company (Version 2)   Canadian "Mann Made" LP

February 9, 1966
Machines   "Machines" EP

February 21, 1966
Somethings   +UNRELEASED

February 24, 1966
Driva Man   see 2/28/66

February 28, 1966
Driva Man (overdubbed)   US "Pretty Flamingo" LP

March 11, 1966
It's Getting Late   US "Pretty Flamingo" LP

March 18, 1966
Come Home Baby   US "The Best Of Manfred Mann -
                                                          A Definitive Collection" CD

Pretty Flamingo   UK single

[**NOTE:** After full research, the following tracks that were listed as by Manfred Mann in US EMI tape listings are in fact <u>not</u> by Manfred Mann: **Here I Stand; I Don't Understand; Be Brave; Out Of The Picture; There'll Always Be Another Spring; All Quiet On The Mersey Front**.]

FONTANA RECORDINGS

	First appearance
<u>Date</u>	
<u>June 8, 1966</u>	
I Wanna Be Rich (2 stages)	US single
Let It Be Me	French "Just Like A Woman" EP
<u>June 28, 1966</u>	
Morning After The Party (original version)	UNRELEASED
Eastern Street	UNRELEASED
<u>June 30, 1966</u>	
Just Like A Woman (2 stages)	US single
Trouble And Tea	French "Just Like A Woman" EP
<u>July 20, 1966</u>	
Dealer Dealer	"As Is" LP
Superstitious Guy	"As Is" LP
<u>July 22, 1966</u>	
Box Office Draw (1st stage)	see 8/12/66
<u>August 12, 1966</u>	
Box Office Draw (2nd stage)	"As Is" LP
Mohair Sam	UNRELEASED
Lovebird	UNRELEASED

August 22, 1966
A Now And Then Thing   "As Is" LP
Each Other's Company   "As Is" LP
Morning After The Party   UK single
Another Kind Of Music   "As Is" LP
Acoustic Guitar Instrumental   UNRELEASED
[**NOTE:** A fragment of the above track is part of the released song "Another Kind Of Music."]
As Long As I Have Lovin'   "As Is" LP
Autumn Leaves   "As Is" LP
You're My Girl (2 stages)   "As Is" LP
Semi-Detached, Suburban Mr. James (2 stages)   US single
Each And Every Day   US single
The Vicar's Daughter   US "The Mighty Quinn" LP
Miss J.D.   UNRELEASED

October 1966
Sunny   "Instrumental Assassination" EP
Wild Thing   "Instrumental Assassination" EP
With A Girl Like You   "Instrumental Assassination" EP
Get-Away   "Instrumental Assassination" EP

December 19, 1966
Happy Families (with Eddie "Fingers" Garvey) (1st stage)   see 3/5/68
Happy Families (with Edwin O'Garvey & His Showband)   "Mighty Garvey!" LP
Each And Every Day (alternate take)   UNRELEASED
Brown & Porter's (Meat Exporters) Lorry (instrumental)   UNRELEASED
Seasons In The Sun (2 stages)   UNRELEASED
Harry The One-Man-Band (original version)   see 8/30/67

January 10, 1967
Brown & Porter's (Meat Exporters) Lorry (vocal)   UNRELEASED
I Love You (2 stages)   UNRELEASED

January 16, 1967
Country Dancing (2 stages)   US "The Mighty Quinn" LP

January 20, 1967
Big Betty (2 stages)   US "The Mighty Quinn" LP

January 25, 1967
All I Want To Do (2 stages)   French "Ha! Ha! Said The Clown" EP
Feeling So Good (2 stages)   UK single
I Want To Be Wanted (1st stage)   UNRELEASED

February 10, 1967
Ha! Ha! Said The Clown (2 stages)   UK single

March 3, 1967
Harry The One-Man-Band (remake; 1st and 2nd stages)   see 3/5/68

March 8, 1967
Sweet Pea (1st stage)   UK single
Last Train To Clarksville   UNRELEASED
Sunshine Superman   UNRELEASED
Keep On Running   UNRELEASED
El Footle   UNRELEASED

April 20, 1967
Sweet Pea (2nd stage)   UNRELEASED

April 25, 1967
Hanky Panky   UNRELEASED
Mellow Yellow   UNRELEASED
Golden Flower (1st stage)   UNRELEASED
Rainbow Eyes (1st stage)   see 5/11/67

May 4, 1967
One Way   UK single

May 7, 1967
Funniest Gig   UK single

May 11, 1967
Rainbow Eyes (2nd stage)   UNRELEASED
Budgie (1st, 2nd and 3rd stages)   see 8/29/67

May 18, 1967
Everyday Another Hair Turns Grey (1st stage)   see 5/22/67

May 22, 1967
Everyday Another Hair Turns Grey (2nd and 3rd stages)   US "The Mighty Quinn" LP
She Once Was My Love   UNRELEASED

June 15, 1967
I Think It's Going To Rain Today (1st stage)   see 8/29/67

June 22, 1967 - June 23, 1967
So Long, Dad (1st and 2nd stages)   see 7/21/67

July 21, 1967
So Long Dad (3rd stage)   UK single

August 29, 1967
I Think It's Going To Rain Today (2nd stage)   UNRELEASED
Budgie (4th stage)   UNRELEASED

August 30, 1967
By Request - Edwin Garvey   UK single
Harry The One-Man-Band (original version; 2nd stage)   UNRELEASED

October 26, 1967
Mighty Quinn (1st stage)   see 11/2/67
Sleepy Hollow (demo)   UNRELEASED

November 2, 1967
Mighty Quinn (2nd stage)   UK single

November 3, 1967
Up The Junction (Version 5)   UNRELEASED
Sleepy Hollow (alternate take)   UNRELEASED

November 14, 1967
Sitting Alone In The Sunshine (1st stage)   see 11/20/67

November 20, 1967
Sitting Alone In The Sunshine (2nd stage)   UNRELEASED

November 1967
Belgravia   "Up The Junction - Original
                                                    Soundtrack Recording" LP

I Need Your Love   "Up The Junction - Original
                                                    Soundtrack Recording" LP

Just For Me   "Up The Junction - Original
                                                    Soundtrack Recording" LP

Love Theme (Version 1)   "Up The Junction - Original
                                                    Soundtrack Recording" LP

Love Theme (Version 2)   "Up The Junction - Original
                                                    Soundtrack Recording" LP

Sheila's Dance   "Up The Junction - Original
                                                    Soundtrack Recording" LP

Sing Songs Of Love   "Up The Junction - Original
                                                    Soundtrack Recording" LP

Sleepy Hollow   UK single
Up The Junction (Version 1 - single version)   "Up The Junction - Original
                                                    Soundtrack Recording" LP

Up The Junction (Version 2)   "Up The Junction - Original
                                                    Soundtrack Recording" LP

Up The Junction (Version 3)   "Up The Junction - Original
                                                    Soundtrack Recording" LP

Up The Junction (Version 4)   "Up The Junction - Original
                                                    Soundtrack Recording" LP

Wailing Horn   "Up The Junction - Original
                                                    Soundtrack Recording" LP

Walking Round   "Up The Junction - Original
                                                    Soundtrack Recording" LP

December 1967
Mighty Quinn (3rd and 4th stages)   UK single

January 2, 1968
Cubist Town (1st and 2nd stages)   US "The Mighty Quinn" LP

Winter 1968
The Charge Of The Light Brigade   "The Charge Of The Light Brigade -
                                                    Original Motion Picture Score" LP

March 5, 1968
Harry The One-Man-Band (remake; 3rd and 4th stages)   "Mighty Garvey!" LP
Happy Families (with Eddie "Fingers" Garvey; 2nd stage)   "Mighty Garvey!" LP

<u>March 12, 1968</u>
Happy Families (with Ed. Garvey & The Trio)   "Mighty Garvey!" LP

<u>Spring 1968</u>
It's So Easy Falling   US "The Mighty Quinn" LP
My Name Is Jack (UK single version)   UK single
My Name Is Jack (US single version)   US single
No Better, No Worse   US "The Mighty Quinn" LP
There Is A Man   UK single

<u>Fall 1968</u>
Fox On The Run   US single
Too Many People   US single

<u>Spring 1969</u>
A 'B' Side   US single
Ragamuffin Man   US single

COMMERCIALS

<u>Summer 1969</u>
The Michelin Theme (Go Radial, Go Michelin)   UK single

<u>Winter 1970</u>
The Maxwell House Shake   UK single

<u>Fall 1970</u>
Ski "Full Of Fitness" Theme   UK single
Sweet Baby Jane   UK single

At this time, no session information is available on other Mann/Hugg commercials, Manfred Mann Chapter Three, Manfred Mann's Earth Band and Manfred Mann's Plain Music.

Endnotes

1. From a recent conversation I had with Manfred, I have confirmed that Manfred's first name is in fact <u>Manfred</u>, and not Michael. This error first occurred in a book by Lillian Roxon, but hopefully I have corrected it here once and for all. You'll also discover that quite a few other band members changed their names before joining Manfred Mann - perhaps it was the thing to do!

2. All UK chart positions are from Record Retailer (now Music Week) unless otherwise noted. The single "5-4-3-2-1" reached #4 on the New Musical Express (NME) chart as well.

3. "I'm Your Kingpin" had such an effect on young vocalist John Kay that he recorded the song during his second US Columbia Records audition with the pre-Steppenwolf group Sparrow in June 1966.

4. "Hubble Bubble (Toil And Trouble)" was slated to be released on Ascot, but only a few promotional copies were released. Prestige was having its problems as well, as they attempted to master "Why Should We Not" from a British single for release as "Blue Brave." Again, only white label promos were released since the poor sound reproduction blocked any further Prestige use of these recordings. Even Manfred was unaware of this record's release! Prestige's retitling of "Blue Brave" was most likely due to their view of "Why Should We Not" as an American Indian melody.

5. The rough edges included an organ solo from Manfred that didn't seem to flow with the song. To get around this difficulty, a tape edit repeated the song's bridge and deleted the organ solo. From a production standpoint, "Do Wah Diddy Diddy" was the first of Manfred's "cut and paste" recordings. This procedure would be used more frequently in the future with varying degrees of success. The long, unedited version of the tune was mistakenly released on the Canadian "Mann Made Hits!" album in 1967. On CD, its first appearance was on the US "The Best Of Manfred Mann - The Definitive Collection" disc.

6. Ascot was in such a hurry to release "Do Wah Diddy Diddy" that they transferred the song from a British single for quick release in the US. This happened even though Ascot had plenty of time to obtain a proper tape!

7. Meeting fan demand in 1964, a special British Manfred Mann photo picture sleeve was made available. The sleeve gave the group's fans a place in which to store their favorite Manfreds 7" records. These were available for about a year, and enabled their proud owners to personally write in the A- and B-side titles of each Manfred Mann record they possessed.

8. Again, a lot of thinking and re-thinking was involved in the making of the album. In early June 1964, the original track lineup of the LP included the songs "Sticks And Stones" and "Ain't That Love?". One last album session on June 5, 1964 produced "What You Gonna Do?" (the B-side of "Do Wah Diddy Diddy") and "It's Gonna Work Out Fine." The Manfreds decided that these two new songs had to be included, and the album's track listing was changed and resequenced. "Sticks And Stones," an exciting cover of the Ray Charles hit, was first released in England on the 1993 compilation "The Best Of The EMI Years." Unfortunately, "Ain't That Love?" has not been located after all these years. This fate has befallen several of the group's unreleased HMV tracks.

9. On the song's original stereo mix (unreleased in the UK), the bass drum countoff appearing on the mono mix was missing. However, the stereo master tape does include this countoff. A complete stereo mix is slated for US CD release in the fall of 1995.

10. The original mono mix of the Manfreds version had a fade-out ending, but the stereo went to a complete (cold) ending.

11. Paul Jones recorded two lead vocals for the song, one for the mono and another for the stereo. The differences are most notable between the ending chorus and the song's fadeout.

12. Paul Jones' intro harmonica track starts slightly earlier on the tune's stereo mix - another variation for the completist!

13. Tom McGuinness' guitar solos on the mono and stereo versions of "Mr. Anello" were different. The mono mix is a touch longer, but the harmonica break that Jones supplied after McGuinness' solo was truncated. The stereo mix of "Mr. Anello" first appeared on the "Soul Of Mann" collection in January 1967.

14. Unfortunately, the original UK album did not express all of the song's power. The unedited mix that later appeared in the US included a slow vocal and piano introduction. After this part, it exploded into the UK album version.

15. The release of the LP coincided with the issuance of two promotional items: an EP with "Do Wah Diddy Diddy" and excerpts of three album tracks ("Bring It To Jerome," "Don't Ask Me What I Say" and "Got My Mojo Working") and an interview LP for radio station broadcast.

After "Do Wah Diddy Diddy" took hold in the US, HMV sent mono and stereo master tapes of the debut album to Ascot Records. Since it was not a British practice to include a hit A-side on an LP (they were usually reserved for EPs), Ascot never bothered to obtain a better tape copy of "Do Wah Diddy Diddy" from the UK for the US version of the album. "The Manfred Mann Album" kept in line with current US standards for albums, which involved using approximately 12 tracks featuring a hit single. To comply with this practice, Ascot replaced "I'm Your Kingpin," "You've Got To Take It" and "Mr. Anello" with the current hit "Do Wah Diddy Diddy."

Ascot saved "I'm Your Kingpin" and "You've Got To Take It" for the next US album ("The Five Faces Of Manfred Mann" - not to be confused with the UK album), but "Mr. Anello" was not released in the States. "Mr. Anello" is planned for a fall 1995 US release.

Other countries created their own "Five Faces Of Manfred Mann" albums: the Canadian "Five Faces" LP, available in mono and rechanneled stereo modes, was identical to the UK album except that "Do Wah Diddy Diddy" replaced "Got My Mojo Working." The Japanese counterpart was issued later in mono only, with the hit singles "Do Wah Diddy Diddy" and "Sha La La" replacing "What You Gonna Do?" and "You've Got To Take It."

16. The March 1965 Canadian release of the LP "The Manfred Mann Return" included the exclusive US LP tracks found on "The Five Faces Of Manfred Mann" and an alternate take of "5-4-3-2-1," which was the exact "Ready Steady Go" TV theme version. This version of "5-4-3-2-1" first reappeared in 1992 on the US CD "The Best Of Manfred Mann - A Definitive Collection."

17. "She" and "Dashing Away With The Smoothing Iron" were finally released in the UK in 1993.

18. Rod Stewart and Cher have also had some recent international success with "Oh No Not My Baby."

19. A completely different version of the song (albeit edited) appeared in the film.

20. The next year (1966), Love, an L.A. area group featuring Arthur Lee, presented a stripped down take of the song and achieved a greater degree of notoriety with it. The pre-Deep Purple outfit Episode Six also recorded a version of the song in 1966 which musically fell between the other two versions, but it was shelved until a 1991 compilation. In addition, Graham Parker's former group The Rumour released "My Little Red Book" as a single, and it followed Love's style.

After "Mighty Quinn" hit in 1968, "My Little Red Book" was dusted off for re-release on Ascot with the bottom side "I Can't Believe What You Say." It sold even less than its original release.

21. The sheet music for "The One In The Middle" reflected the original lyrics, which differ quite a bit from the recorded version.

22. In 1969, British folksters Fairport Convention had a #21 UK hit with a French language version of this Dylan number, entitled "Si Tu Dois Partir."

23. In Canada, the "Mann Made" album was finally released in April 1966, but "Pretty Flamingo" and an exclusive, more relaxed take of "She Needs Company" were included at the expense of "You're For Me," "I Really Do Believe" and "Hi Lili, Hi Lo."

24. "Hi Lili, Hi Lo" was released as a single in Australia and reached #23. In the UK, the song was a 1966 hit for The Alan Price Set, named after The Animals' former organist.

25. For radio station use, a very rare promotional single extracted from the EP included the songs "There's No Living Without Your Loving" and "Tired Of Trying, Bored With Lying, Scared Of Dying."

26. "There's No Living Without Your Loving" was not released in the US until 1974.

27. Fortunately, Paul Jones was aware of "She Needs Company"'s lasting impact and re-recorded it on his first solo LP, "My Way."

28. Interestingly, even though Manfred Mann recorded numerous sessions for the BBC throughout the sixties, their exclusive re-recording of "Pretty Flamingo" has been the only one released so far.

It appears on the 1992 compilation "1 And Only - 25 Years Of Radio 1."

29. "Machines" scored a revival of sorts when theremin and synthesizer pioneers Lothar And The Hand People used Manfred Mann's arrangement as a prototype for their own unique version in 1969.

30. In the US, the song appeared only on the "Having A Rave Up With The Yardbirds" LP, and its most notable cover version was by the group that evolved into Grand Funk Railroad - Terry Knight And The Pack.

31. Stereo album buyers of "Soul Of Mann" were treated to a rechanneled stereo, alternate take of Manfred Mann's first single "Why Should We Not" and the alternate mix of "Mr. Anello." Canada's mono version of "Soul Of Mann" appeared with a modified front cover a few months later, but two tracks were missing: "God Rest Ye Merry Gentlemenn" and "Still I'm Sad."

Other collections were released at this time. In Sweden, HMV issued a unique compilation album entitled simply "Manfred Mann" in 1967. It included most of their hits and some EP tracks. Following the lead of French record companies, Australian HMV had their own way of getting Manfred Mann hits to the fans: EPs. Between their "Come Tomorrow" and "Pretty Flamingo" EPs, HMV enabled fans to get most of the band's Australian hits between "Hubble Bubble" and "Pretty Flamingo."

32. The song's mono mix featured a Klaus Voorman flute track recorded directly onto the mono master tape, unlike the unadorned stereo mix soon to appear on the "As Is" LP. As a rarity, Australian fans also received this unique EP.

33. The mono single mix of "Semi-Detached Suburban Mr. James" had backing vocals that were recorded directly onto the single master, so the stereo mix can never equate with the single.

34. Simon Dupree And The Big Sound (soon to become The Moles and then Gentle Giant) produced an almost note-for-note copy of "Each And Every Day" as the single "Day Time, Night Time," but it did not sell enough to chart. In the US, The Mike Jones Group issued "Each And Every Day" as a very rare 1967 single.

35. "As Is" sported two different cover designs: one with the group standing in an alcove, and the other with the group standing in front of a locomotive in a train yard. It is unknown as to why there were two covers, but the "locomotive" cover has proven to be rarer and more valuable.

36. The first recording stage of "Ha! Ha! Said The Clown" was very confused and had sections that were not present in the final version. On the second stage, the marching drum track was added to the break but the ending was not completed. Further editing used Manfred's keyboard riff and a repeat of the first chorus as the song's ending, and the record finally materialized.

37. Starting from 1961 or 1962, Moody Blues keyboardist Mike Pinder served as one of the mellotron's design consultants. However, Pinder did not use the instrument on record until the album "Days Of Future Past." In late 1966, The Beatles started employing the mellotron on their

latest musical creations. Their first released mellotron recording was "Strawberry Fields Forever" in February 1967.

38. Manfred's vocalization of the title did not appear on the original multi-track tape, as Klaus Voorman appeared instead. The recording was spliced from the middle of the song, with Manfred saying "Sweet Pea" and the first verse was edited on and then faded. A different version of "Sweet Pea" was recorded with different bass and drum tracks, but it was not used. In addition, two vibes tracks were recorded, but only one remained in the final mix.

39. Tony Visconti later became famous producing a wide range of artists, including Mary Hopkin, T. Rex, David Bowie and Thin Lizzy.

40. As with nearly all of the Fontana material, a vastly superior stereo mix of the multi-track "So Long, Dad" tape exists but has not yet been released.

41. The original mix of "Funniest Gig" also had a tape loop of "Just Like A Woman," but this was dropped.

42. "One Way" was originally planned under the title "Ha! Ha! Said The Clown," but the title writing on the front cover was clumsily redrawn before release.

43. In its entirety, "Mighty Quinn" lasted 3 1/2 minutes and had a complete, unfaded ending. To really compete in the singles market, the song was a little on the long side, so it was faded.

44. In the States, "Mighty Quinn" was available on six different Mercury label designs, and it has proven to be a nightmare for collectors keen on such things!

45. The UK and US "Up The Junction" albums sported entirely different covers, and it is not known why this LP was released in the US instead of "As Is," a stronger commercial proposition in the US market.

46. "Sleepy Hollow" was recorded twice before the single version take, but the band was not happy with either version.

47. "What A Mann" included the whole "Instrumental Assassination" EP, but it differed from "One Way" in that it did not contain "I Wanna Be Rich," the hits "Ha! Ha! Said The Clown" and "Semi-Detached Suburban Mr. James," and the latter's B-side, "Morning After The Party." In addition, the Australian issue of "What A Mann" used the same train yard photo used on the UK "As Is" LP.

48. A US acetate exists of the UK version of the album, and the Australian LP was identical to the American issue except for its black and white back cover.

49. Interestingly enough, even though the harpsichord was the main instrument of the song, it was not added until the very end - the third recording stage. In addition, Hugg's drums ran throughout to maintain the song's flow but were selectively mixed out to present the classic mix that remains.

50. "The Vicar's Daughter" had a perfect unfaded ending when originally recorded, but for some reason the ending was not considered strong enough to keep in the final mix.

51. The released version had a continuous tape edit which repeated the final note, instead of the complete ending that the multi-track tape features.

52. After a long run of Australian singles on the Philips label, "Fox On The Run" was the first Oz single to appear on Fontana.

53. In Australia, sales for "Ragamuffin Man" were so strong that the record, which peaked at #4, remained in their Top 40 for 16 weeks, longer than any of their singles! Since there were no Australian LPs from this period, EPs were made available for fans eager to catch up on Manfred Mann's final recordings. The "Mighty Quinn" and "Fox On The Run" EPs covered nearly all their later singles output, and they were nicely packaged. During the '70s, the pop group Paper Lace poorly copied the Manfred Mann arrangement of "Ragamuffin Man" for single release.

54. In addition to the aforementioned Sparrow and Simon Dupree And The Big Sound covers of original Manfreds material, other rare cover versions include The Jaybirds' version of "Hubble Bubble (Toil And Trouble)," "I Need Your Love" by The Jigsaw Band (soon to become simply Jigsaw), and The Patti Smith Group's live version of "5-4-3-2-1." These versions were performed in entirely different ways: The Jaybirds' single was an instrumental, The Jigsaw Band added lyrics to the Mike Hugg instrumental theme from "Up The Junction," and Patti Smith ignored all the words of "5-4-3-2-1" except the title!

55. The song was later re-recorded by Mike Hugg's studio group Full Alert as the disco tune "Sheer Enjoyment" with another arrangement and set of lyrics.

56. "One Way Glass" was a 33RPM mono single released specially in Argentina (translated as "Espejo" - mirror), backed with "Ain't It Sad" ("¿No Es Triste?"). In addition, "One Way Glass" for some reason is in mono on the album.

57. When compared to the original album version, the British and German singles of "Please Mrs. Henry" featured an edited mono remix. This version has not appeared on an album, since it featured Mick Rogers vocals that were not included on either "Stepping Sideways" or the upcoming album.

On US and Canadian singles, another alternate mono remix appeared. This release had exclusive lead guitar overdubbing throughout the song, but it was 8 seconds shorter than the UK and German releases.

"Prayer" also appeared differently on 45, depending on the country. The UK single was the complete version in stereo, while the US and Canadian single featured the entire song in mono. The German disc, however, sported an edited (faded) mono version. The saving grace of the German issue was its inclusion of an art sleeve.

58. The single may have been helped along by the sped-up nature of US and Canadian copies. In addition, only the newly created US stereo/mono A-side promotional copies have the stereo mix on a 45. Regular US copies of the record appeared in mono, unlike the stereo singles released throughout the world.

59. All original copies of the album had gatefold sleeves, but North American albums had black front and back covers, unlike all other issues with white covers.

60. In Singapore, where unlawful records were the norm instead of the exception, an unusual "Swedish Fly Girls" EP was prepared. At the very least, illegal EPs were also pressed for the upcoming "Solar Fire" (two EPs) and "The Good Earth" albums.

61. As a carryover from the start of the Vertigo label, Australian copies of "Messin'" came with the coveted "swirl" label design. For the collector in all of us, all singles of "Get Your Rocks Off" do not include the countoff heard on the LP!

62. Previous reports that MMEB recorded a double album's worth of Holst material have proven to be false. Somehow, Frank Zappa circumvented this copyright procedure in 1967 when he appropriated the same "Jupiter" section that Manfred used as a counterpoint to his Moog solo on "Joybringer." Zappa's reading appeared during the introduction of the track "Invocation And Ritual Dance Of The Young Pumpkin" on The Mothers Of Invention's album "Absolutely Free."

63. The British single mix has still not surfaced on an album, and it is much longer than the heavily edited US single version.

64. North American copies of "Solar Fire" included a longer edit of "Joybringer" in place of "Earth The Circle Part 2." Original LP covers also incorrectly listed "Earth The Circle Part 2," but these were modified soon thereafter.

65. On the single (North American copies went under Dylan's title of "Father Of Night"), the A-side was edited with guitar overdubs at its end. This version is only available on the UK promotional sampler LP "EMI Introduce The New Bronze Age." However, the mix on that album goes to the same length as the single without the fading heard on the 45. The B-side ("Solar Fire Two") was a retitling of the title track, although on US singles it was faded early.

66. Dylan recorded "Quit Your Low Down Ways" in July 1962 for the LP "The Freewheelin' Bob Dylan," but it did not make the final track listing. It remained unreleased until the box set "The Bootleg Series Volumes 1-3 [rare & unreleased]" in 1991, but it was first released in 1963 by Peter, Paul And Mary on their "In The Wind" album.

67. The Japanese issue used the British A-side edit and an edited version of the B-side.

68. Coinciding with the release of the single was a very rare one-sided four-track promo 12" that Bronze issued as an album sampler for "The Roaring Silence."

69. No such version was issued outside of North America and Australia. Especially since the US single was five seconds longer and this was its only album appearance, the revised edition of "The Roaring Silence" has also become an in-demand item for European fans.

70. Despite including album tracks, the album is essential thanks to its alternate mix of "Joybringer," which does not have the guitar overdubs present on the single.

71. "California" was faded early on the US "Watch" LP.

72. The enduring success of "Watch" was reinforced when it became Manfred's first officially released LP in the former Soviet Union, pressed on the Melodiya label during the mid-'80s. Sales were strong enough to warrant a second pressing in 1988. "Nightingales And Bombers" became the second MMEB release in the Soviet republic, first appearing in 1993.

73. A live track from their time in the States, "Spirits In The Night," was released in the US in 1991 on the collection "The Best Of King Biscuit Live - Volume 3."

74. The UK single is edited, unlike the complete US single issued after the album.

75. "Don't Kill It Carol" was available in both regular vinyl and picture disc formats. The latter commands high prices in today's collector market. Later in the year, the unique compilation "The Best Of Manfred Mann's Earth Band" was issued in Australia and New Zealand. Crediting Manfred Mann as "creative producer," the album was an intelligently compiled selection of tracks dating back to 1973.

76. The song's appearance on 45 was very different. The middle section of "You're Not My" was edited, but the song went to a complete ending, unlike the faded LP version.

77. The album version of "For You" had female backing vocals, but Manfred did these vocals himself for the single. The 7" was also heavily edited, and it had a completely different synthesizer solo that worked just as well as the original!

78. Shona Laing's most popular solo recording after her MMEB work was "Glad I'm Not A Kennedy."

79. The 7" sported an edit of the mix on the 12" release. The 3-track 12" also included the previous B-side, "Man In Jam."

80. On the single, the track was edited and mixed differently and the keyboard introduction did not appear on the forthcoming "Somewhere In Afrika." The South African issue of this album did not include the map of the country found on the back cover of all other releases. Instead, one of the characters from the front cover appeared on the back cover.

81. The shorter album version of "Eyes Of Nostradamus" had a Chris Thompson and Steve Waller joint vocal, but it featured heavier guitar and drums than the single. "Redemption Song" also had

a Thompson lead vocal and heavier drums, but the African chanting was reduced in exchange for a synthesizer solo and Trevor Rabin guitar lead. This section also included a snatch of "Brothers And Sisters Of Azania," and crossfaded into African music with chants and synthesizer backing.

82. In Canada, mislabelled singles were pressed with "To Bantustan?" shown on both labels and credited to just Manfred Mann. The correct songs appeared on both sides.

83. Soon after the failure of this record, "Runner" and "Rebel" were issued back-to-back on Arista's Flashback singles label. For the US radio show "The King Biscuit Flower Hour," an ersatz live version of "Runner" was created by recording new vocal overdubs over the existing backing track.

84. Despite what the 12" says, the live beginning of "Davy's On The Road Again" does not appear on the single, so it's not the "full length version!"

85. All of the album's songs were much longer, more fully developed and differently mixed. The only exceptions were "Telegram To Monica" and "A Couple Of Mates (From Mars And Jupiter)," which retained most of their original, basic structure. One example of the downside of the album's changes was the far superior original "Masque" version of "Joybringer," featuring absolutely pretty synthesizer playing during its instrumental passages. Throughout the album, sections like these were edited out, and "Masque"'s continuity suffered as a result.

86. On the original version of "Masque," "Planets Schmanets" provided more coherence by originally following "Start."

87. For the original take, Maggie Ryder sang only the first verse and then a low, processed voice (presumably by Mann) alternated lines with Ryder until sax and piano solos ended the song. On the released version, the low voice replaced Ryder except during the song's choruses. The 7" single mix was entirely different from both of these, using an even different vocal and instrumental combination. The 12" remix issued only in Germany was yet another exclusive permutation.

88. In its final form, the song's melody was simple but its arrangement remained intricate. Sax and keyboard passages that did not fit this mold were edited out. The original version also went to a complete ending unlike the fade on the album, but the "meat" of the song remained intact.

A 7" single with the coupling "Sikelele I" and "Wounded Knee" was straightforward enough, but three separate CD singles were also released. The first contained what was on the 7" plus two exclusive remixes of "Sikelele I": a 7" remix (which was not the mix on the 7"!) and a 12" remix (there was no German 12" either!). Since it was a South African song, "Sikelele" was actually issued on 7" and 12" in South Africa with those mixes. Next up was the second CD single, containing the 7" and 12" remixes of "Sikelele I" plus the album tracks "Sikelele II" and "Medicine Song." Leading to further confusion, the last CD5 was made up of the album version, a 12" remix and the Workhouse Remix of "Sikelele I," and "Wounded Knee." While the 7" and 12" remixes were done by Bobby Summerfield and Manfred in Los Angeles and The Workhouse, the Workhouse Remix was done by Manfred alone at his London studio. Whew!

89. The original mix of "Kiowa" had long, overlapping solos before Manfred's piano finish, but the song works equally well without this section.

90. This disc, a German CD single, contained both the album mix and an exclusive remix, as well as "Wounded Knee." The album version of "Medicine Song" was also included on the sampler album "Perspective '92" on Intuition's parent label, veraBra.

91. Despite its nearly five-minute length, "Wounded Knee" was edited from a longer unreleased version.

92. Most notable about the South African edition is its entirely different front and back cover design, but the music is identical to the German album.

93. At the time, there was a New Zealand folk singer also named Chris Thompson, so Chris used "Hamlet" as his middle name to avoid confusion.

94. "If You Remember Me" and a different take of "Cold Wind Across My Heart" were included on second pressings of the US "Night" album and all foreign pressings. In a mixup of sorts, "If You Remember Me" (from the film soundtrack of "The Champ") was incorrectly credited to Chris Thompson only for its first pressing. Later pressings were billed to Chris Thompson and Night.

95. Stevie Lange, a highly requested session singer, has been featured on her own records, and on the Earth Band's "Angel Station," "Watch" and "Somewhere In Afrika" albums, and Holly Johnson's "Blast" album. "Blast" featured Stevie's contributions on the big UK hit "Americanos."

96. Starship (formerly known as Jefferson Starship) had a major US hit with "It's Not Over" under the title "It's Not Over ('Til It's Over)."

97. Chris Thompson's version of "You're The Voice" was left off "The High Cost Of Living" at the last minute.

98. Faltermeyer and Thompson also wrote "Yes We Can" for a German charity single under the name of Artists United For Nature in 1989. This collection of artists also included Joe Cocker, Carol Decker, Jennifer Rush and Stevie Lange. A 1992 UK re-release of the single was also on the hit album "Earthrise." An extended version of "Yes We Can" included Brian May at the expense of Thompson.

99. In addition to all of Thompson's released projects, his four or five vocals for a Steve Hackett album remain unreleased.

100. A lip-synch appearance of the "This Was" single "A Song For Jeffrey" also marked Jethro Tull's first video appearance on the aborted Rolling Stones/John Lennon British TV special "Rock & Roll Circus." If you look closely, you can spot future Black Sabbath founder Tony Iommi in his short stint with the band.

101. In January 1971, UK Chrysalis advertised the single "Lick Your Fingers Clean" b/w "Up To Me." After realizing that the A-side was not going to be on the forthcoming "Aqualung" album, Chrysalis scrapped the single. "Lick Your Fingers Clean" was later rearranged and re-recorded as the song "Two Fingers" on the "War Child" album in 1974, before the 1988 box set took it under its wing.

The UK market received no singles from "Aqualung," but the US received two: "Hymn 43" (a #91 chart record) and "Locomotive Breath." A quadrophonic version of "Aqualung" made US stores in 1974, and this album is a required purchase. In addition to featuring different mixes of the album's tracks, an alternate (almost solo) take of "Wind-Up" was used by mistake.

Order Form

Fax orders: (516) 352-3037

Postal orders: Crossfire Publishing, P.O. Box 20406, Floral Park, NY 11002-20406, USA

Please send the following book:

"MANNERISMS: THE FIVE PHASES OF MANFRED MANN" by GREG RUSSO

I understand that I may return any books for a full refund - for any reason, no questions asked.

Company name: _____

Name: _____

Address: _____

City: _____ State: _____ Zip: _____ - _____

Telephone: (____) _____

Sales tax:
Please add 8.25% for books shipped to New York addresses.

Shipping:
First class: $3.00 for the first book and $1.50 each additional book
Air mail: $13.00 per book
Surface mail: $7.50 per book

Payment:
___ Money order
___ Credit card: __ VISA __ Mastercard

Card number: _____

Name on card: _____ Exp. date: _____ / _____

Order a copy for a friend!

Order Form

Fax orders: (516) 352-3037

Postal orders: Crossfire Publishing, P.O. Box 20406, Floral Park, NY 11002-20406, USA

Please send the following book:

"MANNERISMS: THE FIVE PHASES OF MANFRED MANN" by GREG RUSSO

I understand that I may return any books for a full refund - for any reason, no questions asked.

Company name: _____

Name: _____

Address: _____

City: _____ State: _____ Zip: _____ - _____

Telephone: (____) _____

Sales tax:
Please add 8.25% for books shipped to New York addresses.

Shipping:
First class: $3.00 for the first book and $1.50 each additional book
Air mail: $13.00 per book
Surface mail: $7.50 per book

Payment:
___ Money order
___ Credit card: __ VISA __ Mastercard

Card number: _____

Name on card: _____ Exp. date: _____ / _____

Order a copy for a friend!